Carlo Michelstaedter and
the Failure of Language

Carlo Michelstaedter in the Boboli Garden, Florence, 1907. Courtesy of the Gorizia Civic Library.

Daniela Bini

CARLO MICHELSTAEDTER
and the
FAILURE OF LANGUAGE

University Press of Florida
Gainesville
Tallahassee
Tampa
Boca Raton
Pensacola
Orlando
Miami
Jacksonville

Library of Congress Cataloging-in-Pubication Data

Bini, Daniela, 1945–
   Carlo Michelstaedter and the failure of
language / Daniela Bini.
      p.   cm.
   Includes bibliographical references and index.
   ISBN 0–8130–1111–6
   1. Michelstaedter, Carlo, 1887–1910—
Criticism and interpretation.
I. Title.
PQ4829.I38Z53   1992
851'.912—dc20   91-28380

The author acknowledges with gratitude the
editors of the following journals for permission to
reprint in the first chapter of the book parts of essays
previously published: *Italica* 63, no. 4 (1986);
Italiana (Rosary College, River Forest, 1988);
Differentia: Review of Italian Thought 2 (Spring
1988); *Romance Languages Annual* (Purdue
University, 1990); and *Italian Culture* 6 (1990).

The University Press of Florida is the scholarly
publishing agency of the State University System
of Florida, comprised of Florida A&M
University, Florida Atlantic University, Florida
International University, Florida State University,
University of Central Florida, University of
Florida, University of North Florida, University
of South Florida, University of West Florida.

Orders for books should be addressed to
University Press of Florida, 15 NW 15th St.,
Gainesville, FL 32611.

To Joe

CONTENTS

Illustrations

ACKNOWLEDGMENTS

This book, conceived in a spirit of adventure, owes its life to a number of friends and colleagues. My interest in Carlo Michelstaedter was first sparked by an article written in 1983 by the philosopher Gianni Vattimo in *La Stampa*. Sergio Campailla then stimulated my interest and curiosity with his extensive studies on Michelstaedter—a source of reference and inspiration. In Rome in the summer of 1988, he personally encouraged me to pursue this project.

My research in the Biblioteca Civica of Gorizia was made enjoyable and rewarding thanks to the hospitality of the director, Dr. Otello Silvestri, and the assistance of Sandra Vogrini and Giulio Nerini. I am especially grateful to Dr. Antonella Gallarotti, the director of the Fondo C. Michelstaedter, who did everything to facilitate my research in Gorizia.

The completion of my work was made possible by grants from the University of Texas Research Institute.

To the Provincia of Gorizia goes my gratitude for having organized the first International Conference on Michelstaedter, entitled "Carlo Michelstaedter: Il coraggio dell'impossibile."

Until a few years ago, Michelstaedter was virtually unknown in America, and writing a book about him in English posed many problems. From the very start, my close friend Prof. Peter Carravetta of Queens College has enthusiastically supported the introduction of Michelstaedter to the English-speaking public. He reaffirmed his faith in the project by publishing my essay "Carlo Michelstaedter: The Tragedy of Thought" in his new philosophical journal *Differentia*. My long-time friend, teacher, and mentor, Prof. Gian Paolo Biasin, who wrote first in English on Michelstaedter in his book *Literary Diseases,* provided constant psychological and intellectual support for this study. He read the complete manuscript, found my errors, and gave me very detailed suggestions for improvement. Two other dear friends read my manuscript with patience and care and offered valid criticism: Prof. Rebecca West at the University of Chicago, and my colleague at the University of Texas, Prof. Millicent Marcus.

I wish to express my thanks to the chair of the University of South Florida editorial committee, Prof. Silvia Ruffo Fiore, who kept me posted at each stage of the reviewing process, and to the editors at the University Press of Florida for their professional help. I thank Mrs. O. K. Stephenson, my typist, who has been an indispensable part of my scholarly life over the years. I also wish to acknowledge my sister-in-law Rita Bini Cirimbilla, who first called my attention to Michelstaedter's drawings, and my cousin Dr. Alessandro Bini, who assisted me in my research in Gorizia.

For his editorial help and above all for his never-failing moral and intellectual presence, my deepest gratitude goes to my husband, Joseph Coleman Carter. It is to him that this book is dedicated.

BIOGRAPHICAL NOTE

Carlo's father, Alberto, born in Gorizia, was the son of Elia Michelstaedter of Germany and Bona Reggio of Italy. His maternal grandfather was the eminent rabbi and scholar Isacco Samuele Reggio, whose valuable library is now in the British Museum. Alberto, however, was not successful in school and began to work as a stockbroker. He later became the director of an insurance company. A self-taught man and a bibliomaniac, he was also a dilettante writer. He often wrote for *Il Corriere friulano,* whose editor was related to his wife, the writer Carolina Luzzatto.

Gorizia and Trieste were then under the Austrian crown and many Italians living there took part in the irredentist movement, a crusade for the return of Gorizia and Trieste to Italy. Alberto was one of them. He married Emma Luzzatto from another prominent Jewish family, who was to endure not only the loss of two of her children but also, together with her daughter Elda, the tragedy of the Nazi persecution. Deported to Auschwitz at the age of 89, she died shortly after arriving. Elda was to die there too in 1944.

Alberto and Emma had four children: Gino, born in 1877, Elda in 1879, Paula in 1885, and finally Carlo, born on June 3, 1887. Not surprisingly, Carlo's closest sibling was his sister Paula. The intensity of their friendship is apparent in the many letters Carlo wrote to her.

In 1897 Carlo enrolled in the Staatsgymnasium of Gorizia, where the instruction was in German and the emphasis was placed on the study of the classical languages. He also studied Italian. While in school he formed strong and long-lasting friendships with Nino Paternolli and Enrico Mreule. Mreule introduced Carlo to Schopenhauer and stimulated his interest in philosophy.

After the Gymnasium Carlo enrolled at the University of Vienna in order to study mathematics and physics, but never actually attended. Instead he convinced his father that he needed the stimulating, artistic environment of Florence. There he went in October 1905, taking with him his paints and brushes. He thought he would stay for a year but remained for four and enrolled at the Istituto di Studi Superiori. In Florence he met Vladimiro Arangio Ruiz and Gaetano Chiavacci, his other two faithful friends; to the latter we owe the first edition of Carlo's writings. Both were to become distinguished scholars in philosophy. Carlo's sojourn in Florence was interrupted only by his trips back home for Christmas and summer vacations.

At the end of 1906 Carlo met Nadia Baraden, a Russian divorcee. He gave her lessons in Italian and painted a moving oil portrait of her. Nadia's suicide in March 1907 marked the onset of chronic, severe psychological depression for Carlo, which was to plague him for the rest of his life. A month before her death, the foremost Italian poet of the day, Giosuè Carducci, died and Carlo went to Bologna to attend his funeral. On that occasion he wrote a sentimental account of the experience in a letter home. The letter was given to Carolina Luzzatto, who published it in *Il Corriere friulano* without consulting Carlo. This was one of the few pieces of his writing published during his lifetime, and he was furious when he found out about it. In this period he did, however, contribute many caricatures to the first and only issue of *Gaudeamus igitur,* a goliardic paper written by the students of the Institute. He divided his time between books and his true passion, drawings.

In the spring of 1907 he fell in love with Iolanda De Blasi, a schoolmate at the Institute. They did not marry because of the strong opposition he encountered in his family. The experience was important, however, since it brought out the complexity and demanding nature of Carlo's personality. He failed in various attempts to publish his essays and to do a translation of Schopenhauer into Italian (he even wrote to Benedetto Croce about it), and his depression grew deeper and deeper.

In 1907 music became a vital part of his life. A new friend, the musician Giannotto Bastianelli, would play Beethoven on the piano evening after evening. Carlo's love for Beethoven developed into an obsession. Argia Cassini, the woman he loved in the last two years of his life, eventually took Giannotto's place after Carlo's return to Gorizia.

In February 1909 he and his family received a telegram from New York announcing the death of his older brother Gino. From this moment he entered the final phase of the depression that was to bring him to suicide.

In the last year of his life he wrote most of what he left: a volume of poems to his beloved Argia Cassini, *Il dialogo della salute,* dedicated to his younger cousin Emilio, his dissertation, *La persuasione e la rettorica* with the *Appendici critiche.* His intellectual efforts and frenetic study brought him to the point of questioning all established knowledge—philosophy as well as science. In the end he refused all books except the New Testament.

By October 17, 1910, the day of his mother's birthday, Carlo finished his dissertation. That morning his mother came to see him and accused him of indifference toward his family. At two o'clock in the afternoon he shot himself in the temple. On October 19 his coffin was carried by four of his friends to the Jewish cemetery and buried next to that of his brother Gino. Two cypresses were planted there in memory of the two young brothers. They can still be seen, standing tall over the tombs that are now on Yugoslavian soil.

Carlo Michelstaedter.
Far di se stesso fiamma
(n.d.). Watercolor on
paper. Courtesy of the
Gorizia Civic Library.

INTRODUCTION

The silence that enveloped Carlo Michelstaedter after his suicide in 1910 can be explained in the light of the Italian cultural climate at the time, dominated as it was by the figure of Benedetto Croce. In Croce's philosophical system, based on the strict separation of the human faculties, there was no space for a personality like Michelstaedter's, whose aim was the abolition of this very separation. He was in fact a philosopher, a painter, and a poet, constantly changing his mode of expression, convinced of the insufficiency of all of them, in an attempt, ever frustrated, to grasp the essence of life and find the perfect form to express it. In this philosophical climate, a large part of the work by the poet-philosopher Giacomo Leopardi had already suffered the critics' censure. So did the entire production of Michelstaedter. What made Michelstaedter unacceptable in the Crocean cultural milieu was precisely that which constituted his originality: his repudiation of a compartmentalization of knowledge and artistic activities. His entire life was a constant challenge to Croce's *distinti* and an attack on systematic thought.

Philosophy had been for centuries synonymous with systematic thought. In his struggle Michelstaedter was, at least in Italy, still alone. The other leading Italian philosopher, Giovanni Gentile, who in 1922 reviewed Michelstaedter's main work, his philosophical dissertation on persuasion and rhetoric, lamented precisely the work's lack of systematic thought, the absence of method; Gentile nonetheless recognized posthumously the young scholar's philosophical mind.[1]

Had Michelstaedter lived in Vienna, where for a while he thought of studying, or had he written his work in German, he would probably not have had to wait until relatively recently for recognition. His sensibility was, in fact, much closer to the pessimism of the North than to the optimism of Italian neo-idealism.

Carlo Michelstaedter was born in Gorizia in 1887 into a highly cultured Jewish family. He was the youngest of four children: Gino, Elda, Paula, Carlo. His paternal grandfather Isacco Samuele Reggio had been a rabbi and a scholar of great renown. Geopolitically, Gorizia was part of the Austro-Hungarian Empire, which ruled a heterogeneous population of Italian, Slovenian, and German origin. Vienna, its capital, though part of the empire, was the center of that cultural area known as Mitteleuropa. Gorizia, however, was culturally isolated, with only superficial ties to the capital. The inhabitants of Gorizia, "depositories of a rather mystical and provincial morality, extraneous to the active disenchantment of the people in Vienna, extraneous also to the cosmopolitism of Trieste," "perceived Gorizia as both a sort of happy island and at the same time as a cage that would shelter their dreams but from which it was necessary to escape."[2] In Gorizia, which counted at that time 4,825 inhabitants, the Jewish community consisted of 274. Its language was Italian; the citizenship, Austrian. The Jews of Gorizia had distinguished themselves by intellectual achievement and wealth, derived mainly from commerce.[3]

Alberto Michelstaedter at the time of Carlo's birth was a stockbroker. In 1900 he became an insurance agent and the owner of an exchange office. There is no record, however, of the religious habits of the family and it is fair to suppose that they were not worshipers. The cultural atmosphere in the house was rather liberal and great importance was placed on intellectual freedom. We know from Carlo's letters that he had no sympathy for any religious cult, let alone Judaism, which, in his opinion, often took the form of fanaticism. His antipathy toward Zionism, openly stated in his letters home, justifies the supposition that the rest of the family probably thought along the same lines.[4] The only interest Carlo had in Judaism was historical and philosophical, witnessed by his study of the Kabbala. It was prompted by his need to verify an idea that came from reading Schopenhauer and Nietzsche: that the Jewish mind lacked mysticism.

Michelstaedter's curiosity was aroused by the discovery of a Kabbalistic literature. His strong belief in intellectual freedom, not religion, was what he owed to the Jewish tradition. "The Jewish commitment is desecrating," wrote Fubini, "it is violation of myths, overturning of idols; it is iconoclasm. Freud, Einstein, Schönberg, Isaac Deutscher, each in his own field, are all iconoclasts. . . . And so is Wittgenstein with his theorization of doubt."[5] If these are characteristics of the Jewish mentality, then in this respect Michelstaedter can be considered part of it. Jewish culture, of course, was by no means the exclusive repository of such critical intellectual attitudes. They were, in fact, shared by a large segment of secular thinkers. Michelstaedter could have absorbed it from Leopardi or Socrates, both of whom he admired immensely. With the Middle European milieu, however, he shared the tragic sense of life, a common characteristic traceable from Nietzsche to Kafka that constituted the core of his philosophy.[6]

He was a self-proclaimed Italian, choosing Florence over Vienna to complete his study. Nonetheless he was not at home in the contemporary Italian philosophical climate, the neo-idealism noted earlier. For this rather optimistic philosophy, based on a trust in reason, he had no affinity.

Reader of Schopenhauer, Nietzsche, and later Tolstoy, Dostoyevski and Ibsen, and an enthusiast of Beethoven, Michelstaedter was intensely aware of living in a moment of crisis, the crisis of reason, and, as Pirandello also believed, of the myths created by reason.[7] Nothing escaped his ferocious criticism: the idealist myth of the absolute, the neopositivistic myths of science and progress, the religious myth of God. In short it was the myth of certainties that had collapsed. In 1905 Einstein published his theory of relativity. Freud in those years was already attempting to bring to the surface from the innermost parts of the psyche, the irrational—to reveal all its powerful force and to legitimize its presence. Schönberg, whose first work was published in 1899, upset standard harmonic rules with his twelve-tone system.

In a beautiful letter to his sister Paula who, like the Paolina of Leopardi, was also his confidante, Carlo made a sapient diagnosis of his times: "It is in part an individual condition, in part the illness of the age insofar as the moral balance is concerned, because we are at present living in an age in which changes in society seem to go hand in hand with a dissolution of all bonds . . . and the pathways of existence are no longer sharply drawn" (*Ep., 158*). He was only nineteen then, but had already analyzed a disease which was historical and for which there was no cure. He was aware of living in the era of God's death, as Nietzsche's Zarathustra had stated, and with the death of God, of the end of all absolutes and eternal truths, the end of all the myths created by man. Schopenhauer had opened the way; Nietzsche provided the accompaniment.

At this turning point in European philosophical thought, it is both significant and appropriate that the influence of its originators was strongly felt. While thoroughly attuned to the development of his own times, Michelstaedter was, beyond a doubt, influenced most profoundly by Greek thought, in particular that of the pre-Socratics. The Parmenidean dualism between being and becoming, as will be shown in Chapter 1, constituted the core of Michelstaedter's philosophy and also of his tragedy. The reality that we live is in constant change. Everything that lives, decays and dies. Being is eternal and immutable; thus it has no part in the world of man. So powerful was the presence of Greek thought in his life that Michelstaedter chose to write his dissertation on the concept of persuasion and rhetoric in Plato and Aristotle, and it is by this work that he is principally known.

Michelstaedter had become interested in the theme of rhetoric in 1908 while working on a term paper analyzing a translation of Cicero's *Pro Ligario*. He confided in a letter to his father, however, that the project made him realize he was not cut out for textual philology: "The only thing that interests me are the observations I could make on eloquence— and on 'persuasion' in general" (*Ep., 321*). His fascination with language and its various uses had begun in high school and grew as he studied various tongues. At nineteen he was reading works in Italian, German, French, Latin, and Greek.

Michelstaedter's dissertation, in examining the concepts of *persuasione* (persuasion) and *rettorica* (rhetoric) in Plato and Aristotle, gives them a very particular meaning; thus I refer to them in Italian in order to avoid the natural confusion that would derive from translating them into English. Rhetoric (*retorica* in Italian, generally spelled with one *t*) is the

discipline of organizing discourse. The word can assume various connotations. The chief goal of *retorica* since the time of the Sophists has
been *persuasione.* The rhetorician speaks in order to persuade and convince through the force of his arguments. *Retorica* and *persuasione,* thus,
go hand in hand. Not for Michelstaedter, however, who considered them
opposites; as embodiments of a Manichean dualism of evil and good. It
should be pointed out, however, that *persuasione* and *rettorica* (Michelstaedter's terms) are not two linguistic but two ontological entities. They
do not exclusively qualify our use of language, but also our way of
living; better, they qualify our language only insofar as language is
strictly connected with our life, insofar as it mirrors reality. In this,
Michelstaedter was undoubtedly a Greek thinker—but a Greek before
Aristotle for whom words correspond univocally to reality.

Rettorica for Michelstaedter signifies misused language, but also hypocrisy, lack of authenticity; that is, of correspondence between words
and actions. Such failures in mankind had their origin in language, and
as we will see, they began with Aristotle. Behavior conditioned by *rettorica* now characterizes society in all its aspects. Thus Michelstaedter
can speak of a *rettorica* of religion, of science, of education, of politics,
by which he means hypocrisy, falsehood, and corruption.

For Michelstaedter, *persuasione,* by contrast, is coherence, authenticity, consistency. It must not be confused with the practice of persuad-
ing others, of which the Sophists were masters. By *persuasione* he means
a perfect coherence between ideals and actions, as the result of an
individual's striving. Achieving *persuasione* is not an easy task and it is
one, as we shall see, that each individual must undertake alone.

Among the Greek philosophers Socrates had a special place in Michelstaedter's world. He was a real model of *persuasione:* he above all lived
his life in perfect harmony with his ideas, pursued truth, and pitted
himself against the *rettorica* of the Sophists, who misused words for the
sake of winning rhetorical contests. In the six *Appendici critiche* to the
dissertation, Michelstaedter examines the origin and growth of *rettorica*
in antiquity. This text (which, in fact, constituted a second dissertation)
has not received the scholarly attention it deserves. In the *Appendici* he
retraced, step by step, beginning with Parmenides, the process whereby
rettorica was born. The turning point was Plato's *Phaedrus* and *Republic,*
where the Greek philosopher attributed ontological status to concepts,

establishing once and for all the separation between knowledge and life (*Appendice* 2).

The detailed, philological analysis of the evolution of such a process in Aristotle, who wrote the first treatise specifically on rhetoric, is developed in *Appendici* 3, 4, and 5. Aristotle created a complete system of abstract nouns and concepts with no correspondent objects in reality. In *Appendice* 6, entitled *On Rhetoric and Dialectics,* Michelstaedter shows to what extreme Aristotle had arrived. "He let words suggest to him ideas, that is, his writing was not prompted by his thinking, but his thinking by his writing" (*Opere,* 302).

Philological analysis reveals the birth of *rettorica* in the *Appendici.* In *La persuasione e la rettorica,* Michelstaedter illustrates the subject with an anecdote: the amusing tale of Plato's air balloon, which he calls "A Historical Example." It was clearly chosen to balance out the example of the "weight" that he uses at the beginning of the work as a metaphor of man's contradictory essence. (We will examine it in detail in Chapter 1.) The nature of the weight, writes Michelstaedter, is to fall, but once it achieves its goal (falling), it also reaches its own end, stasis, and no longer exists as a weight. So it is with man. His essence is to strive constantly and unsuccessfully to achieve the absolute. If man could reach his goal he would cease to be. It is evident that man and the absolute cannot coexist. Paradoxically, in order to achieve the absolute, man must *be* no more. Only in death can his desire be fulfilled.

The story of the air balloon is a lighthearted counterpoint (at least initially) to the heavy logic of the argument of the weight. Socrates honestly and courageously accepted the consequences of the tragic law. He chose death to achieve the absolute. Plato, by contrast, attempted to defy the law of gravity without renouncing "his body," "his life."

> He meditated for a long time and finally invented his macrocosm. The main part of the strange machine was a large rigid globe made out of steel . . . which Plato filled with the Absolute. . . . With this miraculous system he would lift himself without losing his weight [together] with his disciples and reach the sun. (*Persuasione,* 110)

"The departure was joyful and full of hope," comments Michelstaedter. Up in the sky Plato lectured his pupils, explaining to them that whereas things with weight are down on earth, "we are here only because we have lightness." Actually, Plato continued, confusing his pupils even more, "precisely because we are here, we participate in this lightness" (111).

Michelstaedter's irony becomes heavier as it progresses. "Only with the contemplation of lightness, we who possess lightness can see and possess all things not as they appear on earth, but as they are in the kingdom of the sun" (112). The poor disciples were trying hard to see the things their teacher was talking about and did not have the courage to admit they could not see anything. Plato continued to describe the "forms" he was admiring. "Digging out of his memory the most hidden images and, adding to them his crazy fantasies, he nourished himself and the others with words" (112).

> Days, months, years passed—life did not change. . . . The inhabitants of Lightness and Plato himself were getting older; yet the kingdom of the sun was still far away and the reflected splendor of the machine filled with the Absolute gave them neither joy nor force, let alone eternal youth. (112–113)

The disciples had become discouraged and desperate. But one day one of them, more courageous and clever than the others, having learned Plato's logical arguments well, used them on him and managed to bring the balloon back to earth. There he continued to preach the words of his teacher, who had by then become too old and tired for the enterprise. That disciple was Aristotle, Michelstaedter concludes. Plato's system had been deflated like an air balloon. The way was clear for Aristotle to build his own construction, this time on earth, but just as abstract.

Michelstaedter's major text, *La persuasione e la rettorica,* though based on the Greeks, mainly on Plato and Aristotle, takes a personal turn from the very start. In the epigraph to the Preface, he quotes from Sophocles's *Electra,* "I know I am doing untimely and unbecoming things." From the start he takes the role of the antagonist. Yet it is the same role played by those who, in his mind, have throughout history spoken the truth: Parmenides, Heraclitus, Empedocles, Socrates, the author of Ecclesiastes, Christ, Aeschylus, Sophocles, Simonides, Petrarch, Leopardi, Ibsen, Beethoven. Truth is one, eternal, unchangeable. Michelstaedter does not pretend to say anything new. He only wonders how the world has continued after the truth had been spoken, a truth of misery and sorrow. At the onset, he states his pessimistic view of the world and rejects any faith in human progress.

The prophets spoke the truth, but their followers warped and falsified it. He is only repeating a message as old as mankind, trying once more to restore meanings to words. His dissertation, therefore, has a double aim: to denounce the corruption of language, whereby men talk but do not say anything, tracing it back to its origin in Aristotle. He further wishes to show that the corruption of language engendered a process of deterioration of society. He reiterates the painful truth that life is a contradiction in terms: as Leopardi had already explained, it consists in a never-satisfied will. It is a constant tension toward a future that never comes. Men, in fact, do not live in the present, but only in the nonexistent future; thus they do not live. Their so-called life is a race toward death.

In Michelstaedter's elaboration of the concept of *persuasione* we can hear the voice of another philosopher: Arthur Schopenhauer. The Parmenidean opposition of being and becoming is, in fact, coupled with Schopenhauer's idea of suffering that constitutes the only real essence of living beings. For Schopenhauer, as for Leopardi, will is what constitutes the essence of human life. Will presents itself as a constant tension, as a search for what man lacks. "The relationship between human beings is characterized by the effort to satisfy through every other, a desire for that which each lacks; therefore it always is a relationship of exploitation and violence."[8] The will is never satisfied; if it were satisfied, it would cease to be the will, and man's life would cease too. Man lives in a constant state of want; this is his contradictory essence.

Michelstaedter, however, was not satisfied with the diagnosis; he strove constantly against the absurd logic that rules the world. Schopenhauer recognized the primacy of will over intellect and accepted it. Michelstaedter did not, or at least strove with all his energy to achieve the absurd—absurd because impossible—identification of will and intellect. He struggled to achieve a freedom from dependence on outside reality. He strove for the coincidence "of existence and meaning," to use Gianni Vattimo's effective expression, that is, for *persuasione*, for self-sufficiency and autonomy.[9] It was only a utopia for Michelstaedter, who wrote, echoing Nietzsche's Zarathustra, that autonomy is a condition which exists only "in the island of the blessed souls" (*Persuasione*, 42). Man by his very nature cannot obtain it in his life. The only thing he can do is "to assume without reservations the suffering which is a necessary condition of existence."[10] This is also the position advocated by Schopenhauer. But Michelstaedter took it to its extreme, to the point of self-destruction.

Michelstaedter's concern with death, his tragic sense of life, his awareness that mankind was approaching its end and finally his suicide make him into the conscience of his time and the prophet of the world tragedy that was about to explode and that was eventually to take so many, together with his loved ones, to their horrifying end in the Nazi concentration camps. Carlo's mother, Emma Luzzatto, was deported to Auschwitz in 1943, at the age of 89, where she died along with her older daughter Elda and Carlo's beloved Argia Cassini. Of the Michelstaedter family only his sister Paula survived the Second World War and it is to her that we owe what is left of her brother's writings.

In the same year in which he wrote his dissertation Michelstaedter composed *Il dialogo della salute* (*The Dialogue on Health*) and many poems.[11] He had begun writing poems as early as 1905 when he graduated from high school (*liceo*), and he had started to jot down his thoughts. His notes are extremely valuable in understanding the evolution of his personality and philosophy. But above all he left two hundred letters that, thanks to Sergio Campailla, are now available in a critical edition. Michelstaedter's directness and outspokenness make them documents of great value. They also make extremely enjoyable reading, as Michelstaedter—strange as it may seem—was endowed with a strong sense of humor and a gift for the dramatic and for caricature.

Writing in all these various forms did not suffice as a means of expression. His graphic art, up to now almost completely ignored by scholars, complemented and extended the written word. Campailla's outstanding publication[12]—the one exception to the general lack of interest—documents a large selection of his more important works. Hundreds of his drawings, now collected in the Civic Library of Gorizia in the Fondo Carlo Michelstaedter, are important because they anticipate Expressionism, but above all because they reveal, more effectively than do his writings, the core of his philosophy.

Michelstaedter's philosophical works will be examined in Chapter 1, his poetry in Chapter 2, and his graphic art in Chapter 3. This division reflects a teleological approach to his production. He strove all his life to achieve *persuasione,* in order to find authentic language to express his message of truth. He discovered that the language of philosophy could not do it. The abstract, abused words of theoretical systems were dead bodies without souls. He could not find correspondence between them and what they should have signified. It was the language of hypocrisy. Poetry, instead, strove for the synthetic image; the image that does not explain, but evokes; the image that does not claim the assent of theoretical reason, but hopes for that of feelings, through which truth can often speak with a more effective voice. Michelstaedter wrote his poems, too, little thinking of publishing them, probably knowing that his language was still caught up in the elaborate, abstract meanings of philosophy. We don't know how he judged his poetry, but considering his great admiration for Leopardi and his recurrent use of images and even lines taken from Leopardi's poems, dissatisfaction with his own verse is not an unlikely hypothesis.

Poetry, after all, still deals with words. It was in drawing that Michelstaedter was to find his authentic form of expression, the means by which he could finally defeat *rettorica.* With pencil or black chalk, the simplest of tools, he could try to catch the fleeting spark of the soul and with rapid strokes fix it on paper. All of his drawings, in fact, are portraits. His interest is the face and his challenge, the eyes. Between the subject portrayed and the beholder there is no longer any rhetorical mediation. The eyes are the receiver of a message that speaks with the authentic voice of *persuasione.*

SCHOLARSHIP

We cannot judge a thing in itself, but only the impressions that it produces upon us, because the outside world comes to our knowledge in no other way but by means of impressions produced through our senses. . . . Now senses are a completely individual thing. So we can see that already the prime matter of judgment differs in each individual. To that we must add the

different intellective faculty and it follows
that every judgment is subjective and that
there exists only a relative and individual
truth.—Carlo Michelstaedter[13]

EXISTENTIALISM

It was perhaps the mounting wave of existentialism in the 1940s and
1950s that revived interest in Michelstaedter. The cultural climate that
had buried Croce and philosophical systems, that had brought the unconscious to the surface, that had stated the relativism of everything and
had sanctioned the death of God, was now right for Michelstaedter. It
started with Teodorico Moretti Costanzi's 1943 article, "Un esistenzialista ante litteram: Carlo Michelstaedter," which pointed out similarities
between his writings and Kierkegaard's.[14] With Kierkegaard, whom he
may have known through Ibsen, Michelstaedter shared the belief in the
essential contradiction of existence. To exist is to negate oneself as being.
It was the Parmenidean heritage that drew Michelstaedter to something
like existentialism. Of course, there is a basic difference between the two
thinkers. Kierkegaard gave his philosophical discourse a religious dimen-
sion that is totally absent in Michelstaedter's. It is the sin against God for
Kierkegaard that constitutes the negativity of existence.

Soon after, Giuseppe Catalfamo developed further the idea of Michelstaedter as existentialist. Every existence negates essence, and thus negates *persuasione*. "To exist is therefore to contradict oneself, is to live in
the inherent contradiction of life." "The individual wants to be and,
instead, he becomes."[15] On such a premise, however, Michelstaedter can
be called preexistentialist, just as we could call "preexistentialist" Parmenides, the Sophists, Leopardi, Pirandello, and many others.

Catalfamo sees also in the concept of suffering an analogy with the
existential *Angst,* although Michelstaedter was probably indebted to
Schopenhauer for that. If *Angst* is the experience of nothingness, if it
represents the reaction of the individual before this discovery, then in
Michelstaedter it often presents itself as "nausea." The word *nausea*
recurs three times in the *Epistolario* (*Letters,* 360, 394, 408), and twice
in his last poems (*Poesie,* 94, 97). In the *Epistolario* it always appears
in letters to one of his dear friends, Rico; in each instance, nausea refers
to Carlo's condition. Rico was for Carlo a model of *persuasione,* an

example to follow, a Socratic figure. The fourth time, in fact, that the word *nausea* appears, it is uttered by Rico/Socrates in *Il dialogo della salute.* Rico, however, uses it in an ethical rather than ontological sense, to express his disgust for his being so low, that is, for his remaining on an existential level, for his being forever caught in the realm of becoming, for his inability to "consistere" (to persist, to remain faithful to himself). That Michelstaedter could not precisely diagnose his feeling is not hard to understand; after all, it took Sartre's Roquentin one hundred pages of self-analysis to arrive at the understanding of his own nausea.[16]

The feeling of nausea is connected in Michelstaedter, as in many existentialists, with the feeling of inertia. "Inertia" is even more frequently used than "nausea" in the last part of the *Epistolario*. It is the state into which he had sunk in the last year of his life. His incapacity to act, his inertia, and his nausea were connected with the writing of his dissertation, with his longer periods of reflection and the complete absence of action. To Rico, the *persuaso,* Carlo writes in December 1909: "While in this period you have acted so as to conquer inertia which is the enemy of everything, I am still always as you left me" (*Ep.,* 425).[17] If Michelstaedter is far from the transcendent conclusion of Kierkegaard he is close, nonetheless, to Heidegger's dialectics of being and nothing. "For both, in fact the affirmation of nothingness is an act of existence, is the full comprehension of being and at the same time, it is the position of freedom, as it persuades us of the irrelevance of the word as such."[18]

Ioachim Ranke, in his clear analysis of Michelstaedter's "existentialism," for the first time pointed out the main difference between Michelstaedter and Heidegger. Michelstaedter's ethical discourse, on which the ontological search is based and on which it depends, is totally absent in Heidegger, who makes clear that his interpretation "has a purely ontological aim and that it has absolutely nothing to do with a moralizing criticism of existence."[19] It is, in my view, this ethical aspect that makes Michelstaedter a disciple of Greek thought as well as of Leopardi. His adamant refusal to separate *to ón* (being) from *to agathón* (the highest good) derives from Plato's identification of knowledge and virtue.

Ranke well saw the individualistic quality of Michelstaedter's philosophy. The subject is the creator of his destiny. No social institution can help him in his search for authenticity. Each man is alone in the world and must create his life on his own. In this position, Carlo was influenced by Leopardi as well as by Max Stirner's *Der Einzige und sein Eigentum* (*The Ego and His Own*), a text that he quoted at length in one of his letters (*Ep.*, 202).

The similarity with existentialist thought was also pointed out by Giorgio Brianese in an essay where he returns to Ranke's distinction between Michelstaedter's ethics and Heidegger's ontology. Brianese speaks of a "theoretical" rather than "philosophical" affinity between the two that derives from their common philosophical background: the study of the Greeks, of Schopenhauer, and of Nietzsche.[20] Chronology makes it impossible for Michelstaedter to have known Heidegger's work, and it is unlikely that the latter would have known or been influenced by the posthumous publication of the former's work. Yet Heidegger's categories of authenticity and inauthenticity have more than an echo in Michelstaedter's *persuasione* and *rettorica*. "*Dasein* is characterized by incompleteness which can never lack, or *Dasein* would cease to be what it is. Likewise the man of *rettorica* constantly lacks self-possession. Were he to possess it, he would cease to be the man of rettorica and become the *persuaso*."[21]

How much of Heidegger we can find in Michelstaedter is of little interest to us. Existentialism is fortunately the loosest of the "isms." It can easily be applied to thinkers of various schools of thought, because it describes a mental attitude rather than a philosophical system. It opposes the idea of "a school of thought" as such, the compartmentalization of knowledge, the easy optimism about the existence of truths and the certainty of finding them. It is the humble attitude of the responsible individual who is aware of his limits and of the limits of his own constructions. Yet it is at this point that Michelstaedter tries to distance himself from existentialism (of course without being aware of it), in his refusal to accept, in his decision to fight. It is his conscious, useless fight that sets him apart from the other thinkers of the time. Michelstaedter knows that his battle is in vain, yet it is a categorical imperative from which the real *persuaso* can never dissociate himself. If the essence of life is contradictory it is a logical consequence that man's life should pursue a contradictory aim. Reaching the absolute thus necessarily coincides with self-negation and self-destruction.

SOCIAL CRITICISM

If the silence that surrounded Michelstaedter's death was caused by the Crocean cultural monopoly that could not fit him into any of the well-delimited intellectual categories—as he bridged them all—silence or misunderstanding were to surround him even when the cultural leadership passed into the hands of the left. Michelstaedter's lack of political engagement was a cause of suspicion to the followers of the philosopher Antonio Gramsci whose aim was the creation of a popular culture and the bridging of the gap between the intellectuals and the masses. Even Carlo Cattaneo, who otherwise understood Michelstaedter's thought, in an article with the telling title "La rivolta impossibile," ends up accusing him of an inability to understand his own times.[22] Cattaneo's criticisms were based on Michelstaedter's refusing to become politically involved or to act in the name of a social change—for the very sound reason that he did not believe in change. It was hard for Cattaneo to accept the weight of nihilistic and self-destructive thought. As a result he charged Michelstaedter with a lack of understanding. The failure to understand was Cattaneo's.

Only since the 1960s has the attitude of Marxist criticism changed. Muzzioli, in a very interesting essay, echoing Gianni Vattimo, claims that the lesson of the Frankfurt School helped to revise Marxist theory, allowing a more open critical discussion of Michelstaedter's work.[23] According to critics like Benussi, Abbruzzese, Cerruti, and Luperini, Michelstaedter's lack of political involvement does not lessen the positive contribution of his detailed and lucid criticism of bourgeois ideology.[24] Up to this point agreement is easy. What should be avoided, however, is the temptation to see him as "anticipating . . . themes of . . . the so-called Western Marxism."[25]

It should not be forgotten, in fact, that Michelstaedter's thought was extremely individualistic, inspired by a total mistrust of any type of social institution. His bitter criticism against contemporary society, against capitalism and technology, cannot be seen in Marxist terms. He did not leave any political manifestos. Instead, like Leopardi, he was suspicious of all politics and believed that the only revolution man could hope to accomplish must be individual, on his own. In this respect he is again much closer

to Max Stirner than to Karl Marx. As did Stirner, he attacked all systematic philosophies, placed the individual alone at the center of his
vision of the world, and had no faith in either human or natural law.[26]

The pages of his dissertation that lend themselves to a socialist reading are those in the section entitled "La rettorica nella vita" ("The
Rhetoric in Life") and in particular the chapter "La sicurezza" ("Security").
Here Michelstaedter equates work with "violence against nature" and
property with "violence against man." In the description that follows of
the process whereby man becomes a *thing* and is used by another man,
the emphasis is all on human aggressiveness, egoism, abuse. Michelstaedter sees men as being, as Hobbes had said and Leopardi repeated,
hostile to each other even before any type of society is created. It is
precisely the fear of the other that forces men to build this hypocritical
creation that is society, whereby men suppress their urge to overcome the
other in exchange for the promise that they themselves shall not be
overcome. "Each one has seen in the other only the *thing* that is necessary
to him, not the man who must live his own life. . . . But the exchange
that is convenient to both made them safe, though without any reciprocal
affection" (*Persuasione,* 150). Once more Carlo's language is here much
closer to Leopardi's and Stirner's than to Marx's.

Even the so-called altruist, Michelstaedter claims, is selfish. He does
the good of the other in order to satisfy his own desires. There is an
extremely pessimistic page, still unpublished, that is worth quoting in its
entirety. Its force of conviction requires no comment:

> He who has more love for himself than for others . . . thinks of his
> own well-being just as the other. But the world calls the former good
> and the latter selfish and wicked. In my opinion they are both selfish
> because they act to please their will. (It can actually be said, in fact, that
> all our life is not but the fruit of egoism, as it is impossible to imagine
> an act that is not performed in accord with one's will.) As in regard to
> the question who is the better one, I lack the criterion to say it (and
> even if one were worse than the other, he would not be responsible . . .).
> The selfish world follows this criterion: that he who does me good is
> good, he who does not or damages me is wicked. Thus it can be stated
> that the conscience of good and evil is born out of egoism.[27]

Yet the critics who insist on finding in his works a socialistic concern ignore pages like this and look for the few that suit them best. Even his study of part of Marx's *Capital* and the few notes on it he left have been cited as proof of his convictions—as if only Marxists studied Marx's major work.[28]

The short essay "Discorso al popolo" ("Oration to the People") could give the impression of being a socialist revolutionary piece. Michelstaedter wrote it after having read about the following episode in a newspaper. A crowd of workers who protest against a social injustice are distracted by a plane that flies over their heads. They applaud the sign of human progress. Carlo imagines himself present and criticizes this applause. He is then beaten by the workers. The oration to the people begins at this point. Although his words are animated by a spirit of solidarity, Carlo cannot establish a real contact with them. He is the intellectual who must open the closed minds of the masses.

This crowd does not appear to be very different from "that big beast . . . with its stupid and ferocious face" he had described in a letter to his friend Rico a few months before (*Ep.,* 394). He treats them with paternalism in order to teach them that what they cheer as progress is nothing but yet another weapon the bourgeoisie has invented against them. It is the hypocrisy of the bourgeois power that the people must demystify in order to free themselves from their chains.

Carlo's oration concludes with a vision of a future that is more anarchic than socialist. When all the people will have succeeded in unmasking the hypocrisy of the bourgeoisie,

> then you will be invincible, then this vain edifice of bourgeois power will collapse . . . and the world will be ruled by "man," the working man, the man who is healthy in body and mind, the man who will need neither unjust nor complicated laws nor weapons . . . but his faith, his common work and the closeness of brotherly love will be his law and defense. (*Opere,* 671)

The Christian utopian tone of this conclusion is all too obvious. The people he is addressing are the creation of his Chaplinesque fantasy.

The following year Michelstaedter wrote in his notes a few pages that would later constitute the core of *La persuasione e la rettorica.* His ideas about political as well as philosophical revolution could not have been stated more clearly and assertively:

> Every new philosophy is like a revolution that assigns an unjust power in the name of justice, in order to end up installing another one just as unjust. Indeed every power is in itself, for the simple fact that it is a power, unjust and impotent. Every value stated as an absolute value is an abuse of power, and whoever trusts himself in it and attributes to it what is instead his own duty remains forever an invalid. But everyone must create by himself the revolution, must create his own self by himself if he wants to achieve the real life. The only thing that is worthy is individual value. (*Opere,* 700)

Michelstaedter's individualism has by now acquired a Nietzschean component:

> *Persuasione* is the realization of the *Übermensch.* The road to health is not approachable by everyone, has no signs or indications that can be passed around, studied, repeated; but each one has in himself the need to find it . . . each one must again open by himself the road and then he will find himself on the same luminous path that the few chosen ones have undertaken. (700)

These same words will resound with new dramatic power in the pages of Michelstaedter's dissertation.

Chapter 1

THE FAILURE OF PHILOSOPHY

What a disappointment that Epicurus, the
sage I most need, should have written
over 300 treatises. And what a relief that
they are lost!—Emile Cioran[1]

"Philosophy," Michelstaedter writes, "is the path toward the absolute;
the progressive liberation from contingency." The real philosophers are
those who answer man's question "how must I live" (*Opere*, 843).
Michelstaedter thus puts his cards on the table right away. The philosophy he is concerned with is ethics, not ontology. From the start he
proclaims the absurdity of any philosophical system as such that pretends to give answers, to show the truth, to know the meaning of life. He
attacks all past philosophies and philosophers, sparing only Socrates.
The division of philosophy into different branches, which began with
Plato and was well established by Aristotle, is to his mind artificial
nonsense and is the harmful consequence of the separation between
words and things initiated by Plato. The only truth man can discover is
that life is suffering, because it has no meaning.

Michelstaedter's philosophical writing took place in 1910, the last
year of his life. In that year he wrote *La persuasione e la rettorica* (with
extensive *Appendici*) and *Il dialogo della salute,* a Platonic, or better
Socratic, dialogue in which Leopardi's presence can also be felt. Other
writings, mostly dating from the last two years of his life, were collected
as *Scritti vari* (*Various Writings*), and they include many strictly philo-

sophical themes, most of them taken up and developed in his major text.[2] Chiavacci's 1958 edition lists them in a table of contents in two sections: "A: Notes, sketches, dialogues, literary pieces; B: Notes for systematic topics." The separation seems somewhat artificial, as the writings do not differ enough to justify this distinction. Furthermore, Michelstaedter would never have accepted the title given to section B, opposed as he was to systems of any kind. He would have probably preferred a title like *Zibaldone di pensieri*. These notes share with Leopardi's not only similar content and similar views about human nature, society, and life in general, but often even the apodictic tone of many of the romantic poet's late *Pensieri*. Neither of them would ever have written a treatise of any sort, for neither believed in systematic construction of knowledge.

If we now turn to *La persuasione e la rettorica*, Michelstaedter's published dissertation, we immediately notice that the real scholarly work implied by the original dissertation title, *I concetti* [concepts] *di persuasione e rettorica in Platone e Aristotele*, is not there, or is there only marginally. Most of the scholarly work is in his *Appendici*, which he wrote as a separate corpus. They developed individual themes that Michelstaedter had barely touched upon in his dissertation. They could be considered as a very extensive and detailed apparatus of footnotes. The text itself is quite different from a scholarly dissertation. Plato and Aristotle are present only to be put on trial, and their ideas are measured against Michelstaedter's own.

The *Appendici*, however, are of great interest because they clearly show that Michelstaedter's involvement with ethical and metaphysical issues had its origin in his obsession with language—an obsession that found an outlet in his rigorous study of Greek and Latin as well as of German and French. His constant analysis and comparison of languages, and especially his involvement with Greek, made him aware of the falsifications that man through words performs on life. As Campailla pointed out in his edition of *La persuasione e la rettorica*, reflection on classical philology and Greco-Roman culture produced "the most radical and revolutionary speculative positions at the beginning of this century." Not only Nietzsche but also Heidegger arrived at their innovations starting with the Greeks.

"Con le parole guerra alle parole" is the epigraph placed at the beginning of the *Appendici* (*Opere,* 142). It states Michelstaedter's resolution to "give back to words their original meanings." His use of Greek is "an attempt to return to the wisdom of the Ancients." As Campailla puts it, Michelstaedter "does not quote from Greek; he speaks in Greek" (*Persuasione,* 17). The use of Greek is prompted by his need to recapture the authentic meanings that words originally had.[3]

GREEK THOUGHT

In the list of the few *persuasi* in history Christ and Socrates occupy a place of honor, as they alone did not entrust their thought to the written word. "The only power of words is that of the philosopher's live word. . . . Every written thing arbitrarily fixes concepts, whereas only in the meeting of two individuals is the individual value born and established" (*Opere,* 263). It is a very Socratic argument that Michelstaedter uses to attack writing. Socrates had often declared that the written word could not answer his questions. It would lie there, lifeless, fixed and mute forever. The result: ambiguity, misunderstanding, falsehood. Socrates's interlocutor, on the other hand, could always be asked to explain or to express in different words the misunderstood statement. Only from this human exchange would true communication result.

In *Phaedrus* Socrates had said to Phaedrus: "if you, wanting to learn, ask [the written words] to tell you something of what they say, they will show you only one thing and always the same." And this is no sign of certainty and consistency of meaning, as one might think. On the contrary, the written discourse can be used and abused, for it is in "constant need of the father who could defend it, as by itself it can neither defend nor help itself."[4] Following this logic, King Thamus refuses the gift of writing presented to him by Theuth. In offering King Thamus his gift, Theuth pointed out that it would greatly help men's memory and knowledge. The king's reply brings out the ambiguous nature of writing, and leads the critic Derrida to a new reading of the *Phaedrus.* Replying to Theuth, Thamus says:

> You have just exposed precisely the contrary of its [writing's] real effect. Because it will generate oblivion in the minds of those who will

learn it: they will cease to exercise their memory because, trusting the written word, they will not try to call things back to explore their inner meanings. What you offer your pupils is not knowledge, but only the appearance of it.[5]

It is precisely this paradoxical nature of language as writing that is here denounced. Born in order to help communication and knowledge, writing will slowly defeat its own purpose, distancing itself more and more from men. It is precisely this criticism that Michelstaedter presents in the writing of his *Rettorica*.

Analyzing the *Phaedrus* closely, Derrida showed, however, that "Plato's text fails to achieve what its arguments expressly require, the priority of speech, *logos,* and presence over writing."[6] After all Plato needs writing to prove his point, and from writing he draws the metaphors denouncing writing itself. If, following Derrida, it can be said that writing is both cure and poison (*pharmakon*), both "a threat to the living presence of authentic language" and "an indispensable means for anyone who wants to record, transmit, or somehow commemorate that presence,"[7] we must conclude that Michelstaedter saw this ambivalence inherent in language as it evolves: it is the ambivalence of *rettorica;* it is the ambivalence of his own text.

In the course of Michelstaedter's study the concepts of *persuasione* and *rettorica* became an obsession. Leaving Plato and Aristotle behind, he made *persuasione* and *rettorica* two aspects of the basic dichotomy of life versus thought. The very discussion of it is self-defeating; *persuasione,* from the start, is impossible to define with linguistic categories, because it is the very opposite of *rettorica.* It is life, authenticity, self-possession, self-determination. *Rettorica* is the other side of the same coin.

The time Michelstaedter longs for is the time of "naive" expression, to borrow Schiller's use of the word, when man and the world were only one thing and when no distinction existed between names and the things named. Then Heraclitus taught that names are not something accidental, or conventional, but express the *étumos,* that is, the real nature of things. Then no distinction existed between the reality-truth seen out there and the reality-truth spoken of. No distinction existed among ontology, logic, and language. As Gabriele Giannantoni put it:

Every mental content, every vision [was] expressed through a *logos*
(which originally indicated both the "discourse" that expresses a thought
and the "thought" expressed in that discourse) and it was expressed in
it in a univocal and adequate manner. . . . The linguistic sign was the
sign of this Reality-Truth. . . . That which cannot be expressed is
neither thinkable nor real, just as that which is not real is neither
thinkable nor expressible.[8]

Although Parmenides and Socrates are two powerful and positive
presences in Michelstaedter's writings, and although he has been called a
neo-Parmenidean by some recent critics, Michelstaedter was probably
just as strongly influenced by Heraclitus as by Parmenides. The axiom
"Nothing exists in itself, but only in relation to a conscience" (*Persuasione*, 45) is a statement of Michelstaedter's relativism with a clear
Heraclitean origin. Heraclitus's influence is in fact far wider than it may
at first appear.

The discovery that the essence of the world is the unity of opposites is
well exemplified by Heraclitus's fragment concerning the bow whose
name is life (*bios*) and whose action is death. An object thus is named life
but causes death. If the link between names and things is not accidental,
if names do express the *étumos* of things, then this fragment proves that
the opposition is inherent and essential in the thing itself. It is no coincidence, in fact, that Michelstaedter used the image of the bow as a metaphor of the *persuaso*. It well represents, as Brianese noted, the reciprocal
necessity of the incompatible and opposite terms *persuasione* and *rettorica*.[9] It is as evident that Michelstaedter chose the image of the bow
with Heraclitus in mind, as that Derrida had Heraclitus in mind when he
interpreted writing as creation and destruction.

Opposition is the essence of the world: from it things are born and
through it they are destroyed. Thus Heraclitus can say that "life is death
and death is life" because everything transforms itself into its opposite.[10]
The echo of this philosophy will resound even in Michelstaedter's poem
"Il canto delle crisalidi" ("The Song of the Chrysalides"), where he will
make the contradictory essence of life a recurrent and obsessive theme.
Quintessentially Heraclitean is the recurrent image of the flame. Though
common to Eastern thought—and Michelstaedter knew and admired
Buddhist philosophy—it was for the Greek philosopher the principle and

the origin of all things. Fire created everything but fire is also "the translation on the visible level, of that opposition . . . which is the law of thought and of spoken reality."[11] To become fire, to make the self into a flame, is in fact, as we will see, Michelstaedter's obsession.

Parmenides has been considered the diametric opposite of Heraclitus, the latter being (to simplify enormously) the philosopher of "becoming," of flux and change; the former, the philosopher of the *ón*, the *ousía*, of permanence. The two positions, however, can be seen as two aspects of the same reality. When Heraclitus was discovering that opposition is the law of nature, when he was identifying life with death, because each transforms itself into the other, he was looking at what we call reality, the world that surrounds us, the matter that made us and of which we are made. His was the world of "becoming." Parmenides, who wrote not long after Heraclitus, from his opposed perspective, accepted the world we live in as the realm of "becoming," and stated that since "becoming" implies change, and thus nonbeing, "being" must necessarily be a single entity, immobile, with no origin and no end. Furthermore, nothing can be said of it. No attribute can be given to it, for with any "*is* something," we imply an "*is not* something else." In the immutable world of "being," discourse is not possible. Thus nothing can be said about the Parmenidean *ón*. Such an apparently outrageous statement must be considered within the framework of archaic Greek thought which, as with Heraclitus, did not distinguish being as *ón* (essence) from being as predicate. This confusion derived from the belief in the identity of the worlds of thought and language.

Parmenides had thus established for Michelstaedter the identity of *persuasione* and truth. The goddess had disclosed to him the road to being that coincided with truth and persuasion. "What is not," Parmenides had said, "is unknown . . . neither could you ever know it, nor could you express it."[12] The troublesome Fragment 8, for which we follow Guido Calogero's translation, states the identity of ontology, logic, and language: "But to think and thinking that something is are the same thing; you will never find thinking without the *is* in which it is expressed."[13] Outside the verb *to be,* no thought is possible, therefore the only reality we can really express and think of is that of which we can only say "that it is."

In his preface to *La persuasione e la rettorica* Sergio Campailla openly

speaks of Michelstaedter's philosophy as a return to Parmenides. "Living
. . . is a contradiction in terms," for living is will and the will is destined
to be frustrated, never to be fulfilled. Hence "the incompatibility between
being and becoming" (18, 19). Michelstaedter was undoubtedly limited
by this dichotomy. Many pages of his notes are devoted to this very issue,
and he clearly connects this Parmenidean being that is never born (because
eternal, absolute, and has no attributes) with his own idea of being and
with man's desire for it. In these pages the absolute is made to coincide
with *persuasione*. In one we can actually read "essere = peithó." A few
pages later, among various rewritings and deletions, Michelstaedter identifies *persuasione* with silence. "He who is persuaded is silent because he
has no 'motive' to speak."[14] He has complete self-possession. Language,
therefore, seems to coincide with *rettorica*. *Persuasione* seems not to
belong to men.

Not long ago the philosopher Emanuele Severino argued that Michelstaedter's was not an authentic return to Parmenides but a misreading.
Michelstaedter, claims Severino, wants "being" to be immortal, eternal,
one, perfect, absolute, thus transforming the eternity and immutability
of "being" into something wanted, willed. He can therefore speak of the
real *persuaso,* that is, of the individual who wants and obtains perfection. For Parmenides "being" exists a priori. "In Michelstaedter's thought,"
writes Brianese, following Severino, "the immutability of being is willed
not demonstrated." Michelstaedter cannot therefore be considered a real
Parmenidean.[15]

Francesco Fratta contested Severino's and Brianese's interpretations as
narrow-minded. To him Michelstaedter took Parmenides' statements
more loosely than the other two scholars thought he did. According to
Fratta, Michelstaedter could not accept a theoretical absolute, that is, an
absolute which is apprehended through *noũs,* which is grasped intellectually. For Michelstaedter the absolute is not knowable but can only be
lived. Fratta, therefore, argues that Michelstaedter changes the characteristics of this absolute to suit his own theory. Fratta's position is thus
not so far from the one he attacks. Both interpretations recognize the
presence of a heterodox reading of Parmenides owing to Michelstaedter's
strong ethical needs. Their difference consists only in Fratta's praise of
such misreading and his placing it in the context of Michelstaedter's
practical philosophy. What should always be kept in mind is that Michel-

staedter's philosophy is not theoretical but practical. Its aim is to live the life of *persuasione,* not to *know* it. The problem of being, of *persuasione,* in his view, cannot be considered a theoretical problem, but must remain an ethical one.[16]

To conclude, Michelstaedter can be called "Parmenidean" only insofar as he wanted life and thought to coincide; this is what he called *persuasione.* What both interpretations missed, however, is his explicit admission that will and being (*boulé* and *ousía*) are opposite terms. Contrary to Severino's and Brianese's beliefs, Michelstaedter knew very well that "I cannot define *ousía* in any other way than by negating all the attributes of the will. . . . And even if all my individuality points toward the absolute, I am always the negation of the absolute 'insofar as I want it'" (*Opere,* 803). The will to the absolute is reduced to the negation of the self, to *arghía.* And *arghía* is peace, is death.

It is therefore legitimate to affirm that Michelstaedter was "Parmenidean" insofar as he was "Heraclitean"; that is, he needed to believe in an immutable being because he was trapped in the world of becoming. This view is well demonstrated by a single illuminating sentence at the beginning of the section "The Illusion of Persuasion": "Life would be one, immobile, shapeless, if it could 'consist' in one point" (*Persuasione,* 43). This blatantly Parmenidean statement is actually at the same time a Heraclitean statement; the "if" clause openly undermines the Parmenidean quality of it. Life is not immobile, one, shapeless; it is variegated and changeable.

If Parmenides had established the unity of truth and *persuasione,* the Sophists destroyed that unity a century later and introduced relativism. Protagoras had written: "About the gods I am not able to know either that they are, or that they are not, or what they look like; many things prevent me from knowing it: the obscurity of the issue, and the brevity of human life."[17] Thus it is useless to speculate on it, man should concern himself with what is within his range. Things cannot be known for what they are in themselves, but only as they appear to us. Consequently, man becomes "the measure of everything" as Protagoras wrote in his first fragment.[18] Nobody can speak the truth; what appears true to one person may not to another. In the *Thaetetus* Plato has Protagoras defend his position against Socrates, who cannot accept relativism. For the former, true *persuasione* was separate from truth and pursued for itself.

The task of the Sophist, therefore, consisted in convincing not by means of an unknown "truth," but through persuasion. The *lógos* acquired then a divine status. It became capable of persuasion, thus of affecting men's minds and lives.

Socrates was in the vanguard of the fight against the Sophists. In contrast to their rhetoric, which gave the appearance of truth to that which was not true, Socrates' famous question *"Tí estí"* sought the essence of the thing, devoid of any subjective view, or individual interest. What is it? What is that which makes a thing be what it is? The constant, immutable element, the reason of being and of its being known. This was Socrates' only concern. Many of Plato's dialogues present him as the interlocutor of various famous Sophists. Socrates fought against persuasion devoid of truth as against a form of vile deception. Only truth can persuade, and the real pedagogue must be concerned with truth more than with a victorious argument. The Sophists were dangerous pedagogues who brought their pupils away from the path of knowledge and morality. Socrates' battle against the Sophists aimed at reestablishing the unity between truth and persuasion, between knowledge and ethics. The Sophistic rhetoric founded on a *makròs lógos,* a long continuous discourse, had as its end persuasion, not truth. The long, elaborate discourse by its very nature could deaden the listeners' critical capabilities and prevent them from questioning and asking for clarification. The rhetorical structure of the discourse, the richness of its images, would conquer and convince the listener, not the force of its truth. Socrates' *dialégesthai,* on the other hand, consisted in questioning and answering, accompanied by the constant verification of the interlocutor's understanding. His goal, or better their goal, was truth. Hence his polemic against the written discourse, which cannot answer a question. His *tí esti* was an authentic question that demanded an immediate and a precise answer. Truth cannot be imposed on men from above; it is they who must search for and discover it. The Socratic method would in fact lead men to their own discoveries. *Dialégesthai* was Socrates' moral imperative. His death was the ultimate test of his absolute faith in it. Socrates' theoretical and ethical goals coincide; his life was the enactment of his theory. He was a real *persuaso.*

The unity between being and life which Parmenides had advocated, that the Sophists had challenged, and Socrates had reestablished, was definitively destroyed by Plato, or so claims Michelstaedter. "When Socrates was asking *tí esti,* was asking for the value in itself, persuasive, free, good, useful . . . he freed the concept from the finite content given it by men and good only for their particular insufficient lives, and he was asking for the rational, absolute value" (*Opere,* 151). If such an answer was not obtained, the various concepts could then be dismissed as mere names empty of any meaning. This, according to Michelstaedter, was the Socrates of the early dialogues. Yet, as Plato developed his thought he slowly moved farther and farther away from his teacher's moral philosophy, developing in two directions: on the ethical level in the *Republic* and on the theoretical in the *Parmenides* and in the *Sophist.*

In the *Republic,* Plato leaves ethics behind and concerns himself with the material needs of the city. Thus he lays down the basis of a society where, in order to maintain order, the state must think and organize men's demands. Usefulness becomes the first concern. The education Plato outlined in the *Republic* is quite different from that described in the *Gorgias,* which aimed at the justice and goodness of men's souls. Education in the *Republic* consists in adapting (via *mimesis*) one's self to a specific role whose purpose might not even be seen. It must create professionals, very good at a particular job, who cannot see their training and their respective action within the wider range of human life. "But Plato does not have to make men, as Socrates did," Michelstaedter remarks sarcastically, "he must make farmers, shoemakers, blacksmiths, merchants, bankers, warriors, politicians, each of which must perform a function that is necessary to the life of the city" (*Opere,* 159). In the automation of their actions, men lose sight of life's final goal.

Plato's divergence from Socrates on the theoretical level was really the result of the logical development of Socrates' *dialégesthai.* In answering Socrates' *"tí esti"* Plato created his world of ideas, forms, or essences, immutable and eternal, the reasons of existent things and of their being known. In that world he also placed the ideas or concepts (goodness, courage, wisdom, happiness) which have no corresponding objects, but in which individuals participate. It was at this point that the problem appeared with greatest clarity. How can things of this world be said to correspond to the idea, if the idea is immutable and immobile? How could the things of this world participate in the world of ideas? The impasse was caused by the Parmenidean heritage, which had established the incompatibility of the one and the many. "Being" must be one; the many belong to the world of "becoming." Of "being" we can only say that it is itself, for any other attribute given to it would imply that "being" *is not* something else. In order to come out of the impasse, Plato had finally to face the ambiguity of the verb "to be." It was in the *Sophist* that for the first time Plato distinguished "being" as substance from "being" as a predicate. To say that Socrates is wise implies of course that he is *not* unwise, but the *is* as well as the *is not* do not affirm or negate the reality of Socrates, but only of one attribute. Nonbeing thus coincides with otherness, difference.

Michelstaedter, however, did not accept Plato's operation. From it *"Tà pollá* [the many] came out victorious, *to én* [the one] was dead forever and with it the postulate of philosophical honesty" (*Opere*, 191). But if Plato wanted with this argument to move *tò mè ón* (nonbeing) he also created the *éteron* (the other, the different) and made the *mè ón* into a substance. It follows, Michelstaedter remarks, that when I say something, "the other," that is, "nonbeing," is always implicit; I can now pretend that anything I say has substance (or is a real being) (*Opere*, 191). Plato thus gave reality to every idea and every name, and *rettorica* was born. The identity of ontology, thought, and language was forever broken. From then on, being was to be used as a predicate, words were to become technical terms, language was to become a game. "At the price of the loss of life," writes Fratta, "man had conquered for himself the possibility of multiform and infinite speech." The Socratic dialectics was dead and "from its ashes" *rettorica* was born.[19]

Aristotle finished what Plato had begun, and truly completed the creation of *rettorica*. He, in fact, pursued the life of theoresis and not that of *persuasione*. With such a position, based on the separation of the thinking subject and reality, goes the presumption of objective knowledge—as if we could ever see things as they are in themselves. Michelstaedter clearly recognized the naiveté of such belief. In order to see things in themselves, detached from any relation to the subject, man would need to step out of the flux of life. Because this is impossible, so-called objective knowledge can never be obtained. Yet Aristotle continued on that road and established immutable principles that rule and organize our knowledge.

Aristotle, according to Michelstaedter, gave substance to abstractions and made language into an empty sound: "To speak of speaking, rather than actually speaking, and in the spoken words to fake each time a real proof of what has been said." "Words," Michelstaedter continues, "the modes of language . . . become for Aristotle 'things' in themselves: they crystallize" (*Opere*, 234). Aristotle's operation is best seen in the treatment of the verbal forms which, rather than being used to express action or relation, that is, as predicates, are given definite articles and are fixed as solid nouns. Words like "thought, intellect, knowledge, ideas, concepts, categories, principles, syllogisms" become real entities, whereas they are only "the poultice that centuries of *rettorica* have applied to human suffering." "Who could ever take them away from men without also tearing away their skin?" (*Opere*, 165). The intellectual constructions have by now become part of man's nature through an act of self-preservation. It is the fear of the unknown that must be exorcised through its naming. Michelstaedter returns to this idea of words as poultice in an enlightening page of his notes. "Men who have nothing to give rely on words which pretend to give." "Because they cannot make their own world coincide with that of others, they fake words that pretend to contain the absolute world. They signify with words what they do not know and need in order to live—every word contains a mystery and in words they trust themselves" (*Opere*, 725). The attack on Aristotle is developed at length in his *Appendici critiche* and continues throughout.

Aristotle had created *rettorica* which from then on would take over all forms of human life, slowly destroying all authenticity. This process has continued up to today and has built very complex intellectual systems. Religions, scientific theories, philosophical systems are all the modern products of *rettorica* with which man deceives himself, giving names to darkness and nothingness. Modern philosophy, Michelstaedter writes,

> is not exempt from this error. It has presupposed the spirit beyond things: the thing in itself, God, the absolute of the moderns correspond now exactly to Aristotle's substantial *arké*. With this presupposition of an absolute form in everything, Aristotle as well as Hegel and Croce have been able to give a very vast content to thought . . . [a content] which did not exist. (*Opere*, 837)

The world, in fact, cannot be explained. "The world is the world of contingencies, relativity, it 'is' because it 'is,' has no reason, no goal, no beginning, no end: it is the negation of the concept of 'substance,' of 'absolute'" (*Opere*, 843). It is against words and only words that Michelstaedter launches his attack. They alone are responsible for deception. It is pointless to grow angry at the way things are. "Things are as they are, as they cannot but be, . . . each has its own cause for being the way it is." Instead, Michelstaedter continues to be angered by words that confer upon themselves a value and an intent they do not possess. Words like goodness, virtue, right, or wrong should be used as relative expressions because they contain the connotations we give to them. It is deplorable to use them as general philosophical fixed labels (859).

RETTORICA: THE UNAVOIDABLE PITFALL

> It sometimes seems to me that a pestilence
> has struck the human race in its most dis-
> tinctive faculty—that is, the use of words. It
> is a plague afflicting language, revealing
> itself as a loss of cognition and immediacy,
> an automatism that tends to level out all
> expression into the most generic, anony-
> mous, and abstract formulas.—Italo
> Calvino.[20]

We who use language to interpret reality, to invent meanings—where have we arrived? We jugglers of words, creators of schools of interpretations, academic fads, theories (or "plans" as Umberto Eco would now call them) have by now become their slaves. Once simply means to an end, our linguistic or intellectual creations have become the ends themselves. They have become designs to which we try to adapt our lives and the world around us. They are our new absolutes by which we live and judge. It is our need for meanings that prompts our intellect to create new absolutes after it has destroyed the old ones.

As Pirandello's Cosmo Laurentano says in *The Old and the Young*, philosophical systems, like religions and scientific theories, are manmade products. They are all poetry, creation of the human intellect "which on hypothesis, that is to say on a cloud . . . builds up castles, pinnacles and towers," and these are nothing but "churches, chapels, shrines, temples of different styles poised in the air." He continues:

"Breathe, and the whole structure collapses; breathe, and all these castles which tower like mountains crumble, because there is nothing inside them; a void . . . a void and the silence of mystery."[21] "You live on the surface," Lia tells Casaubon in Eco's *Foucault's Pendulum*. "You sometimes seem profound but it is only because you piece a lot of surfaces together to create the impression of depth, solidity."[22] But Lia's statement is not an accusation of superficiality directed toward an individual. It is a philosophical statement about the world. Surfaces are all that the world is about. The abyss does not exist. It is we who want to believe in it; so we create it. As Calvino's Palomar had already taught us, "It is only after you have come to know the surface of things . . . that you can venture to seek what is underneath. But the surface of things is inexhaustible."[23]

Then why write about anything? Why continue to interpret? Why study Michelstaedter? To write about him seems to defeat the purpose from the start, as "this writing about" is what he strongly rejected as the source of falsehood. Better, then, to do like two young writers from his part of the world, Antonio Devetag and Franco Ferranti. They learned his lesson very well: rather than writing *about* Carlo Michelstaedter, they had him speak in their plays as the protagonist. Of course we could object that Devetag and Ferranti have created their own Carlo Michelstaedter.[24] The objection is justified, but outweighed. Devetag and Ferranti have indeed created their own Michelstaedter but they do not pretend to give us the "real" Michelstaedter; neither do they pretend to find in his writings the hidden meaning to be used as the key for every future interpretation. They have read his work and used it as the text of their plays. They have made a character out of the pages he left, and, as Pirandello would say, rather than fixing him in a series of stereotypes, they represented his drama in its making.

Another artist who has given life to Michelstaedter is Giulio Nerini, a librarian in the Biblioteca Civica of Gorizia and a young musician who wrote the music for one of Michelstaedter's poems, "Alba. Il canto del gallo" ("Dawn. The Song of the Rooster"). Devetag, Ferranti, and Nerini, it seems to me, have done more justice to Michelstaedter than most of the scholars who have tried to explain his life and his death.[25]

Then, what am I doing in this chapter? In this book? The very thing that Michelstaedter despised: interpreting. Why? Because as he himself proved with all his written pages, as individuals of the human species we cannot help it. Because, as Palomar says, "not to interpret is impossible, as refraining from thinking is impossible." Because, as Eco repeats, interpreting is in the nature of language.[26] It is the need to find meanings that prompts us to fabricate them. In a way we are all Sherlock Holmes or Sam Spade, in constant search of the nonexistent key that will unlock the existential puzzle.

At the end of *The Name of the Rose,* Adso collects small vestiges of the burned library. "Relics," Eco calls them, purposely giving to the word a religious connotation.[27] He continues his search although Guglielmo had told him that there is neither order nor system in the universe. After eight years and another five hundred pages of intellectual games, Casaubon will tell us the same thing, that "there is only silence out there." But, of course, we will not believe him, and "will look for other meanings even in [his] silence."[28]

Ferdinando Adornato, in an interview with Eco, asked him whether the meaning of *Foucault's Pendulum* could be summarized in the sentence "Intellectual games can be lethal."[29] After Eco's affirmative reply, he asked whether such a statement could be applied to Eco himself. An annoyed Umberto Eco gave an answer that is worth quoting. "Yes, one can die from an intellectual game. What more do you want me to tell you? There are over 500 pages thrown out there as a protest against all those brains, mine included, that rack themselves in search of a Plan, of an ultimate meaning. Is it not enough for you?"[30] Eco is warning against the very thing he is doing, that he loves doing and knows how to do so very well. And this warning is conveyed to us in that very shape and form, or better, by means of what he is warning us against. A paradox, indeed! In it we are caught, in it we try to live. There is no alternative.

It is not by chance that Eco has stopped writing treatises (the whole, inclusive, systematic *corpora* of knowledge answering every question) and he is now writing novels. Better than any other literary form, his novels can express the "principle of encyclopedia," which, Eco says,

does not furnish us with a complete model of rationality (it does not reflect in a univocal way an ordered universe), rather it supplies rules of reasonableness . . . rules that allow us to decide at every step the

conditions that warrant the use of language in order to make sense—
according to some provisional criterion of order.[31]

After all, young Adso had learned this basic lesson. When Guglielmo
reveals to him that the events that brought him to the resolution of the
mystery were connected by chance and that his system was flawed, Adso
is not at all shocked and says that by imagining wrong orders and
systems he had, nevertheless, found something. Having recognized the
insight of his young pupil, the old master comments: "The only truths
that are useful are instruments to be thrown away" as soon as they have
accomplished their task.[32] But woe to those who attach themselves to
them. "One can die from intellectual games," just as one can die by
refusing them.

LA PERSUASIONE E LA RETTORICA

The text *La persuasione e la rettorica* is short and its 150 pages are
unevenly divided between *persuasione* and *rettorica;* ostensibly one-
third of the text is dedicated to *persuasione*. At a closer look, however,
only three pages follow the title "La persuasione" and the other forty-
seven are divided between the section "L'illusione della persuasione" and
the section "La via alla persuasione." *Rettorica* is explained in detail.
Persuasione, on the other hand, is not, and no examples are given except
for the names of the few *persuasi* of history: Socrates, Christ, Leopardi,
Beethoven, Tolstoy, Ibsen. The list, as we shall see, is quite revealing.
Persuasione is defined only negatively or through metaphors. It could not
be otherwise, for it is not an intellectual category, but a moral category. It
belongs to the realm of ethics, and it cannot be explained. As Wittgenstein will say, what gives value to the ethical sphere is precisely that it
is outside the realm of logic.[33] Logical explanations belong to the realm
of *rettorica. Persuasione* can only be lived.

The most powerful definition—or better, representation—of *persuasione* is, undoubtedly, the one rendered with the metaphor of the weight
at the opening of the work.

A weight hangs on a hook, and in hanging, suffers that it cannot descend; it cannot get off the hook, for, being a weight, it pends and, pending, depends.

We want to give it satisfaction: we free it from its dependence; we let it go, so it may satisfy its hunger for what is lowest and independently descend to the point to which it is pleased to descend. But it is not pleased to stop at any point it reaches, and would like to keep descending, so that the next point should be even lower than the one it occupies at any moment. But no future point will please it, and be necessary to its life, so long as a lower awaits; each time it is made present, every point becomes devoid of attraction, not being still lower; thus *at every point it lacks lower points,* and these attract it all the more: it is always held by the same hunger for what is lower, and its will to descend stays infinite.

For if everything were finished at a given point, and if at one point it could possess the infinite descent of the infinite future—at that point it would no longer be what it is: *a weight.*

Its life is this lack of its life. If it no longer lacked anything—but were finished, perfect: if it possessed itself, it would have ceased to exist. The weight is its own impediment to the possession of its life, and its inability to satisfy itself depends on itself alone. *The weight can never be persuaded.* (*Persuasione,* 39–40)[34]

The essence of the weight is to fall, but when the weight fulfills its need (falling), it also reaches its end (stasis), and it ceases to be what it was (a weight). So, for the weight to "consist," to keep its essence, to remain a weight, it must exist in this constant state of unfulfilled tension. "The weight," Michelstaedter writes, "can never be persuaded." So it is with man. His essence is a constant need, a deficiency asking to be filled, satisfied. Schopenhauer said life is will, and Leopardi had already understood that it consists in desire, "in a lack, in a nonbeing, in an infinite and never-ending tension." Were man's desire to be satisfied, he would no longer be; as for the weight, its essence is negativity.

After talking about man in general, Michelstaedter suddenly switches to the first person in order to continue his discourse with a very personal example. The weight is now personified.

I will climb the mountain—the height calls me—I want to possess it—I climb to the top—I dominate it; but how do I possess the mountain? Yes, I am high up over the plane and over the sea; I can see the horizon created by the mountain; but all that is not mine: what I see is not in me, and *in* order to see more "I have never seen": I do not possess the sight. The sea is shining from afar; it will be mine . . .; I will descend to the coast, I will hear its voice; I will sail over its back. . . . I will be content. But now that I am on the sea, "the ear is not satisfied with hearing," and the ship always plows new waves and "a similar thirst holds me": if I dive into the waters, if I feel the waves over my body—but where I am, the sea is not; if I want to go where the water is and possess it, the waves will open up before the man who is swimming; if I drink the salty water, if I exult as a dolphin—if I drown—still I do not possess the sea: I am alone and different in the midst of the sea. (*Persuasione*, 40–41)

The images of the mountain and the sea will return many times. They are a refrain, a constant presence in Michelstaedter's writing. They are also a real presence in his life, as will become apparent, and he will transform them in metaphors of the absolute. The absolute, in fact, is not a theoretical entity, but a nonentity; it is all that man is not and tends to be, a state of perfection, self-possession. One can speak of it only negatively. "I have never known what the absolute is, yet I know it the way the insomniac knows sleep, the way the beholder of darkness knows light. This I know, that my conscience . . . is made up of a lack" (*Persuasione*, 96). Man tends to fulfill his need, namely the possession of the other, without realizing that he will never achieve *persuasione* by going outside himself. He must achieve self-possession and he will need nothing more, since from the others he cannot obtain what he has not already in himself. "The *persuaso* is he who has his life within himself: the naked soul in the island of the blessed" (*Persuasione*, 42). As he wrote in his notes: "*Persuasione* is the present possession of one's own life" (*Opere*, 728).

The very short chapter entitled "La persuasione" is over. Nothing more can be said about it. The nature of *persuasione* is, in fact, its very unspeakability. *Persuasione* can only be lived. Yet it is the condition of the naked soul in the island of the blessed. Thus it is an oxymoron; it cannot be known but must be lived. Because "man's life is inevitably *rettorica*," as Brianese well saw, *persuasione* cannot be achieved in life unless it annuls it.[35]

This extreme position is doomed to be frustrated and Michelstaedter knows it well. Man needs others and the world outside; his being is determined by that of others. Michelstaedter is so certain of the impossibility of achieving *persuasione* that he calls the second chapter of this section "The Illusion of Persuasion." This "illusion" is born when man transforms what exists only for himself, what is good only for himself into objective entities, into the absolute good. "He does not say: 'this is for me,' but 'this is'; he does not say: 'this I like,' but 'this is good': because, in fact, the 'I' for which something is or is not good, is his own conscience, his pleasure, his being, which to him is immobile, absolute, and outside time" (*Persuasione*, 52). Man, therefore, judges things outside only in relation to his own goals. "Everything that lives persuades itself that the real life is whatever life it is living" (52). Man is still the center of the universe. To any individual his own world is the whole world. He can only comprehend what he can grasp. The limits of his world is the extension of his reach. Freely adapting Parmenides' famous fragment (quoted above) that "to think is the same as thinking that something is," he states that my living and the world I live in are one and the same.[36] "Now if," as Fratta says, "my living is will to be—that is, lack of being—the world I live in, the things which are real for me, insofar as they are correlative to this will of mine, will necessarily not be, and I will not acquire any real essence from my relation to them."[37]

Man's constant need of something constitutes his essence. He struggles for the possession of that which, once achieved, would change his person and sanction the loss of his individuality. The example of chlorine and hydrogen which strive for union well exemplifies the idea. Michelstaedter writes: "If we . . . place chlorine near hydrogen, the former will only live for the latter. Hydrogen will be for chlorine the only value in the world: the world, its life will only consist in getting united with the hydrogen" (*Persuasione*, 46). Each lives in order to unite itself with the other, but once this union is achieved, they will both have lost their individualities. The union will give birth to hydrochloric acid; neither chlorine nor hydrogen will be any longer. "Hence their life is death; their love hatred" (47).

This example develops the metaphor of the weight, and gives it a dramatic conclusion. Man's essence is unfulfilled desire; if it were fulfilled he would cease to be. As long as man lives, he *is not;* if he *were* he would exist no more. This is the meaning of the statement "he who sees God dies" (*Persuasione,* 50). The end and goal of man's life is death— only there do being and knowing coincide.

Michelstaedter was to become obsessed with this contradiction, analyzing it over and over without, of course, being able to resolve it; it did nonetheless grow clearer and with this clarity, its tragedy became more evident. No relation is possible between the world and the absolute. "The world of relativity, of the will, as such, can never transcend itself, neither can it ever reach its goal—being—yet life is will to being, will to the absolute" (*Opere,* 838). "Philosophy wants to explain things; it wants to subordinate things to a reason; . . . it wants reason to be the determining motive for actions." Yet, Michelstaedter continues, the absolute is being, outside time, eternal and immobile, whereas the world is "material fact" (838). An absolute world cannot exist, because "if there were one, ours would not be. Neither could [the absolute] have ever been the cause of a world, which is relativity" (840).

Entitled "Road to Persuasion," the twenty pages of his third chapter should lead us to the absolute life. It is the constructive part of Michelstaedter's philosophy, but a great disappointment for the traditional philosopher. As might be expected, there will be no theory of *persuasione,* for it would be a contradiction in terms. Here, more than before, the nontheoretical nature of *persuasione* becomes evident.

Fratta rightly points out that these were pages that must have, more than the others, upset the traditional Italian school of thought. They were probably the cause of Croce's silence and Gentile's criticism. It was impossible for the latter to accept a philosophy whose core was a concept that could never be defined.[38] But if *persuasione* cannot be defined, neither can a method for achieving it be found. Playing with the Latin ablative *omnibus* (everybody) that in Italian is also a synonym for bus, Michelstaedter writes:

The road of *persuasione* is not run by *"omnibus,"* has no signs, indications that can be passed . . . but each one has in himself the need to find it. . . . Everyone is alone and cannot hope for any help but from himself. The road to *persuasione* has only this indication: do not satisfy yourself with the sufficiency of what is given to you. (*Persuasione,* 104)

It is a negative concept, it is the awareness of man's finiteness and limits and the suffering that accompanies such awareness. Nothing more can be said about it. The real task is living it constantly and courageously.

The epigraph that opens the chapter is revealing. It is a quotation from Aeschylus's *Agamemnon,* where the identity of *persuasione* (peithó) and truth is established. We may infer then that the sense of the term as employed by Michelstaedter is older than Aristotle. The chapter begins with a question: "That which you do, how do you do it—with what mind do you do it? Are you or are you not persuaded of what you do?" (67). Michelstaedter shows here that man lives and acts in order to continue to live, with an eye to the future and with a constant fear of dying, so that "every present moment of his life has in itself death." "In fact, where is life if not in the present? If this present has no value, nothing has value." "He who fears death is already dead" (*Persuasione,* 69).

It is at this point that the negative essence of *Persuasione* is stated in all its clarity. "He who wants only for one moment his life, who only for one moment wants to be persuaded, must take possession of the present; see every present as the last, as if, after [it], death were certain" (*Persuasione,* 70). As Brianese well put it, "*rettorica* pretends to flee from time, as constant mutation; *persuasione* presents itself as the will to be, to exist (*consistere*) in the present."[39]

These last pages of the section on *persuasione* are extremely rich. Images, metaphors, parables abound. The Gospels as well as the Greek texts are constantly cited. Statements are presented with the authority of axioms, as absolute truths unshakable and indestructible. Yet (or maybe because of it) they are totally abstract and detached from reality. "Everyone is first and last"; "he must create himself and the world that before him does not exist; he must be master, not slave" (73). They culminate in the maxim "to give is to do the impossible; to give is to receive" (82). Man must affirm himself not just in order to continue to exist, "he must love [the world] not because it is necessary to his own needs, but for what it is, in itself" (82). He must not depend on anything but himself; he must be self-sufficient.[40]

Persuasione cannot be achieved, Michelstaedter tells us, and "the road to [it] is hyperbolic. As the hyperbola approaches the asymptote ad infinitum so the man who by living wants his [real] life, infinitely approaches the straight line of justice" (78). *Persuasione* is the mathematical limit-point to which "one comes closer and closer ad infinitum but which is never reached" (80). Michelstaedter is fully aware that it is impossible for man to overcome his finiteness and that *persuasione* is nothing other than "the ideal-limit which man will never reach," "but for which he will never cease to strive." In this light Michelstaedter's image of the hyperbola assumes its full significance. *"Persuasione,"* wrote Brianese, "is positing the necessity for removing *rettorica,* yet *rettorica* not only is never removed, it cannot be removed."[41] This discourse is similar to that of Fratta who emphasized the ethical quality of Michelstaedter's philosophy. "*Persuasione* cannot speak the theoretical language . . . is not a concept defining something already given, rather it is the formulation of a request for a different reality, which never existed, whose necessity is posited . . . by the painful feeling of the lack of being."[42]

After all, Michelstaedter had clearly stated in a note that "real being [the *ousía*] remains out of my consciousness and out of my life," and that "I do not live the absolute, neither does my *noũs* know it—that which I live and that my *noũs* knows is the nullity of everything that is visible and knowable" (*Opere,* 803). This could be Parmenides; man does not belong in the world of real being.

The need for the absolute springs forth from man's finiteness. It is limit that makes men desire the infinite, and this limit, as Schopenhauer saw, is suffering. It is lack that makes men want completeness. Michelstaedter is fully aware of the contradictory essence of life; he knows that to make himself an absolute being is to negate himself as a finite being, that to make himself as an eternal being, means to negate himself as becoming. He knows that the life of the absolute is the end or death of the finite.[43] "By making his own life richer and richer with negations, [man] can create himself and the world" (*Persuasione,* 84). He will universalize himself, for he will embody the suffering of every living creature and will speak with the voice of the world.

Only when you want no longer will you have what you want, because that which you want is absolute being, and all your will is nothing but contingency: it is not in itself . . . as long as your body will be, it will throw its shadow over things so that you will not be able to see, when you will no longer be, you will be able to see. (*Opere,* 781)

Michelstaedter's suicide seems at this point to have been a coherent and logical consequence, but about this more will be said later.

The section on *persuasione* is over. The closing image is a metaphor used to describe the final achievement. Only the metaphor could, in fact, define *persuasione.*

Alone, he [the *persuaso*] lives the vertiginous immensity and profundity of life. . . . The stability of the individual occupies an infinite time in the present and stops time. Each of his moments is a century in the life of others—until he turns himself into flame and is finally able to inhabit the ultimate present. (89)

In this context the image of the flame acquires its real significance. The flame is the metaphor of the *persuaso* who affirms himself by negating all material boundaries. Fire, in fact, lives by means of destruction. Its strength grows with the amount of matter that it destroys.

The image of the flame is recurrent in Michelstaedter and has been a great source of discussion among scholars.[44] Interpreted by some as a sign of his mysticism, his desire to become one with the absolute, its connotation of strength and self-assertiveness also calls to mind D'Annunzio or Nietzsche.[45] In Michelstaedter, in fact, the humble submission of the individual to one infinite Power is absent. The emphasis of his philosophy is on strength and energy. And of course his primary source of inspiration was his beloved Greek philosophers: Heraclitus, first of all, for whom fire was the symbol of the unity of opposites; and Empedocles who made fire one of the four constituents of the universe. For the Stoics, the *animus mundi* is a divine flame. But the negation of the limit is also Christ's sacrifice, and fire is also the Holy Spirit in which he is transformed to bring the divine message to men.[46]

Like the image of the flame, that of the hawk is recurrent; in fact in this particular context it occurs first. If the flame has an antagonist in darkness, the hawk has it in the crows with their heavy bodies incapable of rising high.

The hawk in the dash of his flight, holding his body stable, bats regularly his wings, and rises confident to the height. So man on his road to *persuasione* maintains at each point the equilibrium of his own person; . . . he has neither uncertainties nor weaknesses; if he does not fear pain he has honestly taken upon himself pain as his *persona*. He lives it in each moment. And as all things share this suffering, in him all things live. (87)

The hawk has become "il persuaso" and the flame. In fact, "where to others there is darkness, to him there is light . . . where to others there is mystery and impotence, he has the power and can see clearly. Because he has the honesty to feel always insufficient" (87). The *persuaso* is he who is conscious of his limits, of his negativity; he who is conscious of the evil in the world. It is a positive concept whose positivity is born out of the awareness of a negativity.

Who more brilliantly than Montale could transform the hawk into a poetic image that symbolizes fleeting, precarious, frail good? The symbol of positivity is born here too out of "the evil of living" (*il male di vivere*). Even Montale's hawk metamorphoses into the sunflower "maddened with light" (*impazzito di luce*). "Dark material things aim at clarity" and in the light their end is to vanish. Michelstaedter's absolute is just as utopic and unreal as Montale's.[47]

In his opposition to metaphysics, Michelstaedter was reproposing metaphysics of a different type, yet still a metaphysics. The man of *persuasione* places himself above time and space; he negates, thus eliminates the material limits of life, defies temporality, and declares his independence from it. Of course, the act is self-destructive, yet his temporal destruction achieves precisely what he had set out to do.

Temporality and finiteness can be overcome only through self-negation. Suicide is, then, the logical and ethical consequence of a philosophy that is still radically attached to "strong thought." As Brianese rightly put it, "the *persuaso* dies in order to live authentically."[48] In his attempt to make "form" and "life" coincide, Michelstaedter collapsed. And metaphysics, a metaphysics of death, still leers at us.

Michelstaedter's life and death are the last tragic act in the death of metaphysics. What is left for us is no longer, as Gianni Vattimo teaches, to strive for "a liberation from appearances in order to possess the authentic being," but to accept, instead, only "a freedom as mobility amidst the 'appearances.'" It is time that we learn to live in and to love our world of appearances, Vattimo concludes, because it is all we have. "Philosophy must not and cannot teach us in what direction to go; it must teach us to live in a condition where no direction exists."[49]

RETTORICA

On the arduous road to *persuasione* man collapses, his solitude overwhelms him. He asks to exist for someone. He needs to be recognized by others. At the same time he needs to attribute objective existence to that which only exists for himself. He is not satisfied with living the external reality, he must also state that he knows it.

All of our experiences, as Michelstaedter writes, are subjective:

> If I am hungry, reality around me is nothing but a collection of things more or less edible, if I am thirsty, reality is more or less liquid, more or less drinkable. . . . If I am neither hungry nor thirsty, if I do not need any definite thing, the world is to me only a collection of grey things. I do not know what they are, but that they certainly are not made for me to enjoy. (*Persuasione,* 122)

There is no objective knowledge, nothing exists outside the knowing subject. If it were to exist, we would not know that it did. Everything acquires a meaning in relation to the need of a subject to which it relates. "In life everything exists only in relation to other things" (*Opere,* 819). "Things interest [the individual] only insofar as they have had and have a relation to him" (*Opere,* 807). "All matter reduces itself completely to the content of my senses. However much I study this matter I will never transcend my senses in which alone matter exists" (*Opere,* 713). It is, therefore, the subject's volition that establishes an order among the outside phenomena. In themselves, in fact, each thing is just as worthy as any other. All knowledge, therefore, is an interpretation. "There is no other reality but the reality of the subject" (*Opere,* 146). (This last quotation was taken from *Appendice* 1, which Michelstaedter wrote in order to analyze this issue precisely on the linguistic level.)

"When one speaks, one states one's own illusory individuality as absolute" (*Opere*, 143). The speaking subject pretends to be an absolute subject in the moment in which it posits any object as an objective entity that exists in itself. Michelstaedter examines the various types of statements, or subordinate clauses, pointing out their dependence on the subject that states them. He does this comparing Italian, Greek and Latin, showing that it is actually language that deceives us, that it is through its use that man begins to find objective correlatives for every sound he utters. Every subordinate clause is nothing but a subjective statement, and a sentence like "I know that something exists" is the subject's fallacy. Only the imperative mode is not

> interpreted reality, but life; it is the intention that is living in actuality . . . it is real as the subject is real, because as the subject, . . . [it] is the will of something. It is the subject that invades with his own life the realm of words: it does not make words, but it lives. Long live the imperative! (*Opere*, 149–50)

Subjectivism therefore means relativism. Objectivity is a word that has no room in the life of man. To the scientists who protest: "But we look [at things] objectively," he replies: "looking is a verb like any other and as such it requires a subject, thus their so-called objectivity is yet another form of subjectivity" (*Persuasione*, 123). Man's consciousness determines meanings: thus life is, by necessity, *rettorica*.

"When man says 'this is,' he affirms his person, he is stating his own reality, because he affirms himself in relation to a thing which is the object of his volition." The thing, therefore, exists as such, relative to the subject's will. But, according to Michelstaedter, when I say "I know that this is," I pretend to attribute objective, independent existence to something that instead exists only in relation to the "I" who wills it (97). The first statement is honest, for it shows the relativity of the living subject; the second, however, is totally insufficient, for it wants to state such relativity as absolute (98).

And so "men talk, always talk and their talking they call reasoning" (*Persuasione*, 98). Their desires, their fears must be given names in order to be exorcised, and objects must be made to correspond to them so that desires and fears be justified. It is an elaborate construction made to fill up the dark void that surrounds us. "Men who have nothing and can give nothing," says Michelstaedter, "rely on words that falsify communication" (*Persuasione*, 99). Words are used as a poultice to soothe suffering; "with words they signify what they don't know and what they need . . . with words they weave a veil" to cover up darkness (99). They ask for life and they are given a name, "the name as conventional sign," as Parmenides called it (*Persuasione*, 100). Man, therefore, speaks of things he does not know; he names them to exorcise the unknown and uses words which have no correspondent in reality.

Although Michelstaedter accuses men of attributing reality to words and ideas, this process of hypostatization is inherent in language itself. It is the risk of thought; it is the threat man has to face constantly as language becomes more complex through usage. Sociology, medicine, anthropology give names to needs and fears; through such a naming process man finds justifications. Dressed in names, the obscure traits of human nature acquire a false transparency and a familiarity that make them malleable and possible to reckon with. Medicine, for example, has created, says Michelstaedter, words like "nervous" or "neurotic" for the weaknesses of human nature, whereby man can cope with the mystery of his dark side. "When objective experience is insufficient to justify an individual['s behavior]," for example, "then this individual is [labeled] 'mad'" (*Persuasione*, 183).[50] A word is thus created for a phenomenon we can neither explain nor understand. Again, Pirandello springs to mind, in particular his tragic characters Enrico IV, Moscarda, and Chiarchiaro in "La patente." The label Chiarchiaro is given by society to name the unexplainable has become the reality, the essence by which he will always be judged. The power of this act of naming is enough to change Chiarchiaro's very nature, and to determine his future actions. At the end he has actually become what the people had unjustly named him. Thus we see how tenuous the border is between Michelstaedter's discourse and that of Pirandello, Calvino, or Umberto Eco. The instinct to interpret takes us to such extremes. We cannot help it. Language as means of interpreting and of naming the unknown creates monsters which take over our lives.

Michelstaedter compares talking men with children screaming in the dark. Both talking and screaming are ways of asserting one's identity in the darkness that surrounds us. "The system of names," he writes, "covers with mirrors the room of individual misery. Men fake in their words [the] absolute act and with words they feed their life's boredom" (*Persuasione*, 99).

Philosophical systems have now replaced religions, but their aim and structure are just the same—to camouflage darkness, to invent explanations and meanings for the unexplainable and the meaningless. In inventing cosmologies, ontologies, and the like, philosophers can be said to perpetuate an act of violence over men and the world. As Musil observed: "Philosophers are violent people who lack an army, and therefore they take over the world, enclosing it in a system."[51]

Michelstaedter had plenty to attack, in close range—Croce, for example. But even when he speaks of Croce, Hegel is the real target. Hegel, he knew well, had elaborated the most complex of all philosophical systems, where every phenomenon had its specific slot. Hegel is the culmination of the development of *rettorica* begun by Aristotle. Croce, on the other hand, imitated Hegel's thought without the benefit of a mind of comparable magnitude. "If I had such a sharp and abstract mind, like [Croce's]," Michelstaedter comments sarcastically, "I would not even have occupied myself with philosophy, but I would have been a jurist. He, instead, makes systems" (*Opere,* 661).[52]

Michelstaedter's criticism of idealism becomes on the social level an attack against the bourgeoisie, against its presumption, certainties and optimism about the goodness of society. The episode of the iron barrel exemplifies well his scorn of middle-class complacency. It is a dialogue between a happy bourgeois, full and content after a large meal, and the author. The fat bourgeois is satisfied with himself because he has found the right slot for everything, even for poetry, literature, and science. What is important, he remarks, is to know where everything belongs. First duty, then pleasure:

one thing is theory, another thing is practice. I, you see, enjoy these theoretical discussions. I get a kick out of the elegant ethical problems and even have fun in exchanging some paradoxical statements. But, let's be careful, for everything has its place and time. When I wear my uniform I am also another person. . . . I think that in the exercise of his functions, man must be absolutely free. . . . And in the antechamber of my office I leave out all my personal opinions, feelings, human weaknesses. And I enter the temple of civilization to perform my deed with a heart tempered by objectivity! (*Persuasione,* 138–39)

To the objection of his interlocutor that life is filled with the unforeseen that can strike us down any time, the fat man answers with a list of remedies for each single unforeseeable event up to his insurance policy in case of death. This man, Michelstaedter comments, is the man Hegel dreamed of, the individual in whom the union of subjective and rational will be realized.

This image of fat, blatant optimism standing before the door of his office, ready to slip into a different costume or mask, suggests another Pirandellian comparison. Michelstaedter's man is content with and proud of his life because, as Pirandello's tragic character in "La carriola" says, he is one of the many who lives and does not see himself living.[53] He, as anyone else, is caught in a form, or mask, and cannot see it. Pirandello's, on the other hand, is a tragic character because he can see himself trapped in the form the world had given him, and he can no longer live. The man in the iron barrel, instead, is happily intoxicated by the content of his own trap. He belongs to an earlier stage of man's history. He is a member of Hegel's happy bourgeoisie. Pirandello's, on the other hand, represents the crisis of bourgeois man through the development of self-consciousness.

LEOPARDI'S PRESENCE

> . . . di molti tristi e miseri tutti, un popol
> fanno lieto e felice ("and of the many sad
> and miserable they make one smiling and
> happy people").—Giacomo Leopardi[54]

The third chapter of the section on *Rettorica* opens with this epigraph. In his analysis of human society Michelstaedter followed closely Leopardi's ideas. Yet the poet's presence is not limited to this topic; it is constant.

The echo of Leopardi's verses can be heard throughout Michelstaedter's writings. It is, of course, more obvious in his poetry, as Campailla has shown, where the influence is not only thematic but also linguistic.

Entire verses or phrases are borrowed from the *Canti*. Many also appear
in Michelstaedter's letters and are proof of his familiarity with them.
They are inserted in the course of his narration as a way to give poetical
shape to an idea or a feeling. At times they just capture the musical echo
of a sound like "sento da lungi i domenicali rumori" (I hear the faraway
sounds of Sunday) or "sento ancora giù nelle strade morire gli ultimi
rumori" (I still hear the dying sounds down the street) and they are
connected with the melancholy and sadness of the passing time and of the
condition of solitude of the poet (*Ep.*, 283, 295).[55] "Il passero solitario"
("The Solitary Sparrow"), for example, appears more than once in his
letters (*Ep.*, 405, 418). Other times, though, the similarity is more profound and involves the principles of their philosophy, as when Michelstaedter speaks to his friend Gaetano Chiavacci against suicide using
Plotinus's argument, the same one Plotinus uses against Porphyry in
Leopardi's *Operette morali*. I shall come back to this in the Epilogue.

In the preface to *La persuasione e la rettorica* Michelstaedter makes a
list of the few *persuasi* of history. In this list that begins with Parmenides
and ends with Beethoven and Ibsen, Leopardi has a place too, perhaps
even a place of honor. It is Tristano's voice we hear in the preface—that
Tristano who, being accused of spreading gloom and pessimism among
men, replied: "This is what I said to myself, almost as if that painful
philosophy were of my own invention—when I saw it rejected by everyone. . . . But then, thinking it over, I remember that it was as new as
Solomon . . . and the most ancient poets and philosophers."[56] Michelstaedter borrows Tristano's words in order to justify his task. Both he
and Leopardi realize they are repeating things that have been said over
and over, because there is but one truth: that life is suffering. They make
of their courage their first ethical virtue, that which helps them "to look
intrepidly at the desert of life, not to dissimulate to [themselves] any part
of human unhappiness, and to accept all the consequences of a philosophy that is painful but true" (*Operette*, 489). As Campailla pointed out,
it is the "heroic" Leopardi that Michelstaedter admires. His "Postille
leopardiane," in fact, was inspired by the 1826 *Canti*.[57]

The other side of this ethical behavior is contempt for the plebeians
for their arrogance and cowardice, for their easy optimism ruled by
ignorance. Man believes in appearances, does not care about substance
and proceeds by self-deception. The polemic against progress is com-

mon to both. Tristano's sarcasm against "the profound philosophy of the newspapers, . . . masters, and . . . lights of the present age" recurs in the *Operette* and in the *Zibaldone*.[58] It is the same polemic Michelstaedter brings against *rettorica,* established knowledge that, ignorant of reality, dresses it up in names to which nothing corresponds. "It is to satisfy oneself with the conventional sign that hides darkness" (*Persuasione,* 101) because Leopardi had said "the world is satisfied with appearances . . . and . . . does not care about substance" (*PP,* 2:38).

In both writers, the discussion of human society is connected with that of human nature. Both individualists, they were concerned not with men as a collectivity, but with the individual. They were both convinced that society institutionalizes the abuses of power of the stronger over the weaker and that it was ludicrous to think of a happy society made up of unhappy individuals. Michelstaedter knew well that after Hobbes, and along with Hegel's master–slave model, Leopardi had pointed out with great precision the violent selfishness of human nature. This selfishness, he said, is "inseparable from man" whose "major danger" is his fellow-man because "naturally any animal hates his fellow-creature and is ready to offend it whenever this is required by his own interest" (*PP,* 2:33). Michelstaedter is in full agreement with Leopardi in denouncing man's basic "hatred against man," and the hypocrisy of the definition of civil society. "The affirmation of one's own individuality," writes Michel-staedter, "is always . . . violent. . . . Insofar as one affirms as just what is just for himself, he negates all that is just for others" (*Persuasione,* 77–78). "The individuals of what we call society," writes Leopardi, "are each at war . . . against everyone else, more or less openly, and against all together" (*Z,* 1:485). Socialistic hopes and utopias do not engage them. "The human species," Leopardi continues, "is divided into two groups: those who abuse their power and those who suffer the abuse. Neither law nor force of any kind, no progress either of philosophy or of civilization will ever prevent man from belonging to one or to the other group" (*PP,* 2:22). Michelstaedter echoes: "everyone [sees] in the other only the thing that it is necessary to him, not the man who has himself a life to live" (*Persuasione,* 150). Organized society justifies the use of violence by assigning different roles to individuals.

Michelstaedter defined "civil society" as the kingdom of *rettorica* where the "sign that hides darkness" is the very term "civil society." What men call "civil education," he writes, is nothing but "their hunger." What they call ethics is nothing but "their fear," and "the sword of justice" is nothing but "their violence" and "their selfish hatred." Men, he continues, "have made a strength of their weakness. . . . This is the realm of rettorica" (*Persuasione,* 144). "It is from reciprocal fear and arrogance (*prepotenza*) that the conventions of social morality are born; and it is from everyone's deficiencies and inabilities . . . that the division of labor is devised, whereby each one is at the same time master and slave" (*Opere,* 351).

Their polemic continues and moves on to include the sciences. The attack against so-called scientific progress is ferocious. The lapidary sentence "all progress for society is a regress for the individual" (*Persuasione,* 156) is echoed in dozens of similar expressions in Leopardi. Michelstaedter, though endowed with a strong and athletic body, attacked furiously "every progress of technology that dulls that part of man's body" making it weak and finally powerless (*Persuasione,* 156). Leopardi, who rightly lamented the weakness of his own physique, had written a century earlier: "One who is weak of body is not a man but a child; indeed worse, because his fate is to sit and watch the others live (and he at the most can chatter), but life is not for him" (*Operette,* 491). He prefers ancient times, when "physical weakness [was thought of as] disgraceful." "With us, [instead] . . . and already for a very long period of time, education does not deign to care for the body, which is too low an object. It cares for the spirit" (*Operette,* 491).

Leopardi's bitter sarcasm shows all his contempt for the stupidity of his age that thinks that spirit can flourish independently from the body, "without noticing that by ruining the body it in turn also ruins the spirit" (*Operette,* 491). Machines are cursed as the cause of the deterioration of the body. Man is losing his physical faculties and soon, concludes Michelstaedter, his "eyes will stop seeing . . . [his] ears hearing . . . and the body of man will disintegrate" (*Persuasione,* 159). Machines will not save man; he will succumb just the same. Technical progress cannot defeat death; modern man will die more impotent than ancient man, whose strong body could resist death more heroically. Carlo uses the beautiful example of the man at sea—the sea, as will be shown later, is a highly symbolic image in his writings—to prove his point. The old sailor had in his hand the sail and the shaft "and he was the reason for the balance between the wind and the sea," it was he "who struggled to win or to die. The modern sailor, instead, dies just the same, but sinks with the ship without even being able to fight" (*Persuasione,* 158). The image of the ancient sailor can be read as a metaphor of the *persuaso* who fights to *be,* who with all his strength struggles for his real life at sea, whereas the modern man represents the man of *rettorica* who does not live, but lets himself be ruled by outside forces and is determined by them.

The myth of the machine that replaces man and that eventually renders him useless is attacked with vehemence by both. Leopardi makes it the object of his sarcastic polemics when he announces through the Academy of Syllographs the contest for the construction of three machines: the machine of the ideal friend, that of the artificial steam men, "programmed to perform virtuous and noble deeds," and finally that of the ideal woman (*Operette,* 83). Such a contest was prompted by the realization that men cannot cure their evil and that, therefore, they should "little by little withdraw themselves from the business of life," letting machines take their place (*Operette,* 79).

Such naive trust in human progress has given rise to a plethora of artificial constructions to which men cling as if to absolute truths, capable of giving an answer to each question. "But long live statistics," Tristano exclaims, "long live economic, moral, and political sciences, the portable encyclopedias, the manuals and the many beautiful creations of our century! And may the nineteenth century live forever! Maybe very poor in things, but extremely rich and generous in words, which has always been an excellent sign, as you know" (*Operette,* 499–501). Leopardi's irony becomes caustic sarcasm in Michelstaedter's definition of science as "the workshop of absolute values" (*Persuasione,* 181). "The roots of science," he says, "have taken hold on to the deepest of man's weaknesses and have given stable and eternal basis for the *rettorica* of knowledge" (*Persuasione,* 130–31). The *rettorica* of sciences is a new form of religion. Scientists give to their modest opinions the sanction of absolute laws, "on which men, without knowing, lean [for support] . . . and without knowing them, so they pass them on" (*Persuasione,* 135). *Rettorica* becomes the art of names stripped from any meaning.

This false education begins at an early stage and it is much more harmful—and Michelstaedter's attack consequently more violent—because it is inflicted upon children. It is more vile and cowardly because it acts upon virgin, naive soil, on the child's trust and credulity. Leopardi was in complete agreement on this topic. It is with children that the first successes of *rettorica* are obtained. These successes treacherously sow in their souls the seeds of that separation between essence and appearance which will allow them to accept and to universalize the rule that "one thing is theory, another is practice" (*Persuasione*, 189). The child is abused. His fear of the unknown, of the future is exploited; rules are given to him as unshakable truths. From an early age he will live the separation of life and thought.

This striking similarity between Leopardi's and Michelstaedter's social ideas can be explained with their similar, basic philosophical principles. For both writers, nature is ruled by mechanical laws. No hidden design has been imposed upon it by a supernatural mind. Because man is part of nature just as any other living being, no special place was assigned to him, and therefore it is absurd for him to search for meanings. This is the whole truth that can be discovered about life. Suffering is man's fate. Because no answers can be given, the only task the philosopher has is to teach man how to live. The only philosophy is, therefore, moral philosophy. This discussion, however, will coincide with the theoretical discourse that the absolute—man's constant objective—is not "being" (*to on*), to be grasped and known, but precisely the absence of it. Reaching for the absolute, thus, means to live this absence, fully aware of it, without self-deception. Modern philosophy must coincide with heroic ethics.

MICHELSTAEDTER'S *OPERETTE MORALI*

In his introductory essay to *Il dialogo della salute e altri dialoghi*, Campailla points out that this dialogue must be read against Leopardi's pages on pleasure and happiness in the *Zibaldone*. Furthermore, although Socrates is the model of *dialéghestai* that Carlo has in mind, the Leopardi of the *Operette morali* is present here, as in other short dialogues. The dialogue epitomizes, Campailla continues, *La persuasione e le rettorica*. All the main themes of Michelstaedter's dissertation are present, with the difference, though, that the latter was a required scholarly work, thus already bound to become rhetorical, whereas the former was the product of an inner quest for *persuasione*. The opening of the preface to the dissertation, in fact, begins with the words: "I know I speak because I speak, but I will not persuade anyone; and this is dishonesty, but *rettorica* [he adds in Greek] forces me to do so" (*Persuasione, 35*). The audience of this work will be a group of university professors, ministers of *rettorica*. Michelstaedter seems to be saying that a work of *rettorica,* by definition, cannot persuade anyone; his failure, therefore, is sanctioned from the start by its very nature. Thus, what he cannot do with his dissertation, that is, convey the message of *persuasione* which was his constant objective, he will attempt through the Socratic method and with someone who has not yet been contaminated by *rettorica. Il dialogo della salute,* in fact, is born from a need to show the road to *persuasione*. It is dedicated to his cousin Emilio, five years his junior. Because metaphysics is nonsense, because theoretical life is pointless, because nothing can be discovered in the world outside, apart from suffering, man must be concerned with his moral life. This is what Carlo does and wants his cousin to do.

Carlo had tutored Emilio for the matriculation exam (*maturità*) during the academic year 1909–10; Emilio had been ill and had had to withdraw from school. Emilio, to whom he was deeply attached, represented nature still uncontaminated by *rettorica*. He represented authenticity. Carlo probably felt toward his younger cousin like a wise Socrates toward his pupils. Carlo's care and affection for his cousin must have been profound as he dedicated this dialogue to him—this, in order to complete his pedagogical task, to help his protégé to become a *persuaso*. He had emphasized on several occasions the importance of teaching young minds, an activity he considered the noblest in life. The dialogue is dedicated to "his" Emilio—for Carlo certainly felt he had helped to form his young mind—and "to all those young souls who have not yet placed their god in their career" (*Dialoghi, 27*). That is, to all the unselfish, authentic souls who have not yet been spoiled by the *rettorica* of life.

The dialogue is constructed on the Socratic model. The two interlocutors are Carlo's best friends: Rico and Nino, the former performing the role of Socrates / Carlo, the latter that of Emilio. In asking his questions, Rico, as Socrates always did, leads Nino toward the answer he has already in mind through the use of the Socratic analogy. Death is the subject and it constitutes the structural frame of the dialogue, opening and closing the text.

It begins in a cemetery, the realm of the physical death that everyone fears. At the exit of the cemetery the guardian wishes the two friends good health. The wish sounds like a mockery. A long dialogue starts. In it the signifiers *health* and *death* constantly change their signified. The health that the guardian wishes the two friends is obviously physical health. The respondents, however, attribute to it a different signified. The fear of death at the beginning which constitutes our life and coincides with it is the real death, but the death, at the end, of him who asks nothing and fears nothing is the beautiful death that constitutes the real life. The opposition life–death, which obsessed Michelstaedter, found in "Il canto delle crisalidi" its poetic voice. As often occurs in his works, an oxymoron is given form by an image producing a "paradoxical synthesis."

Echoing the philosophers of the *Operette morali* and the Socratic dialogues, Michelstaedter states that "outside pleasure, nothing has value to us," and that our actions are motivated by pleasure alone (*Opere*, 336). Leopardi, for his part, at many stages in the *Zibaldone* had stated that the desire for pleasure is the spur that moves man and makes him act, and he had elaborated consequently a real doctrine of pleasure, as he himself wanted to define it. Though its roots are in eighteenth-century materialism and sensationalism, it nevertheless presents elements with relevance to our century.

Its beginning statement is well known: "the human soul . . . has constantly the desire for and aims solely . . . at pleasure, that is, at happiness, which, if we consider it well, is the same thing as pleasure" (*Z*, 1:181–82). The analysis then moves on to the nature of such desire, which is the essence of human nature. Torquato Tasso's Familiar Spirit explains to him that nobody knows pleasure "by experience, but only by theory"; pleasure is a theoretical subject, "not a real one," which is like saying that pleasure does not exist in actuality, but only in the imagination. As the Familiar Spirit specifies, it is a "sort of feeling man conceives in his mind but does not experience" (*Operette*, 173). Better yet, it is not even a feeling but a concept. The Familiar Spirit offers Tasso the proof of this by making him realize that man always says "I will enjoy" or "I did enjoy," but never "I enjoy." "Thus, pleasure is clearly either past or future, never present" (*Operette*, 175).

Michelstaedter brings forth the same discourse in his dialogue between the souls of Diogenes and Napoleon. The Greek philosopher is here

acting as the Familiar Spirit in Leopardi's dialogue while trying to convince Napoleon that his satisfaction and enjoyment in life were not in the
actual success of his military and political achievements, but in anticipa-
tion of the things to come. Now that he is only a soul detached from life
there is no more enjoyment, for he can well see the outcome of all his
deeds. In certainty there cannot be any enjoyment. The voice of the
Passerby in another of Leopardi's dialogues can here be heard—the voice
that tells the Almanac Peddler that "the life that's beautiful is not the life
we know, but the life we don't know; not the past life, but the future"
(*Operette,* 481). Notwithstanding this constant frustration, pleasure
(that is, happiness) is the goal of man's life. Consequently "our life,
always missing its goals, remains continuously imperfect," and it is a
perennial violent state (*Operette,* 175).

The example of the weight exemplifying the contradictory essence of
Analyzing human nature in *Il dialogo della salute,* Michelstaedter
writes that "life consists in a lack, it is lacking everything . . . and
desiring everything" (*Dialoghi,* 39). In his dissertation he elaborates
upon this concept. "I want my enjoyment," that is, "I want myself
enjoying (because enjoyment is nothing but the correlative aspect of my
will, it is my very being)" (*Persuasione,* 107). Compare Leopardi's words:
"And this love for pleasure is a spontaneous and necessary consequence
of self-love and of self-preservation." It "has no limits, because it is
inherent and congenital with existence" (*Z,* 1:196, 182).

The example of the weight exemplifying the contradictory essence of
human nature that opens *La persuasione e la rettorica,* and returns in *Il
dialogo della salute* (330, 339, and 346), finds its perfect counterpart in
Leopardi's famous example of the horse. "If you desire a horse," he
writes, "you think you are desiring it as a horse and as a definite pleasure,
but actually you desire it as abstract, unlimited pleasure." "When the
soul desires a pleasant thing," he explains, "it actually desires pleasure as
such and not a specific pleasure," which is like saying that the soul
desires desiring (*Z,* 1:182, 183). After the metaphor of the weight,
Michelstaedter writes, "I know that I want and I do not have what I
want" (*Persuasione,* 39). Man's essence, therefore, as in the example of
the horse, consists in a lack, in a nonbeing, in an infinite tension and in
never arriving. Man desires an absolute pleasure that does not exist;
better, it exists only as aspiration, because, as in the case of the weight, if
it existed, it would cease to be absolute.

Man's essence consists in a lack. The human tragedy is inherent in his contradictory essence. The satisfaction of the need would bring about the end of him who is desiring. "This is the dear, sweet life: lacking everything, and desiring everything. This is life: if we did not turn to the future, but had everything in the present, we could no longer live" (*Dialoghi,* 39).

Leopardi returns over and over to this topic, and tries to reason on this contradiction of human nature. His reasonings culminate in the famous passage at the end of the *Zibaldone* where he negates the principle of non-contradiction on which Western logic had rested for centuries: "one thing cannot at the same time be and not be." Such a principle appears absolutely false if one considers the contradictions that are in nature; first of all, the contradiction of the human essence. Man *is* and at the same time cannot but be unhappy. "Now being, united with unhappiness, and united to it necessarily, by its very essence, is a thing directly contrary to itself, to the perfection, and to its proper end which is only happiness, damaging to itself, and an enemy to itself. The essence of human beings, therefore, is in natural, essential, necessary contradiction with itself" (Z, 2:924).

Human beings are part of nature and the absurd logic that rules over man is inherent in the absurd logic of nature that destroys in order to create, feeds on corpses, and prospers through destruction. To the Icelander who reproaches her for having created man to suffer, Nature answers:

Did you think by any chance that the world was made for you alone? Evidently you have not considered that in this universe life is a perpetual cycle of production and destruction—both functions being so closely bound together that one is continuously working toward the other, thus bringing about the conservation of the world, which, if either one of them were to cease, would likewise dissolve. (*Operette,* 199)

It is "the continuity of the race" that nature cares for; nature consequently is indifferent toward the individual (*Persuasione,* 177). Why should man place himself above other living beings and thus put nature on trial? Perhaps because he is endowed with reason that causes him to think, to ask questions, to need answers. Yet, what is reason but another physiological function just as limited by its material circumstances as any other?

Michelstaedter wrote an amusing short dialogue between the "I" and "the foot" in his first Appendix. It was probably inspired by a fall he had in one of his wild climbs on the San Valentin, and by the consequent injury to his foot. The quarrel between the "I" and "the foot" is caused by the presumption of the "I" that represents reason, in considering itself the master of the foot (representing passion) and therefore in attempting to boss it around. "The foot" then tries to make the "I" realize that its will can do very little if the foot is, for some mechanical reason, unable to move. Thus it tries to explain to the "I" that in order to be what it is (namely, a reasoning "I"), "I" needs "the foot" together with all the other parts of the body. At the final refusal by the "I" to accept such logic, "all the parts of the body disassembled . . . in the middle a feeble 'oimè' was heard dying away. Then everything was silent" (*Opere,* 173). Michelstaedter's pessimistic materialism cannot but bring to mind the end of Leopardi's dialogue between Nature and the Icelander. Man's presumption is punished here too by his disappearance. And it is yet more cruel insofar as the Icelander cannot even finish speaking—the utter nonsense of his words!—and because we are not even sure of the cause of his end. Maybe it was the wind that carried him away together with his words, or it was two lions "who were so worn out and starved that they barely had enough strength to eat up the Icelander, which they did and thus managed to get enough nourishment to survive for the rest of that day" (*Operette,* 199). Leopardi's contempt for human presumption receives here the most cruel sanction. Man's great "spirit" is barely enough to keep nature alive for a few hours.

Leopardi's influence is also evident in "Il dialogo tra la cometa e la terra" ("Dialogue between the Comet and the Earth"). The direct echo is "The Dialogue between Earth and Moon" where Earth is also on the losing side. Leopardi's Earth is not too smart; in fact, she is rather gullible as she herself admits. Earth represents men's presumptuousness, their view of themselves as the center of the universe. (Leopardi will develop this theme further in the dialogue "Copernicus.") Michelstaedter's Earth represents the status quo, rule and order as it proudly declares, and is suspicious of anything that might put it at risk.

The similarity between the two dialogues, however, ends here. Leopardi's Moon elicits a different discourse from Michelstaedter's Comet. The former's message is the discovery of universal suffering; thus, the Moon and the Earth find in this basic element a similarity between their otherwise very different natures. The Comet, instead, represents something completely different, but something that Leopardi would have also liked. It is a symbol of independence, unpredictability, creativity, all of which are emphasized by contrast to the dependence, bourgeois caution, and fear of the new, represented by Earth. It can almost be read as the dialogue between the artist and the bourgeois who wants to have "tranquil sleep," who "asks no question and does [his] duties, day after day, month after month, year after year" (*Dialoghi,* 114). The Comet, instead, does not take anybody's orders, shines with her own light, and runs through the sky scaring the wits out of the other planets.

Michelstaedter's imagination was charged by the appearance of Halley's Comet between May 18 and 19, 1910. The episode had created incredible excitement and even fear in people's minds. To some it signified the announcement of the end of the world, and even writers like Svevo and Canetti recorded on paper the excitement that the incident had stirred. Michelstaedter was, of course, on the side of the comet, "the unpredictable celestial body that loves and creates risks, that carries with itself light rather than expecting it from others" (*Dialoghi,* 20). The event that shook up the tranquil sleep of his bourgeois fellow creatures was, of course, welcomed with cheers.

There is something very unlike Leopardi—to return to our point of departure—in *Il dialogo della salute.* What really differentiates it from the Socratic and the Leopardian dialogues is that Rico and Nino are actually the two sides of Michelstaedter. Campailla, in fact, talks of a dialogue that really is "the dramatization of a monologue" (*Dialoghi,* 12). The close reading of this text shows inconsistencies and confusion. The main purpose is to lead young minds along the path of *persuasione,* and thus to teach them not to depend on future expectation, to free themselves from needs and dependence and, finally, from the fear of death: real death is to live with fear.

Yet Rico, who delivers this message of *persuasione,* also speaks a more humane language. "He who has lost the flavor of things is ill . . . since flavor is nothing but the feeling that something is useful to one's health"

(Dialoghi, 46). Developing this theme later, Rico arrives at this conclusion: "those who look for the pleasure of the body, that is, for the meaning of the existence of their bodies, [they] lose its entire flavor, so those who look for other pleasures signifying a vaster existence, lose the taste of everything and do not know anything any more. They are empty" (64). Rico seems here to advocate an active rather than a contemplative life. Looking for meanings does not bring about happiness. On the contrary, it alienates the world from the individual whose mind and body are so drastically separated that no further union is foreseeable.

Salute is here synonymous with *persuasione.* It is mental and physical integrity and authenticity. Disease is a typical twentieth-century literary theme that in Italy found its spokesman in Italo Svevo and Pirandello. It is the consequence of the obsessive use of reason at the expense of the body. Sharpness of mind often goes hand in hand with physical weakness. Yet weakness is often welcomed and, as in Svevo's case, even prized for it is a sign of self-awareness and of a critical mind.[59] Svevo's awareness of the incompatibility between physical strength and intellectual life made him accept the impossibility of obtaining both. Having opted for sharpness of mind, he learned to live with his physical ailments, even to laugh at them, and retreated to the realm of thought and writing. Michelstaedter, instead, though just as much aware of such incompatibility, could renounce neither a strong body nor a sharp mind. His idea of *salute* is utopian and does not coincide with that of contemporary philosophy. *Salute* is, to him, the perfect accord of mind and body, the absolute coincidence of thought and action. *Salute* is authenticity, *persuasione.* Yet Michelstaedter had repeated over and over that only he who does not depend on anything, who finds everything in himself, is a real *persuaso;* thus we cannot but call such a concept of *salute* paradoxical.

After twenty years of working with Michelstaedter's texts, Campailla first raised a doubt about his health in the preface to the dialogues. Had a real pathological condition been deliberately kept in the shadow for all these years out of respect for the family? A careful reading of Michelstaedter's letters, Campailla claims, would bring to the surface the "progressive loss of a balance, [and] not only of a psychic balance" (18). The line quoted in the text from Simonides, "no good of any type comes from knowledge if we lack venerable health," acquires, for Campailla, a tragic connotation.[60]

It is, of course, pointless to debate such an issue, useful though it might be, for example, in the attempt to explain Michelstaedter's suicide. An act as complex and mysterious as suicide demands a rigorous analysis in which such speculations could hardly be admitted as evidence. What this dialogue shows, however, is a great confusion of contradictory feelings and ideas and the suffering that they must have caused to a mind which, though sensitive to the changing times and capable of the most profound analyses, probably could not cope with the heavy ethical consequences: the loss of foundations. His obsessive return to the theme of self-possession, independence, "consistency" in the desert of life belies a deep and profound feeling of uncertainty and psychological imbalance.

In 1905, he wrote this short, previously unpublished page in his diary. Probably not intended to be seen, it is a lucid example of self-analysis that verges on the borders of masochism.

> Since I started studying—my inner self—neither a motion of the heart nor the most hidden instinct, neither the innermost recesses of my thought nor that of my feelings, in any instant of the day, in any instance of life has escaped the merciless scanning [*scandaglio*] of cold reason. And so I destroyed the spontaneity, the authenticity of my feelings, I destroyed the youth of my soul, I damned myself to eternal misery. You don't know the torture of feeling in oneself those motivations that one despises in others, the rage caused by feeling oneself pushed by them toward the things that the intellect scorns. You have not felt the supreme torment caused by self-contempt, by the nausea for this mud that surrounds us and constitutes our own essence. You have never felt the overpowering desire to escape from your own self, cruel and ferocious judge. . . . My ideal would be to free myself from myself, to cease this horrendous splitting of my being in two that will drive me mad. Only in sleep have I peace but I do not enjoy it, precisely because I am not aware of it.[61]

Two themes are at work in this dramatic passage. The first is the theme of dichotomy, feeling–reason. Reason with its merciless analytical tools brings into the open, examines, scrutinizes and eventually nullifies the innermost feelings by confronting them with the nothingness that surrounds us. The complete awareness of one's emotions blocks any spontaneous act and eventually dries out the instinctive part of human nature. Man remains at the mercy of analytical reason.

The second theme at work here is the discovery of evil in one's inner self. Self-analysis not only destroys emotions by considering them vain reactions against the nullity of existence, it also destroys naive faith in the goodness of the instincts. Man discovers the mud that constitutes his being, a mud into which no divine breath has been infused.

As he wrote in another page of his diary in the same year, this merciless self-analysis exhausted him:

> I am horribly tired, my mind is broken by this inane effort of suggestion. Everything is useless. My impressions do not stick onto my soul. They vanish as soon as they come closer. Their vanishing gives me an infinite anguish. Everything flees before my brain, making me dizzy. Or is it my brain that is vanishing? It seems to me that I am a different person at every instant, I lost the feeling of continuity of my "I." Only tenacious and deep suffering unites me with the past. Suffering is the last link of the chain that ties me to life. I believe I will become mad.[62]

The following year, in a letter to his sister Paula, he diagnosed his existential malaise. His sadness, he tells her, has no specific object, hence the tragedy of it; hence the *Angst*.

> I suffer because I feel cowardly, weak, because I see myself as incapable of controlling the ideas that race through my head . . . the way I have no control over my passions; because I have no moral balance . . . because I have no intellectual equilibrium, which would bring thought straight to its goal . . . because . . . everything is slipping through my hands . . . and more and more I am convinced that I am nothing but a degenerate. (*Ep.*, 157)

The awareness of his mental unbalance, of his incapacity to control his thoughts and the fear of becoming insane return with the obsession of his obsessed mind. Two years later to his dear friend Gaetano he will write a similarly revealing letter that is a literary jewel and to which we will soon turn. Mental illness, it appears, is still with him. He reiterates

his anguish because he cannot control thoughts and feelings. "The consequence is that I feel I . . . that is, I cannot feel myself. This is all (I have
just stopped writing, pen in hand), in the effort to say clearly what I am
feeling, and I have understood that I really do not feel myself. I can no
longer find myself" (*Ep.*, 330).

MICHELSTAEDTER AND PIRANDELLO; OR, FOLLY

> The ontologically insecure person[s] . . .
> have come to experience themselves as pri-
> marily split into a mind and a body. Usu-
> ally they feel most closely identified with
> the mind.—R. D. Laing[63]

It was precisely in order to exorcise this sense of loss of the self, of alienation of the "I" that Pirandello kept his pen in his hand and wrote, wrote
obsessively, throughout his life.[64] Because writing is on the side of contemplation, Pirandello immediately made his choice; a choice prompted by fear
of a violent instinct which he succeeded, through writing, in controlling.

Carlo was nineteen when he wrote the letter to Paula quoted above.
At nineteen Pirandello had also written to his sister a letter describing his
existential anguish:

> Meditation is a black abyss, inhabited by dark ghosts, guarded by a
> desperate distress. A ray of light never penetrates it, and the desire to
> possess it sinks you more and more into darkness. . . . We are like
> poor snails that, in order to live, need to carry with them their small
> shells. . . . An ideal, a feeling . . . an occupation—here is the small
> shell of this big snail, or man—as they call him. Without it life is im-
> possible. When you arrive at not having any more ideal because by
> observing life you see it as a big puppet show . . . without meaning
> . . . when you, in a word, will live without life, think without mind
> and feel without heart—then you will no longer know what to do: you
> will be a traveler without a home, a bird without a nest. I am so.[65]

Michelstaedter in another letter will compare his brain to a wave-filled
sea whose "bottom remains murky and dark" (*Ep.*, 330). The dichot-

omy of life–thought, or action–contemplation, was clearly established from the start, and it was precisely its obsessive presence that brought Michelstaedter and Pirandello to the verge of insanity. Pirandello, however, used writing as a real *pharmakon* to exorcise the power of his unconscious. Michelstaedter, instead, was overwhelmed by such dichotomy.

The one and only time Pirandello mentioned Michelstaedter—in an interview for *Quadrivio* only a month before his own death—he referred to him as an example of those unhappy thinkers who "wanted to make form and substance coincide absolutely and in every instance and were overwhelmed."[66] With this statement Pirandello recognized an affinity on a basic philosophical point: the contradictoriness of life whose essence is flux but that must be fixed if it is somehow to be grasped. It must give itself a form. This form, however, is death; it stops the life that it tries to define. Pirandello shares this belief with Michelstaedter, but considers the pursuit of such coincidence (of "form and substance") totally inane, insofar as it has only two possible conclusions: suicide, as in the case of Michelstaedter and Otto Weininger, or madness, as in the case of Nietzsche.[67]

Michelstaedter too mentions Pirandello only once, but unfortunately less revealingly—at the end of a letter home where he records that he has written to his brother Gino and sent him a story by Pirandello. He omits the title of the story and any word of comment. His matter-of-factness justifies the assumption that he must have been familiar with Pirandello's works. By 1907, the date of the letter, Pirandello had already written dozens of stories and had published his most famous novel, *The Late Mattia Pascal.*

Fourteen years earlier Pirandello theorized in his essay *Arte e coscienza d'oggi* about the existential crisis he had diagnosed in his letter to Lina and placed it in historical context. "The old laws having collapsed, the new ones not yet established, it is natural that the concept of the relativity of everything has widened so that . . . nobody is any longer able to establish a fixed, unshakable point." The same truth is delivered by that incredible character, Anselmo Paleari, in *The Late Mattia Pascal* when in a lighter tone he exclaims: "Darkness and confusion! All the big lanterns have been blown out. Which way are we to turn?"[68] The lanterns are metaphors for human ideals, absolutes, laws. They have all collapsed and man has lost all fixed points of reference.

Perhaps Michelstaedter had not read *The Late Mattia Pascal,* but in his letter to Paula he is writing of the same existential malaise:

In part it is individual, in part, though, it is the disease of an epoch in regard to moral balance, because we are in a transitional epoch of society when all ties seem to be loosening . . . and the paths of existence are no longer clearly traced . . . toward a culminating point, but they get all confused together, and vanish, and it is the task of the individual to create for himself his luminous path in the universal chaos. (*Ep.,* 158)

Yet Michelstaedter, like Pirandello, sees that part of his crisis is also personal, subjective, probably connected to his oversensitive nature.

As for the rest, the problem is mine and takes away from me the strength of my thought, the enthusiasm of any initiative, the clarity of any conception, and I remain groping in the dark, floundering to rise to the surface. This I feel profoundly and I know I will neither be happy nor will I do anything good, and if I don't become mad I will torment myself and suffer until I die. (*Ep.,* 158)

Darkness, sinking, madness are all themes we find repeated ad infinitum in Pirandello, and, as Laing has shown, they are the symptoms of the schizoid personality.

Had Pirandello known Michelstaedter's letter to his sister, he would have had yet another proof of his diagnosis. He seems, in fact, to be speaking of Carlo when in the same essay he wrote that the youngsters "are all affected by neurosthenia and are morally inane." A great confusion had taken over their conscience. They no longer knew "in what direction to go; they are lost in an immense labyrinth, all surrounded by an impenetrable mystery. Many are the roads but which is the true one?" (*Saggi,* 900).

The crisis both authors are analyzing is in part historical, in part personal, but, for both, it is also the essential condition of human beings. Neither of them, in fact, had any hope that social or historical changes would come to the rescue. "Life has no rest, just as the sea has none" (*Saggi,* 903) and life is desire, never fulfilled. Michelstaedter's and Pirandello's voices are here speaking in unison. "Possession will never correspond to the desire, man will never free himself from his chain," said Pirandello (903). The tension of Michelstaedter's "weight" can still be felt.

In his *Pirandello la follia,* Gioanola makes brilliant use of Laing's essay *The Divided Self* to analyze most of Pirandello's production and prove that the threat of insanity was his constant companion and that his wife's tragic illness was to him a mirror of his own "latent psychotic potentiality."[69] Michelstaedter was also obsessed with the idea of becoming mad, as we have seen. Both authors, as did the psychologist Laing, found the origin of this obsession in the drastic separation of the mind from the body.

Laing, who followed the psychiatrist Minkosky in his analysis, was convinced by the latter that this separation was the trait of schizoid patients who "maintain judging capability, but lack the life instinct."[70] Pirandello, after all, was fascinated by the mysteries of the psyche and was very familiar with Binet's *Les altérations de la personalité* (1902) and Marchesini's *Le finzioni dell'anima.* Many are the characters of his stories and plays in whom this opposition is embodied. The epitome of the dichotomy is represented by the writer Silvia Roncella and the cameraman Serafino Gubbio. Silvia "lives" in order to write. She is detached from the life she describes in her books to the point that she is unable to bring forth a new life, to procreate. Actually her capability as a writer is inversely proportional to her attachment to life. Serafino, whose arms and hands have become part of the camera that shoots life in segments, that is, stopping it, will lose all his humanity. In the end, he will, just like an automaton, continue to shoot a real human slaughter.

Pirandello, who created characters in order to give a body to this obsession, theorized about it with great lucidity in his famous essay *L'umorismo (On Humor,* 1908). "Life," he wrote,

> is a continual flux which we try to stop, to fix in stable and determined forms, both inside and outside ourselves. . . . The forms in which we seek . . . to fix in ourselves . . . this constant flux are the concepts, the ideals to which we would like constantly to comply.

Yet inside us life continues "indistinct under the barriers and beyond the limits we impose."[71] But if these forms can easily collapse just with a breath, as Cosmo Laurentano has told us, what can happen to them when "moments of flood arrive, and the river overflows"? "Everything is submerged," exclaims Moscarda in *One, No One, and a Hundred Thousand*.[72] Life rushes through and tears down all our artificial constructions.

We cannot but think of *Il dialogo della salute* at the moment when the ridiculous form of the philosopher that Carlo/Rico had built for himself is shuttered by the floodtide, as Pirandello calls it, that suddenly comes to the surface and tears down the neat construction in an instant. The wise Carlo who talks of balance and virtue cannot even control his own bad temper when his brother comes to his room and disturbs his profound philosophical reflections. The virtuous philosopher simply slaps his brother in the face. And Carlo remains stripped by his artificial creation, alone with his naked truth. Yet, Pirandello continues, "one cannot be in the abstract. Being must happen, must create its own appearance to itself: the world. The world is the activity of being, it is appearance, illusion, to which being itself grants the value of reality." "Life is being that gives itself a form. It is the infinite which becomes finite. In every form there is a purpose, an end. Every form is death" (*Saggi*, 1274).

There is no way out of this impasse, no possible synthesis to such opposition. Although life cannot be known and man can only sense it, he will forever and ever need concepts, ideas; in short, abstractions, forms— and Michelstaedter will repeat this in his dissertation—in order to make sense out of the chaos. At least so he thinks; just as he needs a form, an appearance for himself, says Pirandello, in order to acquire an identity for himself and the others. The attack against names, ideas, truths becomes, for both authors, the attack against systems of any kind, be they philosophies, sciences, or religions. They are abstractions, screens as Michelstaedter had said, that cover a dark void. Science has now taken the place of religion. "Don't we call nature today what in the past we called, more poetically, God?" The scientific definition of nature "as a symbol of mechanical connection" does not help us to understand it any better (*Saggi*, 1056). "Science extracts life and almost destroys it in order to anatomize it" (1058). What remains? A series of neat abstract formulas with which we can only play a game.[73]

Michelstaedter sees the course of events moving toward a future where each word uttered or action performed will be mere appearances, an empty shell devoid of any content. Words like "virtue, moral, duty, religion, goodness . . . will, too, become *tópoi koinoí* [commonplaces] and they will be as stable as the scientific ones" (*Persuasione,* 174). Darkness will be completely veiled to everyone's eyes in the same way, for men will then be all domesticated in the same way.

If human language is made to coincide with *rettorica, persuasione* will be achieved only through silence. "Language," writes Michelstaedter, "will reach the limit of absolute persuasiveness—what the prophet reaches through a miracle—that is, it will arrive at silence when each act will be totally effective" (173). "True contact between beings," wrote Cioran, "is established only by mute presence, by apparent noncommunication, by that mysterious and wordless exchange which resembles inward prayer."[74] Born out of the need to communicate, language must finally yield and accept its defeat.

Michelstaedter's ferocious criticism of the violence inflicted upon children at the end of *La persuasione e la rettorica* is justified by the fact that it is the cowardly way of perpetrating *rettorica.* The child learns right away that "one thing is theory; another, practice" (189); he is forced to learn theories and principles that have no relation to his needs and desires. He knows that his obedient behavior, though meaningless to him, will bring him some gain; a prize, a gift, a promise, and he acts accordingly, organizing his life into two separate spheres. When the child becomes a young man in college he is told "to do a study on Plato, [for example], or on the Gospel" so he might become a famous scholar, and he is warned to be objective and detached from the object of study (189). He works without ever asking what is the meaning and the purpose of all he is doing—he has been trained to do this from an early age.

This outpouring of acrimony and bitterness by Michelstaedter is clearly a self-indictment. He is here questioning and repudiating his own work. And, of course, he cannot go on.[75] His scholarly dissertation was by its very nature a self-defeating task. It represented everything he was combating. It was the celebration of *rettorica.* He had not been able to remain faithful to the original topic. It happened to him as it happened to Eco's last hero Casaubon with his dissertation on the Templars. The works that had started as scholarly dissertations had changed in the process of being written. At the end, both were questioning the very nature of the undertaking. Yet there is no escape from *rettorica* and

Michelstaedter knew it (and Eco knows it too). The same afternoon he mailed his dissertation to Florence, he killed himself.

Had he run outside that afternoon to find solace in the green waters of his Isonzo or to climb his beloved San Valentin, perhaps nature would have offered him a taste of *persuasione,* enough to make him go on living longer. Michelstaedter knew that nature would never lie to him. Neither would it address him with the language of *rettorica.* His passion for physical outdoor activities was the most genuine way he could communicate his love and devotion to nature.

The San Valentin (now known as the Sabotino) was the destination of many of Michelstaedter's climbs, often undertaken in the company of his few, faithful friends. It was also a symbol of purity and authenticity. Climbing San Valentin to the top was almost an act of penitence and purification with, at the end, the Cross of sacrifice and rebirth (a wooden cross actually stood at the top). He and Nino when climbing the mountain felt as if they had performed a religious rite (*Ep.,* 431). The sanctity of the mountain was confirmed in Carlo's request to Paula to send him a rock taken from it. He then thanked his sister and treasured it as a sacred relic.

Just as the psalmist looks up at the hill to acquire the strength that comes from God (Psalm 121), Michelstaedter conquers the mountain in order to identify with the absolute. His is not a philosophy of contemplation, but of action and creation. On this mountain he had written some of his last poems, in a desperate effort, perhaps, to defeat the *rettorica* of words with the purity of the surroundings. Even in his letters to his friends, the mountain is a powerful presence. There, too, its purity is evoked in contrast to the obscurity of intellectual activity.

After the tragic death of his brother Gino he writes home: "In the moments when I feel a little enthusiasm in my arid work I feel I am fighting for life and for the sun against the aridity and obscurity of academic philosophy. I feel I am fighting for the sun, the air and the purity of the rocks of Monte Valentin" (*Ep.,* 355). In this image of uncontaminated life he sees himself as the hawk that protects the purity of the top of the mountain from the baseness of the crows.

In 1908 Michelstaedter wrote a legend about Monte Valentin; a piece of "poetic prose" Campailla called it, a romantic story with a medieval setting.[76] The piece has all the characteristics of young Carlo's style.

D'Annunzio's presence can be felt in the formal aestheticism, in the sensual atmosphere of the setting as well as in the hymn to joy and physical love. Yet this legend is also a testimony to the energizing power that nature had for him. Nature was authenticity, *persuasione,* whereas the philosophical discourse of his writings was *rettorica.*

Is it pure coincidence that Eco's masterpiece of *"rettorica," Foucault's Pendulum,* ends with the image of a hill? (Nature is otherwise almost absent in the novel.) To the image of the hill is juxtaposed the disbelief created by the intellectual constructions that disrupt men's lives, giving them neither comfort nor peace. The hill had appeared at the beginning of the novel, before any plan had been conceived, before the human mind had started creating monsters and mazes in which to plunge to damnation. "Yet the hill is so calm tonight, a summer night now," totally untouched by the insane plot the human mind is about to conceive.[77] And so it will be at the end, still there, stable, always the same, a stronghold against the dizziness the human mind has created.

"So I might as well stay here . . . ," says Casaubon at the end, "and look at the hill."

"It's so beautiful."[78]

Yet the human mind, Svevo warned us, has become capable of creating *ordigni* (bombs) that will erase even the beautiful hill and with it, the rest of the earth;[79] similarly, in Leopardi's words,

> so too of the entire world, and of the infinite vicissitudes and calamities of all created things no single trace will remain; but a naked silence, and a most profound quiet will fill the immensity of space. Thus, this stupendous and frightening mystery of universal existence before it can be declared or understood, will vanish and be lost. (*Operette,* 379)

Even Leopardi's "crow" will cry no more.[80]

THE *EPISTOLARIO;* OR, ABOUT *PERSUASIONE*

> We begin to live authentically only when
> philosophy ends, at its wreck when we have
> understood its terrible nullity, when we

have understood that it was futile to resort
to it, that it is no help.—Emile Cioran[81]

The dichotomy of life–thought, or body–mind, tore Michelstaedter in two. In his very person the two parts in fact seem to have been equally strong and powerful, defeating the conventional wisdom that one always acquires strength at the expense of the other. Did Michelstaedter's futile attempt to balance them contribute to his final act?

If his philosophical writings are the place to examine his intellectual search in its unfolding, in his letters his concern with nature and the physical aspects of his being is openly stated. Furthermore letters have, or at least should have, a quality of authenticity that derives from the spontaneous urge to communicate with immediacy an idea or a feeling that would normally be expressed orally were the receiver of the message present. The idea or feeling is generally recorded, left there without further reflection or connection. Campailla writes in the introduction to the *Epistolario,* "the letter is for Carlo a sort of magical ritual; it promises to rescue a threatened intimacy, the descent to secret depths; the day is organized around it, condensing [in it] its essential meaning" (*Ep.,* x). Carlo's letters are the pages of a diary where he constantly tries to assert himself with all the good and the bad; and where he strives for *persuasione.*

The hundreds of letters written home and to his intimate friends clearly show the intensity of his sensuality and physicality, which he did not attempt to restrain. It is evident how much he treasures and cultivates this side of himself: his exhausting mountain climbing, his passion for dancing ("a physical pleasure, an unmatched voluptuousness" he calls it [*Ep.,* 98]), his long swims in the rough waters of the Isonzo which made him famous and proud, and his frustrations when an injury to his foot kept him at home for some time. He was constantly pushing himself to the limits of his capabilities, and nature was his beloved playground. There he had the illusion of reaching that absolute that as a social being he never could even approach.

A letter describing the funeral of the poet Carducci brings out better than others this aspect of Michelstaedter's nature; its force springs from contrast. The main subject, in fact, is death, yet its end is a hymn to sensual life. He loves Bologna for its richness, abundance, fullness of life. The qualifiers he chooses to describe it are self-explanatory:

I think of Bologna again, of the past three days; they appear to be an oasis of a superior sun and life, so intense, that I'll be scarred by it for the rest of my life. But then, I love Bologna, with its porticos, its beautiful dark-red palazzos, its beautiful vast piazzas, its imposing San Petronio church, its lively movement . . . of happy people everywhere in throngs to see and to be seen enjoying life. I love the generous and sincere cordiality of the people, I like the teeming public places, full of life and warmth, and . . . more than anything else, I love its women, opulent, radiant with life, who smile when smiled at, and who seem to give themselves entirely through the glance [sguardo]. (186)

One of Michelstaedter's greatest pleasures was taking long walks alone or with his close friends to the outskirts of the city. It was his habit in Gorizia as well as Florence: hours and hours of excursions in the countryside and climbs to the top of the hills surrounding the cities. When in Florence it was not unusual for him to decide in the middle of the night to walk to Fiesole and see dawn from the surrounding hills. He loved the impression that nature made on him at night. Even a sudden rain that could at times accompany his walk would not spoil it. He wrote home one day that "some thick dark clouds blocked the view of dawn from a height of 1,000 meters and made us pleasantly wet on the way home. We walked eight hours" (Ep., 189).

Summer, the season of energy and power, excited him immensely. To his family he wrote: "We suddenly plunged into a fiery summer . . . that kills and makes everybody cry, but that makes me live a life one hundred times more intense." Walking through the streets of Florence he could smell the strong scent of summer. "Thursday I walked two hours under the sun, alone in the countryside, to go swim in the Arno" (Ep., 213). And spring excited him with its joyfulness. "It grabs me by the throat," he wrote to Paula, "if I do not move, if I do not expand, if I do not live—I suffocate. It is like being drunk" (Ep., 303).

Already at age nineteen he had celebrated his closeness to nature in his answer to a question in a family game ("Where would you like to die?"): "where and when infinitely beautiful nature suspends my individual life and makes me palpitate through her and makes me feel the need of uniting with her."[82] Carlo seems to be proud of his exceptional physical qualities, of his being unique, of his being nature's special son, and he wonders why "I do not live always outdoors, why do I make myself sad with books, and with these mummified creatures [his professors], risking also to become mummified" (*Ep.*, 302). In order to feel good "at least relatively, [he] would need to walk at least 12 hours" (*Ep.*, 389).

From early on, Michelstaedter analyzed the incompatibility of thought and feelings. To another question ("Which is your favorite entertainment?") he had answered, "I enjoy all those things that make me feel so strongly as to silence my thought."[83] The opposition of thought and feeling is openly stated and the reciprocal war declared. Writing home after a long walk to Piazzale Michelangelo he describes the emotion that the nocturnal view of Florence gave him as "a wave of beauty running through my body . . . I became one with nature. Nothing in such a moment is more of a hindrance than thought. I enjoyed that three-hour walk immensely" (*Ep.*, 102). He knows that even the description of the emotions felt would kill them, and he limits himself to relating the occurrence.

Likewise when writing to Gaetano and describing his physical activities at Pirano, his swimming, sailing, dancing, he states that he refrained from talking in order to live more intensely the life of nature (335). And we could add, borrowing Pirandello's words:

> Life was pulsating in his throat, with the taste of so many inexpressible things, which made him almost cry from the fullness of the joy that he felt and in seeing that the others were enjoying it too. . . . But he had the strange fear, that not only with saying it, but even only with thinking of it, it would vanish. (*Saggi*, 1272)

"Life cannot be explained," Serafino Gubbio will say, "it must be lived" (*Romanzi*, 2:662).

A year earlier, back home for the winter holidays, pampered by the attention and love of his family, he had written to his dear friend Gaetano Chiavacci: "My spirit fluctuates deliciously in a sea of good and sweet things so much so that I feel I am getting stupider and stupider by the day; just as deliciously, however, and progressively I am becoming a bourgeois." At home, vacationing, Carlo is simply living: "Imagine, that since Monday I have no longer thought; I left a piece of my brain on each cliff of the Apennine." Nature and thought do not agree with each other.

Carlo lives the life of nature and keeps Plato, Kant, Homer "religiously" closed on his desk. "I sleep like a pig, eat, drink. . . . I practice fencing, I dance, walk, talk" (*Ep.*, 266). At times one seems to be reading Svevo's pages to Livia with their expressions of fear that the superficial happiness of the good bourgeois life will turn him into an idiot. We seem to hear the voice of Zeno Cosini, although Zeno, unlike Carlo, accepts the incompatibility of reason and feelings, deciding at times to follow one or the other according to his own personal whim.

Although aware of the dichotomy he was living and of the equal power the two elements exerted on him, Michelstaedter, as a good Romantic, was critical of reason and had always positive words for feeling and nature. Thus he is constantly concerned with his physical well-being. After a physical illness and several months of study in preparation for his exams, he feels that his inertia is ruining him also morally, making him more nervous, more irritable. "I need to lead a purely physical life for many months" (321). And what joy only two weeks later when, feeling better, he writes home with the former intense exuberance:

> The pains in my knees are almost gone. . . . actually today . . . I feel free. I run, jump, do fencing, I feel reborn: I skipped over every bench I found on the road, I climb again the stairs three by three, I get on the trolleys while they are running, I started again to beat up all my friends and to upset those who live on the first floor. I have become a man again. (*Ep.*, 324–25)

The joking tone shows that he is thriving physically again. It reflects his mood after having taken and passed the boring exam in Italian literature that had turned out to be a painful work of historical and philological research. In the same early letter where he had written about his illness and his depression he had told his father that he was not made for this type of study. The connection of his physical state with his extremely abstract and theoretical work is evident. To Paula, too, he wrote: "Above all, I think of my body, it is important to me." And a few paragraphs later: "I must stop talking about myself, because I must stop looking into myself—it can be intellectually useful but it's not healthy" (305–6). Again it is Zeno who comes to mind with his theory that thought and self-analysis make action impossible. Zeno, however, makes his choice and accepts its consequences: he will be a paralytic thinker. Of course, at times, he will decide to follow an impulse, for example, to pursue a woman. But then he will follow it without trying to rationalize it, giving reason a deserved break. And he will even laugh at his own weaknesses and cleverness. Carlo cannot. He can neither laugh nor can he accept the necessity of compromise. In his Nietzschean dream of asserting himself as the *Übermensch,* he prefers death to compromise. His is the insane urge of someone who wants feeling and reason to coincide.

To his father on January 17, 1907, he wrote that he could never be satisfied with only a contemplative life. "Too many things tie me to life." "And so I constantly fight against that contemplative tendency of mine" (*Ep.,* 170). "I have to repress the disgust that I feel at this mincing operation on the part of thought, at this fragmentation of the ideal unity that I feel inside me" (*Ep.,* 171). His preference for the instinctive part of man is justified by its superiority. Man's instinct and nature do not lie, they are authentic, they are the voice of *persuasione.* Only when a "man lives (not when he reflects outside of life) does he feel the absolute universality of the concepts of good and evil" (*Ep.,* 230). If good and evil are inside, as part of one's nature, then it is possible "to project them as a universal law onto the others . . . but not as an abstract good outside [one]self" (230).

It is clear, then, that *rettorica* derives from abstraction, from reasoning, from theories, never from nature. It must have been tragic for Michelstaedter to realize that nature, which is authenticity itself, and never lies, could in his own person become low and even evil. These realizations he, characteristically, verbalized.

Often in his letters home Carlo apologized for his actions and words that might have hurt the feelings of those who loved him. He hated himself for this violent aspect of his nature that nothing seemed able to control, not even his enlightened, superior mind. The violent outbursts, to which his family was probably by then accustomed, are to him an a posteriori cause of great remorse and suffering.

> By now you have probably forgotten . . . but I am instead still under that impression and cannot control my melancholy. I am really sorry for having been so unbearable with you all, especially with you, Paula. I can feel that I was really hideous. . . . I would slap my face now if I

could see me as I was—all those airs and not wanting to hear anything, that acting so presumptuously and wanting always to be right; a real swine. (*Ep.*, 246)

Michelstaedter's capacity for introspection was great. He turned upon himself the lens of the scientist, the scalpel of the surgeon. Pitilessly he tore into the weak and evil fibers of his soul. The result of a painful operation was the exposure of all the weaknesses that the real *persuaso* should overcome. After taking advantage of his aunt Irene Bassani who admired and loved him dearly, Carlo felt self-contempt. "I went there to enjoy myself (to eat at her expense), to sponge on her, faking an affection I did not and I do not feel. . . . I made fun of her in every way and I have done it even a moment ago; and the poor old lady wrote me a very affectionate letter" (*Ep.*, 288). Of course, nothing of what Carlo discovered inside himself was outrageous or particularly wicked. In this respect, he was just an average human being with many petty traits and some good ones.

But he never accepted his being like other human beings. After all, he continued to criticize them for all their pettiness and ugliness. By doing this with such acrimony he placed himself upon a pedestal above the masses of the miserable as if he were the Solon of mankind. In such a context, the realization of his own pettiness and ugliness could not be accepted with humility; he responded with bursts of rage.

Yet there were more serious episodes that made him realize that the identity of theory and practice, the coincidence of thought and action was a total illusion. There is a moving page at the end of *Il dialogo della salute* that is self-explanatory. Rico, the main interlocutor, is Carlo himself here performing an act of self-confession.

I, who would walk on the streets or in the mountains with one of my friends talking of virtue, fortitude, courage and of the "vanity of everything," of life and death, I—the very same—would then give a profound and philosophical slap on my brother's cheek, if he dared to trouble the peace of my sanctuary where I was fabricating wisdom; or I would slam the door in my mother's face. . . . My mother remained silent, at times she would cry; my brother once rather than protesting noisily, stiffened, clenched his fists, and left without a word. I went after him, I looked at him and saw in his contracted face such a deaf rebellion, such a hatred in his surly eyes, such a desperate flame, that it terrified me. I grabbed him and tried to hug him, but he freed himself with disgust. Ah the tears he did not weep, I wept! Freedom, justice, imperturbability! What's the use, when one is the slave of a door that opens and with the same hand that has made great gestures to inflate long sentences, slaps a child to defend "the peace of his own thoughts," in order to be able "to think" ahead in the blind impotence of my lost peace! And notice, please! On my brother I was naturally applying pedagogical theories. And then after doing it, immediately aware of the infamous injustice, the first gesture: a caress, to beg for my brother's forgiveness. In "terror" because I had seen in such a mirror the vanity of my words, the nullity of my person, grabbing hold first, hoping with that easy act, to gain the comfort from a child's weak condescension, the comfort that would put my heart to rest. Coward! And then, after recognizing even this last act of cowardice because of his fortitude, the crown of drama, the tears. Can you see that heap of flesh sobbing and dissolving itself in tears? That is the philosopher! Nausea! Nausea! (*Dialoghi,* 82–84)

The analysis could not have been more pitiless. It must have left Michelstaedter crushed in the ruins of his artificial constructions.

It had started with the death of Nadia. Nadia Baraden was a Russian divorcée some years older than Michelstaedter. He had met her in Florence at the end of 1906 and had given her Italian lessons. A strong friendship developed that perhaps became more intimate. She was a cultured woman, and he shared her artistic and literary interests. He even painted her portrait in oils, one of his most moving. Carlo was only nineteen and although we do not know the details of this relationship, it is likely, as Campailla says in his biography, that he might have behaved with the superficiality characteristic of his young age. The episode did not last more than a few months. On April 11, 1907, Nadia took her life, while Carlo was in Gorizia for the Easter vacation. He ran back to Florence, haunted by unanswered questions.

Within a few weeks he was writing love letters to a girl at the Institute where they were studying, with whom one of his friends was also in love. This intense, brief infatuation was censured by his parents, who must have written him letters of criticism and parental moralism, judging by his replies. Carlo felt unjustly judged by his family and wrote voluminously to explain his behavior and to reassert the strong moral principles his parents taught him. Still, he must have been filled with doubts as to the honesty of his actions if he could write to his dear friend Gaetano:

> I have been torn by strange problems and I still am, so unable to dominate them that I even ignore their actual weight and what the consequences of the various solutions can be. . . . Everything has sunk into materiality, and the whole construction of my dear and proud dreams has fallen into the most despairing skepticism. . . . I no longer believe in my faith. . . . All the painful things that happened this year and especially the one you know [Nadia's death] and which I thought I could easily overcome, are tearing me apart. And most of all I am tormented by a doubt about the honesty of what I did . . . you know what I am referring to. And I despise myself like a dog. Everything, everything is collapsing . . . I ask myself why I am living, and I find peace only in sleep and in the most violent exercises. (*Ep.*, 244)

Nadia remained in his thoughts. At the end of 1909 he wrote a dialogue between Carlo and Nadia with a Greek title ("He who attaches himself to life has been already judged"), reminiscent of Dido and Aeneas. The doubts about his honesty that he had confessed to Gaetano become here open accusations. Nadia is dead and accuses Michelstaedter of being a selfish individual, just like any other human being, miles away from that *persuasione* that constituted the object of so many of his discussions and so few of his actions. "You have loved neither me nor anyone else, but in every person only yourself," Nadia tells him.

> —Nadia, I still love you.
> —Don't talk. Only he who "is" can love the person who no longer is and cannot love him.
> —But you have never loved me.
> —I would have loved you if you had been such to love without asking to be loved. (*Dialoghi*, 98)

Nadia is here speaking with the voice of *persuasione,* that voice she probably heard so many times coming out of Carlo's mouth—but only as a sound.

> —Poor Carlo! . . . No one can love the one who only loves the love that he needs, for, if he needs it, it means he does not possess it. You have nothing, and nothing you can give, but you will always ask, more and more miserable, you who "are" not and cannot love, but you ask for love in order to delude yourself into thinking that you are someone. But nobody can love him who "is" not.
> —Nadia, I shall kill myself! (*Dialoghi,* 98)

It was still only a cry on paper.

Michelstaedter resorted to physical exercise in moments of mental depression. The more his mind was confused and upset the more he felt the need to exert his body to the utmost. From Gorizia he wrote to Gaetano a list of physical activities for the days to come and of his intention to participate in a street demonstration for irredentism. Excited, he wrote: "Imagine if there were really a chance to exercise my hands—what pleasure!" (*Ep.,* 328). Yet, three weeks later the tone had changed completely, and his mental depression had taken over again. In the same letter where he describes the days spent vacationing near the sea, at Pirano, in the company of Paula and the Cassini sisters, he explains his torment to his friend. Its power derives from the contrast between nature and mind. The intense life of nature that Michelstaedter leads at Pirano opens up the dark abyss of his psyche.

The days spent at Pirano are days of physical activities: walking, climbing, swimming, sailing, dancing. Even talking is purposely reduced to a minimum in order to live the life of nature, intensely. Carlo's personality appears here completely split. The son of nature has found his perfect habitat and achieves fulfillment in all his activities. To Gaetano he describes this stretch of the coast as a sailor or fisherman would, and he is proud of the offer made to him by fishermen to remain with them and live at sea. He seriously thinks that it might be the best solution to his indecision. Yet Carlo is also a creature of thought. The beautiful comparison of his brain to the sea conveys all the power and intensity of his chaotic needs and feelings:

> My mind is like an undulating sea that reflects all lights, that mirrors . . . all the skies . . . but that shatters them all at the focal point—but the bottom remains murky and dark . . . certainly I have what the sea has not: I have the uninterrupted torment of bygone intentions and of future commitments, of the different and unfulfilled yearnings: the consciousness of my meaninglessness [*nullità*] in this world regulated by actions as well as by thought and art; of life dissolving, awaiting what? In the illusion of a progressive shaping [*formarsi*] that does not exist. (*Ep.,* 330)

The image could not have been more effective. The sea, symbol of force, vitality, infinity, and the freedom of nature, is here made to coincide (or at least Carlo is trying to make it do so) with the intellectual, spiritual absolute. But this attempt is bound to fail; the two can never coincide.

Michelstaedter's brain is like the sea with its strength, force, freedom, but also with its dark, irrational, turbid side. The brain–sea image proves his refusal to be only like the sea or the fisherman, and his need to be everything: nature and spirit, action and ideal to a degree of perfection. Frustration follows frustration. "I realize with growing terror that I am condemned to remain outside the intensity, passion, greatness of life, and that I will never have a way of living it within me." And in his depression he admits: "There would be nothing left for me to do but lead a physical violent life, go wandering on horseback through the plains and rest at night in a tent counting the stars" (*Ep.,* 331). His ultimate negative response to this rhetorical proposition is powerful. As for the Leopardian shepherd, the life of nature is not enough for Carlo, yet intellectual fulfillment escapes him. Even reading no longer satisfies him.

> Everything passes through rapidly as if my brain were a point or a mass of points. . . . There is no possibility for me to embrace a larger whole, actually even before trying I already feel the void. . . . So I no longer am able to think, to write or to paint; I feel disgust toward myself. (*Ep.,* 336)

His mind and feelings are openly at war. Although he likes Fulvia Cassini and enjoys her company, he writes to Gaetano:

> my heart must be like a sucked pear—I feel something very special for her, I wish to be with her more than anything else, yet I do not think it is love. . . . This means I am no longer capable of feeling love, that even this now escapes me like everything else, actually with it all the rest is escaping. I thought how happy I would be if I were really in love, and I had this love in everything I do. Instead I am no longer good for anything. (*Ep.*, 335–36)

In the pursuit of perfection, of the coincidence of mind and body, Carlo has lost both. He now knows that his refusal to pursue only one term of the dichotomy and his attempt to realize both has ended in total failure: "Gaetano, my friend, how unhappy I am and how scarce the probability I see that in the future something can change, if not for the worse, while chains of every kind are approaching" (*Ep.*, 337). And the natural consequence of this dissatisfaction with himself comes out as aggressiveness toward others. The imitator of the great *persuasi* of history is not even exempt from the most common and lowest weakness of human nature: turning against others the contempt he feels for himself.

AN EXAMPLE OF *PERSUASIONE:* ENRICO MREULE

The short list of the *persuasi* of history that Michelstaedter makes at the beginning of his dissertation starts with Parmenides and ends with Ibsen. Among his famous contemporaries Michelstaedter does not seem to find anybody. Yet he found one *persuaso* very close to him: his intimate friend Rico Mreule. One year older, Rico emigrated to Argentina in 1909—a gesture, as we will see, of profound significance for Carlo, who transformed him into a modern Socrates in his *Il dialogo della salute.*

The eight letters to Rico in Michelstaedter's *Epistolario* reveal more or less his tormented soul, but all have a spark of *persuasione,* which was probably lit by this friendship. In his first letter, written in April 1909, Carlo expresses his feelings after having heard Beethoven's *Eroica.* He tells his friend of his need to run outside, to climb the San Valentin and to feel like the hawk that reaches the top of such elevated purity. In the second letter, written precisely two months later, he discusses a terrible play he had gone to see, lured by the critics' florid comments. The description of the evening is extremely revealing and changes direction as it proceeds. Michelstaedter, in fact, was disgusted by the public applause that greeted the end of the play and began to boo and whistle with all his might. To the indignation of the audience, he laughed louder and louder at the "stupid and ferocious face" of that "big beast made out of one thousand people" (*Ep., 394*). Although the commotion continued outside the theater, "no blood ran" on the streets, he remarks. At this point the tone shifts abruptly. The irony, sarcasm, laughter, and jokes that Carlo the actor had produced before his public died out when he was left alone on the street at night: "I stopped laughing and was taken over by a nausea of myself who had behaved just like the public, in an inadequate manner" (*Ep., 394*).

The episode was to Carlo another sign of his own vanity. In the same letter, continuing a discussion he had started in the April letter and that Rico had likely continued in his answer, he expresses his ideas about the real *persuaso*. The examples are Christ, Buddha, and Leopardi, but also Plato when he was looking for the absolute, which to him coincided with the highest good (*agathón*). The *persuaso* "climbs the mountain (Calvary) in order to die, not to adjust himself to life." "There is no 'after' for him who has lived in one moment all times" (396). Lately, Carlo writes at the end of his letter, he had "learned to know Christ and Beethoven and all the rest [was] waning" (398).

Carlo openly identifies his friend with Christ in another letter: "a Christ wounded and dirtied by the slander and wickedness of those around you" (404). It is a difficult letter that begins with a statement about the strength of their pact of friendship. It is a rapport founded on negations and reactions, thus unbreakable. It acquires its strength and eternal quality by the tragic truth of the nullity of everything. "And the more tragic the conditions the more the friendship flourishes, our friendship which feeds on negative forces" (403). The contradictory essence of Michelstaedter's philosophy is exemplified here. The positive force of the tie between the two friends derives from the negative force of the universe in which it lives. We can stretch the image a little further; it also derives from the opposition between the two types: *homo persuasus* and *homo retoricus*.

Rico is surely Carlo's alter ego. He is the meter against whom he measures himself. The letter proceeds with a discussion of Plato and Aristotle, which Rico continues in his reply. It is one of the very few letters to Carlo that have survived. Rico agrees with his friend on the matter of Plato and Aristotle and reveals his profound relativism and subjectivism. Rico's other replies to Carlo must have been extremely powerful and profound if the latter writes, after reading them, such merciless self-analysis.

> All you wrote in your last one is true, and it is as much true as it is sad. For me it is the almost material contact with that truth that tells me: "you have failed, all your hope is in vain, whatever you do or say is a dishonest attempt." (*Ep.*, 407)

Michelstaedter is tormented by his fickleness. For him who professes the necessity of "constancy," of being always faithful and coherent to oneself, his instability was a source of desperation.

> Before the things of life I do not have a steady reaction, but flare-ups of enthusiasm that quickly burn out. . . . And I am at times cold, at times ardent, always split in two, while one part skeptically observes the inconsistencies of the other and always has clear the sense of its own limitation, of nausea. (*Ep.*, 407–8)

Michelstaedter can examine himself so profoundly and mercilessly because Rico is before him as the other self. "But you, instead, are always the same . . . the realization of such difference between us puts me in immediate contact with my life and with life in general" (*Ep.*, 408). It is the presence of "the other" that produces self-consciousness.

At the end of November, without telling his family, Rico boarded a ship for Argentina. Nino Paternolli, their common friend, accompanied him to Trieste. A few hours later Carlo is already at his desk, writing his dear friend one of his most moving and telling letters.

The opposition between the "I" and "the other," between Carlo and Rico, is established at the opening: "While I write here in the light of my lamp in my usual place as you see me—you, I think, you will already be in the open sea" (*Ep.*, 420). The contrast between thought and life is clear. Carlo, as usual, can only sit, think, and write about that life, "the open sea," that Rico is instead living. The image of the sea is as recurrent in Michelstaedter's writing, perhaps more so, than the mountain, and we will examine it at length in his poetry. They were both used at the beginning of his dissertation as metaphors of *persuasione*, that which one strives for and can never possess (*Persuasione*, 40). In "I figli del mare," the most famous of his poems, the harbor that Itti and Senia (the "children of the sea") are struggling to reach is not a shelter away from the tempestuous sea, but it is the very fury of the sea on which Rico is now sailing. As a real *persuaso*, Rico is crossing the treacherous ocean but his "soul will remain clear and immutable" (*Ep.*, 420). Carlo diagnosed his disease and discovered the reason for his attraction to Rico: it is the reason that darkness is attracted to light:

> With your action . . . almost with concrete arguments bearing alone the weight of the theoretical arguments, with which you in our conversations would open to us the path to the right evaluation of things, you have accomplished for us the only benefit that a friend can offer a friend. (*Ep.*, 421)

Carlo continued to write praises of his friend, though he realized that they could never substitute for actions. "But it is useless that I produce so many words in my comfortable room" (*Ep.*, 422). With his long letter Carlo is following step by step his friend's journey. He proceeds through sentences while Rico is proceeding through waves; Rico's nautical knots cannot be matched by thoughts on paper. Carlo knows each move of the ship. "By now you will no longer suffer the cold, since you will be off the coast of Brindisi. From the agency we found out that the ship will touch only the ports of Almeria and Las Palmas in Europe" (422). At the close of the letter, in a desperate gesture, he tells his friend that he has just climbed up in Nino's attic, where the three friends used to spend so many hours together, to ask the sun at what point in the sea his dear friend was. It is all Carlo can do—a pathetic climb toward a light which he can reach only vicariously. "But when you receive this letter you will be 'abandoning' the Mediterranean and will be sailing over the open sea" (*Ep.*, 424).

The thought of Rico becomes obsessive and with it Carlo's self-analysis and feeling of inadequacy. In December he writes to Rico:

"While you in this time have acted so as to conquer inertia, which is the enemy of everything, I am still the same as you left me, different from myself. Therefore the more I hear and desire to hear from you, the less I feel like talking to you" (*Ep.*, 425). Two months later, there has been little change, and he can still write:

> As for me, I am always there, as you know "at the point when the moment is no longer for waiting, but for acting" and always immobile. As when one must rise and constantly dreams of having risen . . . and little by little realizes that he is still lying in bed . . . and he neither rises nor stops dreaming that he is rising, and continues to suffer from the live image that troubles the peace of his sleep and of the immobility that makes the dreamed action vain. (*Ep.*, 431)

As time passes Carlo's depression increases. Lack of recognition of his intellectual activity adds to it. His writings, which he sent to various journals and publishers, came back with courteous and cold rejections. Not only can he not live as Rico could, he is not able to write. He shares with Nino his impression after reading Rico's letter, commenting: "Rico's letter set fire inside me, when I think of us, who envying him, are prevented from wanting to join him by the same things that prevented us from leaving with him" (436). But Carlo belongs only in part to "the race of those who remain on land." And this was to be his tragedy.[84]

In a letter to Gaetano, who suffered a similar depressive crisis, Carlo speaks with the words of Rico to comfort his friend. He has learned or at least memorized his lesson, and now he repeats it to Gaetano: "Why are you worried? What do you fear? Nobody will ever be able to take anything away from us. Life is not worth our tears. But let's always go ahead and try to be self-sufficient in everything; there is nothing that is too severe, no position really unbearable" (*Ep.*, 438). This is Rico's voice speaking, the same voice we hear in the opening of Carlo's last letter to Rico. Rico's authentic life is so intense that he can still live among and with his friends even now when he is so far away. "Whereas I," Carlo laments, "cannot live with you but only insofar as you think of and care for me even from afar. I have the impression of no longer having any voice, so much this sad nightmare of weary inertia oppresses me" (*Ep.*, 440). Carlo had not written to Rico for four months, four arduous months in which he was struggling with his dissertation. It was no longer possible for him to write as a *persuaso*. Neither could he write "without conviction empty words just to be able to present a written paper" (441). "In order to do my work as I wanted, I needed that voice that comes from free life; I had hoped I could find it; instead I found myself wishing only for silence, having lost every interest in what I had proposed to say with enthusiasm." Silence is the only honest action. And he is silent even with Rico.

By the end of June the struggle is three-quarters over; the prospect of the sea at the end of his chore gives him a last burst of energy. Yet all these months he has been only writing, playing with words, creating *rettorica*. "One year has passed since we have shaken hands here in my house . . . since then how much you have done, and how your words have become action! I am, instead, still nourishing myself with words and I feel ashamed" (442). Those were to be the last words Carlo wrote to Rico. The nourishment of *rettorica* was no longer sufficient to keep him alive.

LETTERS TO HIS FAMILY

Michelstaedter left Gorizia for Florence at the end of October 1905. Although enrolled in the school of mathematics at the University of Vienna, he had obtained permission from his father to spend some time in Florence, to study art, his real passion. Leaving for Florence meant crossing the border into Italy, and he experienced many of the problems foreigners have in such circumstances. Sending letters home was not one of them. It is amazing to see the efficiency of the mail service in those days. Letters would always arrive at their destination within twenty-four hours. A journey to Florence then as now was a cultural pilgrimage that every intellectual would make. In this period another of Michelstaedter's famous compatriots, Scipio Slataper, was living in Florence, as was the poet Umberto Saba from Trieste, of whom Michelstaedter left a portrait in pencil.[85] A few years later yet another poet, Giulio Marin, was to enroll in the same Istituto Superiore where Michelstaedter studied between 1905 and 1909. Slataper and Marin were active in the *La Voce* movement, with which Michelstaedter as far as is known, had no contacts.

A month after arriving in Florence, Carlo received permission from his father to enroll in the Istituto di Studi Superiori in order to obtain a free pass to all museums and libraries in Florence. Alberto Michelstaedter,

a self-taught man of letters, understood the importance of his son's
experience in Florence and tried to facilitate it. From Carlo's letters of
this period, we know that he was studying physics and mathematics on
his own to prepare himself for the exams at the University of Vienna.
Carlo spent a little less than thirty months in Florence between his arrival
in October 1905 and his final return to Gorizia at the end of June 1909.
There remain 130 letters written to his family. In the first months he
sometimes wrote home twice a day. Campailla has pointed out the
importance of correspondence among the Jewish community, "a way to
show solidarity, to maintain the unity of the group, and to overcome the
opposite dangers of isolation and assimilation" (*Ep.*, xi). Carlo wrote
hundreds of pages home. Most of his letters are addressed generally to
Carissimi (My dearest ones), many to his sister Paula, sixteen to his
father, and only seven to his mother. In the most prolific period of his
correspondence home he never wrote a personal letter to his mother; the
first to her was dated May 22, 1907.

To the family, Carlo wrote almost a day-by-day diary of his activities.
Places visited, lessons attended at the University, criticism of boring
professors, study habits, walks, acquaintances, nuisances, even his daily
diet, with the most accurate list of expenses; everything was recorded
and found its way in his letters home. There are also amazing pages that
reveal the great amiability that tied the members of the Michelstaedter
family together, and the strong affection Carlo felt for them. The insistence on his desire to be with them, on how much he missed everyone is
almost overwhelming. The letters home, as Campailla notes (*Ep.*, xii),
signal Carlo's "temperamental charge" and intense nature. Statements
like "I desire you overwhelmingly" or "I cannot think of you without
crying . . . I could never have expected to suffer so intensely from the
separation" (12, 14) are indicators of "a neurosis" that was already
"meandering" inside his psyche (*Ep.*, xii). Together with the power of his
feelings these letters also reveal his profound sense of humor. They are
never boring; some are amazingly funny. His closeness to all the family
members manifests itself in the form of affectionate insults, jokes, anec-
dotes, and the use of dialect in many dramatic descriptions. Michelstaedter loved the theater and in his letters he often plays different roles
to make the characters come alive.

The letters to Alberto Michelstaedter are just like all the others Carlo addressed to his family. The only personal element was at times the request for money or the expression of his gratitude for money received—typical of letters to a father. In none of them, however, did Carlo reveal his intimate self, with the sole exception of a group of five letters, all written between the end of May and July 1, in which he tried to explain his love for his schoolmate Iolanda de Blasi and to defend himself from the accusation of being a superficial, selfish young man. Nadia Baraden had committed suicide a few weeks earlier, and a friend of his was already in love with Iolanda, so his behavior seemed callous and inappropriate.

The letters from his father to him are unfortunately lost, but from Carlo's combative and proud self-defense we can infer that their content and tone must have been extremely severe. After all, we have "the paternal sermon" Alberto gave his son on the eve of his departure for Florence. The stereotype of the father figure is complete. The insistence on honesty, rectitude, and honor runs through the whole piece, whose leitmotiv is, however, the pursuit of the golden mean, that is, "measure," the avoidance of excesses and the necessity of striking the right balance. It is a letter that besides revealing much about Alberto—who was only typical of the time—tells even more about Carlo. The insistence on measure and self-control reveals a legitimate concern: namely, the concern with Carlo's violent temperament, with a nature that easily yields to rage, incapable of dominating passions.[86]

In these few self-revealing letters to his father, his main objective is to gain back his family esteem and trust and to assure them of his mental and emotional stability. It is, therefore, interesting to find statements about himself that are the opposite of those made a few months earlier to Paula. To her he had written, "I suffer because I feel cowardly and weak, for I cannot control things, people or ideas . . . as I cannot control my passions, because I lack moral equilibrium" (157). And to his father: "I assure you that I feel strong and healthy and I feel I can control ideas and things" (222). Of course, it could also have been a moment of passing optimism. The only intimate pages to his father, therefore, had a forced quality. Never again would Carlo open up his inner self to him.

Paula was his confidante—like Leopardi's Paolina—Gino and Elda being too old for sharing entirely their experiences with their youngest sibling. And to Paula, Carlo wrote long letters, not only confiding in her, but also counseling her in moments of hardship. Their loyalty to each other was total, and their love very intense. In it one can detect the presence of elements which, though typical of lovers, are nevertheless often present in a brother-sister relationship, including possessiveness and jealousy. It is not a coincidence, in fact, that in the most difficult sentimental period in Carlo's life, precisely the one mentioned above, of his infatuation with Iolanda after—and maybe even before—Nadia's death, he never wrote to Paula.[87] Iolanda had taken her place. Four months of silence followed. When finally on June 4, 1907, he starts to write to Paula again, Iolanda has disappeared. He must apologize for his silence and defend himself from his sister's accusations. Naturally she would have wanted to be the exclusive confidante of Carlo's love-story and it is likely that his justification—not writing because "I thought papa would have read you my letter"—could not but have hurt her feelings. In Carlo's self-defense we can clearly perceive the smothering intensity of Paula's feelings.

> I would like to have you close to me now to be able to hug, caress and kiss you and to make you feel all my love that has never undergone, and never will, any changes. . . . You think that I have changed. I don't know in what way. You think that I am undergoing a phase of imbalance, madness, dissatisfaction, and who knows what not. Instead I assure you that I have never been calmer, more serene and aware of what I feel and want, more satisfied with myself. (*Ep.*, 226)

As time passes Paula fears that Carlo is growing away from her. His silences are interpreted as betrayal, his words are often misunderstood, and he feels justly offended that she who knows him well could so misread his letters: "After all it is ridiculous that I must reconfirm my love to you every so often. . . ." He expects more understanding at least from the people in his family.

> As soon as I do not write, for some personal disposition, and then I write not precisely the way you expected . . . I immediately must be told that I have changed, that I am no longer me, that I no longer care about you and all the many nice things you write me. But for goodness' sake, if I have been all my life in a certain way, how is it possible that

you think, that now, all of a sudden something can have radically changed me? Don't you understand that it is extremely irritating for me to hear this, whereas I would like to expect you to say, if a letter of mine may seem strange to you: "he wrote a strange letter," "he is in a crazy mood," . . . instead of threatening me with anathema as if I were the lost son. (*Ep.*, 319)

Yet we can also understand Paula's feeling, considering the intimacy of their relationship.

In April 1909 Carlo did not return home for the Easter holidays. Paula went to visit him in Florence. She stayed for a month and he did all he could to give his sister a pleasant time. When she left he did not tell her goodbye at the Florence station, but rode on the train with her as far as Bologna. There he took a train back to Florence while Paula proceeded north. On the train that was taking him back Carlo wrote a loving letter to her.

My Paula, I am again on the train in this sad station, and I am feeling again the awful impression I felt as I saw your tearful face through the steam of the departing train. . . . I left the station like a sleepwalker with the impression that I always had to think of something or to wait for someone, and this something and someone was you, my poor *pasticcio,* and when I became aware of it and said to myself "I have nothing to wait for, I have nobody to take care of, Paula has gone," I felt as empty as a cave; inside I was lacerated by the painful meaning of that ugly impression. After a month of such united life it seems to me I have no goal, no reason for doing one thing rather than another. It seems to me that everybody seeing me must say "what animal is this? For what use is it made?" and must read on my forehead: "animal without goal." (*Ep.,* 366)

Paula remained faithful to Carlo's memory for seventy years until her death in 1972 and even wrote a moving but very discreet biography of her brother. It is thanks to her that most of his writings are now safe and available to scholars in the Fondo Michelstaedter in the Gorizia Civic Library.[88]

EMMA MICHELSTAEDTER; OR, *LA PERSUASIONE*

In his letters home Carlo often complains about the laziness in writing displayed by the members of his family; most of all by his mother. Several times in his first year in Florence he asks the question, "Why doesn't Mother write?" "But what's bothering Mother? She never writes a line" (*Ep.*, 114, 102). In time he became less demanding and no longer wondered so intensely about those silences, especially his mother's. If at the beginning he felt neglected, with time he seemed to learn more about her and to understand the reason for her silences. Of course, I am merely speculating; Carlo never openly commented on this matter. Yet, it is a hypothesis that has solid ground in his philosophy.

Carlo wrote only seven letters to his mother, fewer than to anyone else of his family and friends. The first we have was written in reply to one from her after his involvement with Iolanda. Although we do not have Emma's letter, from Carlo's we infer that, though she is disappointed about her son's actions, her words must have been filled with tenderness and understanding. Carlo opens up completely to Emma and lets his feelings speak. The last paragraph is worth citing in its entirety.

> You, Mama, who know how I was in Gorizia, you who have seen so well and so deeply inside me you cannot but be happy, you cannot but love this little girl, who can love me so much and can do me so much good with the feeling she has awakened in me. I kiss you with all my love and give you the kiss that she always tells me she would want to give you. (*Ep.*, 219)

Michelstaedter can take for granted his mother's complete sympathy by virtue of her absolute, unselfish love for him. Emma feels with Carlo for he is still part of her flesh. His feelings are her feelings. Reason has no place in this type of understanding.

Carlo wrote a second (surviving) letter on the occasion of his mother's birthday—he was extremely good at remembering important family dates. After a brief reflection on the passing years and his feeling himself always unchanged, he describes to her his daily activities and briefly talks about the family. It is again the end of the letter that interests us.

> Mama, I am writing to you in a very silly manner, I act like the one who, feeling very emotional and not wanting to express anything,

speaks of superficial matters. But you understand this, and you feel all the affectionate things that I would always want to tell you and I don't know why, we at home feel almost ashamed to say, and today more than ever. I should also have told Paula to give you some flowers on my behalf. But, after all, they are all superfluous things between us. . . . It is truthful, though, the commonplace that all I can wish for you coincides with all that would make me happy. (*Ep., 258*)

He is again underlining the unity between mother and son that needs no words and cannot be expressed through words.

After a short note written at the end of November 1907, there is a long, amusing letter (April 8) that must have delighted the whole family. Carlo is here making fun of his big American cousin Joe, who is visiting Florence—a typical example of a large, strong, healthy body attached to an empty head. He recounts Joe's visits and his silly chats. Joe's judging things in terms of size rather than quality and his constant concern with his bodily functions annoyed Carlo. In his letter he plays his cousin's part and records or invents excerpts of conversation decorated with plenty of linguistic mistakes for the amusement of his readers. It is interesting to see that in the midst of this comedy, still in a comical fashion, he inserts a comment about maternal love which rejoices at any manifestation of her child's essence, even in his urine, "because a little brat does not have to do anything for the moment but to be and live, and the simple fact that he is made by her and is her ideal object gives her joy" (*Ep., 308-9*).[89] No one better than Emma could have understood Carlo's humorous, yet very profound remark. Where maternal love was concerned, Carlo knew that the quality of the object was of no importance. A mother loves her child for what he or she is. The child is love that has become flesh. As he takes leave of her at the end of the letter he writes: "If you were here you would do me so much good" (*Ep., 310*).

Six months pass. On October 16, the eve of Emma's birthday, Carlo confides in his mother as he had never done before.

Mamma mia, I continue to talk to you as I was doing that evening when Paula interrupted us. As I could not talk then in front of her and could not talk in front of anyone else, so I beg you, please, to burn this letter as soon as you have read it. Do not show it to anyone. I was telling you the reason why I had been such a pest with you and not only sometimes, but often, and for little things. You see I have gotten used to thinking of you as the person who loves me for myself, who loves me as I am, with every defect and wickedness. I feel that it is not necessary that you sacrifice your will in order to want what I want, and that you make an effort of intelligence to understand what I feel in a given moment. I feel as if you were never outside me, but that we are still always one only person . . . like twenty-one years and five months ago. And this is after all the mother-son relation as nature defines it. The mother is the only person who can love just like that without need to affirm her own individuality and without feeling it as a sacrifice. And for the son this is the only affection that does not infringe on his freedom. It is the love that must grow and intensify itself and become pure as man grows in awareness and intellect. Until the moment in which he arrives at renouncing life—then even this love will dissolve in universal love. (*Ep.,* 341)

Carlo had looked for love outside. Except for the letters to Iolanda that reveal some excesses characteristic of his young age, none of the other love letters, if there were others, remains. There is, of course, his dialogue with Nadia where love is discussed and where Carlo is accused of the same selfishness he sees in others. At the same time he will always find the love of other women inadequate, selfish. His desperate attempts to find the equal to mother's love are bound to fail. His words for Iolanda are one of those desperate requests—another he will make to Argia—for a love that must be equal in strength and magnitude to that of his mother.

Iolanda . . . do you feel you can love me not for my smile, for my joy, my triumph, my faith . . . but for this struggle that is in my soul, for my sadness . . . for what in me is rebellious and hostile . . . [do you feel] you can love even in defeat, love me beyond life, beyond the human boundary? That you can love me as I am in my becoming, and not as I should be and . . . maybe will never be . . . ? (*Ep.,* 209)

His mother's presence is so real that a few lines later he writes: "my mother would love you, actually already loves you, without knowing, I am certain." Iolanda's image here coincides with that of Carlo's mother.

And this identification is conscious; he is here asking Iolanda to be a mother-bride. From her he asks for absolute love.

Yet Carlo did not find this love in anyone else, and to his mother he returns.

> As long as man lives, the love for his mother is the greatest, the strongest, it is what resists against everything, what always remains the safe shelter, the small harbor where man can come back and feel pure and calm, where the small miseries of life do not reach. (*Ep.*, 341)

Paradoxically he is here using rhetoric to express an absolute truth.

Carlo started this confession as a request for forgiveness. During that summer his temperament had deteriorated, as had his mental state. More than once he had exploded in violent scenes with family members, in particular with his mother. "You must feel," he tells her, "that I feel with all my soul what I say, that I have the intimate 'persuasion' of it, and the pain I have caused you in these months and the doubt I read in so many of your sentences must disappear" (*Ep.*, 341). Again Carlo is justifying his behavior with her on the basis of an intimacy between them that he takes for granted. With her, at least, he should not have to pretend. With her, at least, he can be himself, even his ugly self when circumstances are against him. And she should not misunderstand him, she should not misread his actions. No, this he cannot accept from her.

> It is natural . . . that when I felt lost internally and when I was leading a superficial life while I could not master myself or the consciousness of myself, [it is natural] that I could be indifferent and the same with others, but I would show myself to you as I really was; only that instead of explaining my illness to you, I made you feel it in all my irritability and in my rude and wicked manners. You were close to me and more than anyone else you suffered the consequences. (*Ep.*, 342)

The verb "to feel" recurs many times in this letter and it often takes the place of the verb "to understand." Emma must feel what Carlo feels and this sympathy does not need reason as an intermediary. Reason is what we resort to when we cannot have that *sympatheía* that is the only authentic way of communicating. It is with the use of reason, in fact, that man's problems arise. The natural bond between mother and child needs no logical explanation. It is when the bond is severed that communication must resort to logic.

Yet there is a precarious moment in this letter.

> After this state of affairs, when you would finally say things about me and would blame me as the others can do, who do not know me, I suffered because I felt you far from me, I felt you did not understand me and that you had no compassion—and as usual rather than understanding that after all the fault was mine, I became irritated and caused you more suffering. (Ep., 342)

What, then, is this *sympatheía*? Where did the unity of feeling go? Why did Emma misunderstand Carlo? But did she really? Or was it rather that she just wanted something different from him, that she was not sharing everything he felt? Carlo had created an image of the ideal mother and Emma no longer matched it. How is this possible? Can a mother's love be selfish too? Are then mother and son two beings and not one? By admitting his fault, Carlo is stating his right to be different from his mother's wishes. Then how can he still demand total understanding if there cannot be sympathy? Through Emma's censure, Carlo has been confronted with a moral condemnation that has sanctioned the severing of the umbilical cord. Yet he still tries to fight against it. In his final apology he strives for the union again.

> Now I condemn that silly young man who made you suffer and I find for him only one justification: that he was suffering too, that he was suffering even more; now I feel that you are the most sacred thing to me, and that the best that there is in me consists in this feeling. (Ep., 342)

Carlo still hopes that his "becoming and being what I want and feel I must be" can coincide with his mother's desires; he hopes that his and her desire still can be one.

Only one of Emma's letters to her son remains. It was written at the beginning of September 1910 and prompted the famous answer Michelstaedter wrote on September 10, the answer that was to be his last letter.

Emma's words are filled with sadness and melancholy. They are the lament of a mother for the lost union with her child. It is the painful acknowledgment of his becoming an adult, of becoming the "other." It is the sad "longing" for an age which is now gone forever.

> My Carlo, this tedious rain makes me melancholic and I think of you with more insistence than usual. I would like to have you near me and take care of you as when you were little. To cover you and dress you as I want and above all to be able to make you happy with any little thing. Instead I can do nothing. . . . You no longer understand me, you don't understand a mother's satisfaction in caring for even the basic needs of her loved ones.

Emma longs for that time of unity when mother and son were one; she longs for her Carlo's lost childhood and must acknowledge that he is an adult—and not the one she expected.

> If you only knew, the other evening on the Corso seeing so many youngsters who seemed happy with their families . . . my thoughts ran to you and I saw you so much alone, I saw you better than any of the others; yet I felt tears in my eyes, because I might be stupid, but I suffer, because it seems you are a stranger to me. In the past I was so proud of you that I felt almost pity for the other mothers comparing myself to them. Now everything has collapsed. But enough with bothering you. I kiss you, my Carlo, so very much.

In a postscript she added: "Do not misunderstand me."[90]

It is clear from these few lines that Emma no longer understands her son and that she is fully aware of it. The separation from him though natural is painful, and she still asks him to understand her in the name of that mother's love which is taken for granted because it is universal. And Carlo will understand her, as he will also remind her about universal maternal love. On September 10, Carlo answers his mother with his most moving letter. It is a literary piece, as Campailla pointed out, and it could be considered part of an ideal *Epistolario,* together with Leopardi's and Kafka's letters to their fathers. The way it is organized and constructed makes it also a quintessential piece of rhetoric. I am using this word on purpose not in order to catch Michelstaedter in a contradiction, but rather to point out the existence of a positive rhetoric in his writings. His last letter, in my view, is in fact an example of the sublime, defined by Longinus as the echo of greatness of soul.[91]

The letter begins with an extremely long rhetorical question (18 lines) that is made up of an introductory subordinate clause generating a series of subordinate clauses that reiterate intensely the same idea. Maternal love here is generating infinite activities, which are, however, all similar and whose repetitive quality is conveyed by the stylistic devices here employed.

> When you covered me if I was cold, fed me if hungry, comforted me when crying, played with me when bored, when you stayed awake at night near me and worried about me during the day—tell me, did you do this as a little girl does with her doll, who can repeat endlessly day after day the same game, did you do this as a nurse or a wet nurse, who does it as the daily work of her life, who gives her care to new patients and new babies, or did you do it as my mother who fed and protected me so that I could grow strong and healthy, because in the small, tender stupid thing in need of everything, lacking defense and security before any little event, you were dreaming of the man, the strong man secure of himself before anything, who no longer needs anything that he could not obtain by himself, so healthy that nothing could any more worry him? (*Ep.*, 448)

The main rhetorical figures are all present. The long rhetorical question is organized as a hyperbaton (or inversion) which, by delaying the climax, builds up emotion and suspense. Repetition through asyndeton and accumulation of similar elements mirror the endless, generating force of maternal love that manifests itself through repetitive action. The main clause, namely the real rhetorical question, is delayed by a series of false ones that increase the emotional tension. The answer arrives in the second paragraph. It is the obvious answer that a rhetorical question entails yet it is also a reminder, for Emma, of what the ideal mother must be. In case Emma might act with some selfish motivation, as the letter she had sent him could imply, here Carlo is teaching her a lesson in maternal love. The fact that he does it through a rhetorical question involves her in his discourse and makes her unable to distance herself from it. The ideal behavior of a true mother is what he expects and has had from her in the past. How could she back out now?

> You were not playing the mother game, but you truly were the mother, and the sweet taste that all the little cares, sufferings, sacrifices had for you were this distant hope, this distant vision of the man who was to bloom out of your frail body. You did not take care of me in order to continue to do so in the future—you did not take care of me with the hope that I would remain an eternally frail and impotent object of care—but instead you did it in order not to care for me any more, so that I would no longer need anyone to take care of me. For this you have suffered and hoped for me. (*Ep.,* 449)

This answer is organized in the same way as the opening rhetorical question. He replies negatively to the first questions, leaving for last the real answer. In the adult Carlo, Emma will no longer love "an uncertain future" but "the live present." "It is now time that I act, it is time that you receive and that I give . . . that I be, through my action and my deeds, the man you have dreamed of" (449). Carlo thinks back on his year of "inertia" as he calls it, the year of his dissertation, and names it "the price of liberty." A high price, for it delayed his action and immobilized him with rhetoric.

In the moments of depression Michelstaedter must have gone through while writing the dissertation, it was his mother's thought that pulled him away from the verge of the abyss. In what follows there is, still hidden, that which was going to be, a posteriori, the haunting accusation Emma would have to live with for the rest of her life.

> If you [only] knew, Mama, how many times in this . . . painful life I have bordered on the abyss, how many times I gave up hope of ever reaching life, and I closed my eyes which saw only darkness all around, and I was just on the verge of giving up completely. In those moments, I do not know by what intuition, every time you made precisely that gesture, you said that very word, you came near me in that way that gave me new strength—so I was able once more to pull myself up by the hair. (*Ep.,* 450)

A month later, on October 17, Emma was neither going to make that gesture nor to say the word that would have given Carlo the strength to pull himself up once more.

Carlo feels guilty for this year of inertia, but he knows and tells his mother that the end is now near. Replying to the comparison Emma had made between him, nailed to his desk, and the other youngsters happily walking on the Corso in the company of their families, he proudly accepts the fact of being different. Their life is empty, they only worry about a career which is imposed on them by others, they live idly through meaningless jobs and activities and even their family and relations with friends are empty. Carlo, instead, places himself away from and above the others. The last page of his letter could be called his spiritual testament, his commitment to a life of *persuasione,* his ethical statement. In just one page he compressed the whole of *persuasione* that he had tried to theorize in his dissertation. His words to Emma condensed all the themes he had treated in those twenty pages called "La via alla *persuasione*" (*Persuasione,* 67–89). He knows by now that a dissertation is by nature the very opposite of *persuasione;* he knows that *persuasione* cannot be spoken about but must be lived; he knows that with his dissertation he had defeated his purpose. Thus he is here committing himself to a life of *persuasione.* This is what adulthood means to him; this is what he tries to explain to his mother. He is no longer one with her. He has grown and has severed the tie. This operation, though painful, is the only one that allows a real life. "I know, now, what it means to be a man. . . . I am confident and tranquil because whereas others naively expect a lot from things from people, and depend on them, I know that I cannot expect anything from anybody, thus I have nothing to fear from life" (*Ep.,* 451). And to his mother, a last gift: "When I do something for me it will be for you as well, you will be near me even if we are separated; you will know everything about me and will be able to see how I will accomplish what I feel I should . . . and instead of your cares, you will give me 'only' your love and trust" (*Ep.,* 451).

An enlightening postscript closes Michelstaedter's last letter. Reminding his mother of the intimacy and secrecy of their correspondence, he concludes: "I want to have spoken with you alone; it is precisely because it is so difficult to do it in person that I am answering you in writing" (*Ep.,* 452). As Derrida had said, speaking about Plato's *Phaedrus,* writing is both cure and poison. Michelstaedter resorts to it because he needs the necessary detachment from an intensely shared sentimental situation. Writing allows him to see his passions as if they were outside himself. Recording them helps him to cool them and makes it possible for him to describe them as objectively as he can so his mother can read them as they should be read. Yet Michelstaedter, better than anyone else, knows that the written word is a double-edged sword. As Socrates had said, it is dead, lifeless, and cannot defend itself from subjective and arbitrary interpretations. The very reason that makes it a helpful tool also sanctions its risk.

Only a week earlier Michelstaedter had written another spiritual testament: the letter to his cousin Emilio, to whom he had just dedicated *Il dialogo della salute,* his *operetta morale.* This letter replies to one from Emilio, a letter that had brought to Carlo, who was alone in Gorizia working on his dissertation, the pure air and sun of the mountains and the lake where Emilio was vacationing, together with his own light and purity. Carlo does not answer him right away, because "then you needed neither me nor my words which would certainly have been darker and more wrought than your air, mountains, and lake" (*Ep.,* 446). He is here openly juxtaposing reason and nature; undoubtedly light and purity are on the side of the latter. Only from Pirano, his beloved sea retreat, does he feel he can offer his young cousin some of his own light too. He needs nature to charge him, and he writes his letter in the solitude of a little beach facing the rough sea. "My solitude here is not that of my life in Gorizia which you know—it is not the desert—the voice of the sea is here not the dreamed distant voice that [only] passion pulls near—but it is here always in all its strength and makes me part of its life" (*Ep.,* 447). His little boat is safe in the small abandoned harbor while the waves beat violently on the shore. Literal and metaphorical images are woven together in this discourse so that the coincidence between life and language can occur; and language here is speaking with the voice of *persuasione.* Real life is not that of the sheltered harbor, but the fury of the sea. This metaphor, which is recurrent in Michelstaedter's writing, will rise to a level of sublimity in a series of poems to which we will return. It is the main idea of his dissertation (87, 128); it is the core of his ethics (*Opere,* 784).

The sea has a dense psychoanalytical connotation; it is easy to make the connection between it and Carlo's intense love for his mother. Yet his almost categorical imperative to go out to sea, rather than return to the mother, should be seen as the affirmation of his individuality, self-sufficiency, and independence. The sea is a metaphor for life, which must be faced and not avoided, which each of us must live on his own. Nietzsche's *Zarathustra* resounds throughout Michelstaedter's last words.[92]

> The harbor is not where men build harbors as shelters for their life of trepidation. The harbor for him who really wants his life is the fury of the sea so that he can hold straight and secure his ship toward the final destination. You too will soon begin to sail and I know you will not look around worried to find a calm harbor. I know you will not choose the dull life of inertia that is given to those who yield. (*Ep.*, 447)

Michelstaedter wrote this letter the day before going back to Gorizia. He knew he would see Emilio the next day, yet he felt the need to give him in writing something that will be permanent: his spiritual testament. Once again writing is used to convey a message of *persuasione*. And it is the same message that Carlo had left for Emilio in *Il dialogo della salute*.

Michelstaedter's formidable attack on *rettorica* undoubtedly places him next to Nietzsche. "To the extent that man has for long ages believed in the concepts and names of things as in *aeternae veritates*," Nietzsche wrote in *Human—All Too Human*, "he . . . thought that in language he possessed knowledge of the world. The sculptor of language was not so modest as to believe that he was only giving things designations, he conceived rather that with words he was expressing supreme knowledge of things."[93] Reduced to language, the reality experienced becomes oversimplified. It acquires clarity but it loses truth, which is ambiguous and murky. Musil called this phenomenon "the failure of language" and "it caused [his Törless] anguish, a half-awareness that the words were merely accidental, mere evasion and never the feeling itself."[94] If Musil's Törless ascertains the existence and the value of a realm of experiences that cannot be expressed through language, Wittgenstein will theorize that not everything that is experienced and understood can be said. There is a realm about which we cannot say anything. And it is to Musil's richly metaphorical language that we turn again:

True, there is a simple, natural explanation for everything, and Törless knew it too; but to his dismayed astonishment it seemed to tear off an outer husk, without getting anywhere near laying bare what was within that other, further things which . . . he could always see glimmering underneath.[95]

Must language, then, withdraw before the undefinable? Only the language that "rests on the metaphysical distinction between the sensuous and the suprasensuous," the Japanese tells us in Heidegger's "Dialogue on Language." If language wants to survive, it must "leave undefined what is really intended, or even restore it to the keeping of the undefinable." It must enter into "that country" where "thinking encounters its neighborhood with poetry."[96] Having rid ourselves of a century-old prejudice "that thinking is a matter of ratiocination" and exclusively "a means to gain knowledge," we must now listen to Nietzsche's voice and repeat with him: "Our thinking should have a vigorous fragrance, like a wheatfield on a summer's night."[97]

Chapter 2

THE TRIAL OF POETRY

> The poet was truly beyond good and
> evil; the philosopher instead was an
> exemplary victim of that discontent of
> civilization which he had intrepidly
> unmasked.—Claudio Magris[1]

If philosophical discourse is destined to produce *rettorica,* if *persuasione*
cannot be spoken of, but must be directly lived, perhaps only art could
give it a proper form of expression. Art alone could be authentic, disin-
terested, independent of contingency. Through art, perhaps, Michelstaedter would be able to give voice to his message of *persuasione.* In
order to accomplish this, art must represent honestly the absurdity of
existence, the gap between needs and their satisfaction.

The great teaching that art can accomplish is "consciously to accept
plurality, conflicts, and ambivalence" that exist between individuals and
between individuals and the world. This is the thrust of Cristina Benussi's
monograph on Michelstaedter.[2] Benussi tells us that, like Leopardi, Michelstaedter was interested in the individual in isolation, not in man as a
social creature. The goal of art, therefore, will not be that of re-creating
"harmonization between oneself and the world," because the world is not
knowable and is therefore incomprehensible. The goal of art, its ethical
task, instead consists in representing the crisis, the awareness of the
exclusion of the individual, of his essential extraneousness to the world
around him and others. "The task of art is not to smooth out the

symptoms of discomfort, but in fact to point them out in order to grasp their contradictoriness."[3] Benussi, however, misses Michelstaedter's emotional incapacity to accept the conclusions of reason. If he, in fact, arrives at them, forced by a stringent logic, he does so in a state of pain and of *Angst,* lacking the emotional control of a philosopher like Gianni Vattimo, for example, who is capable of elaborating such intuitions into a vision. Analyzing Heidegger's modernity and paraphrasing him, Vattimo makes a statement that can very well be applied to Michelstaedter: "The work of art can be the 'actualization' of truth because truth is no longer a metaphysically stable structure," and such actualization "is achieved not through a conciliation and perfect assimilation of internal and external, idea and appearance, but through the continuation of the conflict . . . within the work."[4]

It was Henrik Ibsen who led Michelstaedter to the top of the mountain. His poem "Paa Viddeone," which Michelstaedter read in the German translation ("Aus dem Hochgebirge") and rendered in Italian as "In alto," was also a source of inspiration for another Giulian writer: Scipio Slataper. It is surely no coincidence that these two writers, geographically close, were also so profoundly fascinated with their mountains and both influenced by the Norwegian playwright. These twin passions are revealed in Slataper's autobiographical novel, *Il mio Carso,* as well as in his doctoral dissertation on Ibsen. The two students seem to have met in Florence at the Institute, but there is no evidence of close contact between them. After Michelstaedter's death Slataper wrote a review of the little volume published in 1912 that included *Il dialogo della salute* and a few poems. He also wrote a few notes in his diary where he seems to have been influenced in his reading of Michelstaedter by the thesis of his philosophical suicide. The name of Michelstaedter, in fact, is mentioned together with that of Weininger.[5]

Ibsen's poem "In alto" celebrates the ethical ascent of his hero who severs all ties with society and starts off on a spiritual journey into the purity of icy heights. He is Brand's poetical father. Michelstaedter read this poem in the summer of 1908 and called the experience a real catharsis.[6] He had reached Ibsen's poems late, having first read (between March and April of the same year) almost all his plays. We learn this from the letter Carlo wrote to his mother on April 8, 1908, from Flor-

ence. He concluded it with the enthusiastic exclamation, "That is a man!
. . . He made me think and still does. Certainly after Sophocles he is the
artist who had most penetrated into my soul and has absorbed me" (*Ep.*,
308). He read him in the German translation and wrote many pages of
commentary to various plays.

The great models were once more his beloved Greek writers, mainly
the playwrights, then Leopardi, and more contemporaneously Tolstoy
and Ibsen. Of Tolstoy, he wrote: "he revealed himself as a philosopher
and an apostle only insofar as he was an artist" (*Opere*, 651). Art thus
appears to be the only form through which the truth can be delivered.
Furthermore, Michelstaedter continues, only he who lives the truth can
communicate it: "As in every great man, in Tolstoy's art, life and thought
are one indivisible unity" (*Opere*, 652). Of the two, Tolstoy and Ibsen,
Michelstaedter felt closer to the latter. In the same article on Tolstoy
written for *Il Corriere Friulano* (September 18, 1908) he explains the
different ethical conceptions of the two:

> Ibsen wants man to become capable of breaking the circle of lies that
> ties him, he wants him to want truth and to be able to make it triumph;
> he must fight against the lie that is in himself and educate his will to
> fight. . . . Tolstoy does not ask man for struggle but for devotion; he
> must resist society's temptations . . . he must . . . repair the evils
> society creates for the lower classes, by doing good deeds, by helping
> and counseling. (*Opere*, 653)

Ibsen's works, therefore, center on a few great individuals, while Tolstoy's novels center on society; they speak with a choral voice. Both
writers share, however, a faith in truth and an equal contempt for
hypocrisy and falsehood.

IBSEN AND THEATER

As I have noted earlier, Michelstaedter was extremely attracted by the
theater. He knew the Greek writers; his preference was for Sophocles.
Electra's words begin *La persuasione e la rettorica*. He used to go to plays

whenever he could afford it. His letters home make reference to his many evenings at the theater and numerous pages of his diary are devoted to comments and criticism of plays he had seen.

After a brief period of enthusiasm for D'Annunzio, Michelstaedter became progressively disenchanted with him for frequently reducing his characters "to rhetorical expressions devoid of content" (*Opere*, 645). The discovery of Ibsen and Tolstoy made him aware of the abyss between them and D'Annunzio. The latter, like most contemporary writers, he remarked, is satisfied with minor details, superficial sensations; whereas Tolstoy and Ibsen "search deeply into man's soul in order to bring to the surface its highest chord. Each clashed openly with his society suffocated as it was by hypocrisy and each shouted to its face: 'Truth! Truth!'" (*Opere*, 654).

The discovery of Ibsen had been a revelation for Michelstaedter, who probably identified with several of his characters. Furthermore, Ibsen had written plays; therefore his characters, like Pirandello's, were not reducible to the page of a text, but were real beings acting out their ideas and emotions. The individualism of Ibsen's characters and their one-man battles against society attracted Michelstaedter who shared this view in full. According to him Ibsen created "human types who know how to live their dream of authenticity to the extreme consequences, and pay the highest price for it."[7] "I simply know that Ejlert Lövborg had the courage to live life after his own mind. And now—this last act, filled with beauty! That he had the strength and the will to break away from the banquet of life—so young," exclaims Hedda Gabler.[8] It is all that counts. This dramatic sentence must have made a strong impression on Michelstaedter, as he copied it in his diary (in German) (*Opere*, 678). Of course, Hedda's dream will immediately be shattered by the pettiness around her. After all, she must pay for her sins too. Yet her statement is the core of the whole play and Ejlert Lövborg was indeed the authentic individual she wanted him to be.

Ibsen remained for Michelstaedter a source of inspiration during the composition of his best poems—with his mountains and even more with his sea. These two images never left Michelstaedter's imagination. They opened the door to *persuasione,* at the beginning of his dissertation, where they are both used as metaphors of it. The mountain and the sea are before us to be conquered; our efforts are endless and hopeless, yet

this is what the road to *persuasione* consists of: constant struggle, per-
severance, courage in the face of the impossible. This is Brand's final
ascent and sacrifice. A new Christ, he too will die because of the ignorance of those around him.

The theater is perhaps the art form that best embodies the idea of
persuasione. Its very nature is, in fact, action rather than reflection; it is
poetry that becomes drama; it is the union of life and the ideal; it is the
realization, the coming to life of the ideal. Hence, Michelstaedter's
fascination with the theater and with Ibsen in particular. Besides Brand
and Peer Gynt, which are even in their structure dramatic poems, the rest
of Ibsen's theater presents characters who are the poetic distillation of
ideas, poetic symbols who act out what they represent.

Michelstaedter never actually wrote a play, although, as we have seen,
he did write some short dramatic dialogues. But he certainly contem-
plated doing one, as he wrote to his father:

> Do you remember, Papa, that time after lunch when I spoke to you of
> the idea of a tragedy I had in mind? You then replied, "This is not a
> drama; it is pure philosophy." You were absolutely right. But I did not
> succeed in making this idea felt through life, through the events! I was
> not able to make it vibrate in real, true characters. . . . That idea,
> therefore, remains useless, incommunicable, like many others, inside
> myself. (*Ep.*, 170)

A real drama, instead, must bring to life the philosophical ideas that it
contains. They must become action. Real art achieves this union between
life and the ideal. Before writing these words Carlo had described to his
family his mental state. It was a state of abstraction provoked by his
intellectual activity, of which he well saw the dangers.

> When I have formed a group of ideas around anything I have the
> impression I have done everything, and my mind refuses to apply it to
> reality, in the union with which this group of ideas has a life and reason
> to exist, without which it is a dead body, built on air, useless, incom-
> municable. (*Ep.*, 170)

The risk of *rettorica* is always present, and he knew that studying does nothing but increase it. He realized, therefore, that he could not write dramas and limited himself to that most concise of art forms, the poem. With it he hoped to give voice to *persuasione*.

MICHELSTAEDTER THE CHARACTER

Only a few years ago two young writers from his region paid Michelstaedter the highest honor. Each, independently, wrote a play on *persuasione* and the central character, the living embodiment of it, I should say, is Michelstaedter himself. They both tried to give life to an idea of truth and authenticity and gave it the name, face, and voice of Carlo. As we have had occasion to note in the Chapter 1, Antonio Devetag and Franco Ferranti, having learned their lesson well, did not write an essay on Michelstaedter, but, as Pirandello would have done, made him into a character who will "live forever." They redeemed him, on the one hand, from his dissertation and philosophical writings and, on the other, from his final act. "Man will die, the writer will die," wrote Pirandello in "La tragedia di un personaggio" ("The Tragedy of a Character"), but "his creature will never die."[9]

Carlo Michelstaedter the character will live the idea he represents forever like Hamlet and Don Abbondio (though perhaps more modestly). "One is born to life in many different ways," said Pirandello through his character Dr. Fileno,

> and you know well that nature uses the instrument of fantasy in order to continue her work of creation. And he who is born by means of this creative activity that resides in the spirit of man, is ordained by nature to a life that is far superior to that of those who are born from the mortal womb of woman. . . . He who is born as a live character . . . never dies! Man will die, the writer will, the natural instrument of creation; his creature, never.[10]

Art overcomes life. Of course, even Michelstaedter's poems and his graphic art have remained and will remain. Yet he will also live as a character and express better than anything else the idea for which he lived and died: that *persuasione* is the unity of mind and body and that it can never be entrusted to the silent, dead page.

In *La grande trasgressione,* by Antonio Devetag, the first scene is a pantomime of characters acting like puppets, each one with a specific social role. The stage fills up with them. They are grotesque caricatures who bow to the public. Meanwhile the narrating voice speaks the words of *rettorica.* The second scene is a dialogue between "Primo Sapiente" and "Secondo Sapiente" (the First and Second Wise Men), abbreviated PS and SS in the text. (I could not help thinking of the Italian police abbreviation for Pubblica Sicurezza and of the Nazi SS police.) At the beginning of the play Michelstaedter has already committed suicide and his gesture, the wise men fear, especially the First Wise Man, will become a bomb and will generate enthusiasm in young people and ignite a spark that could raise a revolutionary wave. The Second Wise Man, however, tries to calm his colleague. He has a plan. By transforming Michelstaedter's ideas into *rettorica,* he will empty them of all their explosive content. By talking about, celebrating, repeating them, they will be transformed into mere sounds. At the end of the first exchange a decision is made: to build a monument in his honor, to be placed in the public gardens—a toy for children. "Geniuses," comments the Second Wise Man, "especially the dangerous type, must be immortalized in stone. They make the city beautiful and become harmless."[11] What the wise men are here advocating is the petrification of Carlo Michelstaedter.

The second act is called the "Dream of Existence." Michelstaedter comes to life and gives his own long monologue where he narrates the journey to *persuasione* by means of metaphors. The monologue, however, is soon interrupted by the voice of *rettorica,* trying to tempt Carlo back to life's pleasures. But neither his father's reproaches nor his mother's love can hold Carlo in the life of *rettorica;* in the final act he speaks with the voice of *persuasione.* He remains alone on stage. To the others he is the different one, the unique one, the insane man. This Pirandellian play lacks, purposely, any real dialogue. Communication among men is no longer possible. *Rettorica* has taken over. Words no longer have any content; actions have no meaning. He who alone rebels against this state of affairs and shouts the truth in others' faces is ostracized and rejected by society as mad.

Franco Ferranti's work, on the other hand, is a real play with few very brief monologues. Whereas Devetag's Carlo is undoubtedly the figure of a new Christ, an example of absolute virtue, the personification of *persuasione,* Ferranti places the emphasis on the human and weak aspects of his nature. It is the dramatization of the last days of his life, and Carlo is seen interrelating with his mother, with Paula, and with Emilio. The father figure, however, is totally absent, though from Emma's words we can infer that it is everyone's expectation that Carlo take on that role: that of the mature, responsible male who must provide for his future and fulfill his parents' expectations. But Carlo fights against them; he is not a great, strong man. He does not want to be loved for what he should or others think he will become. He wants to be loved for what he is, another example of human weakness, wickedness, and selfishness. Left alone in his room Carlo looks at himself in the mirror and, like many of Pirandello's characters, does not like what he sees. "I am not solid, I am not good, neither am I capable, I am not serious nor do I want to rise to heaven for these titles . . . and above all I give no advice, let alone wise advice."[12] He, like anyone else, sees the world in terms of himself. Things are insofar as they are needed by the subject experiencing them. And not only things but people as well. We recognize them, we attribute reality to them insofar as they are necessary to us. They would not exist otherwise. We reduce people to objects for our use and consumption. This is what we call love; the reciprocal need of the other. Not even maternal love is safe from such accusation in this play. Carlo confronts his mother, accusing her of the same hypocrisy and selfish love as anyone else. To please her he must play his role too, the role she has taught him since he was little:

> I must play my part, my act, as an acrobat, or a fool, whichever . . . double flip . . . and your son finished brilliantly his course of study . . . And to the public, please, applause! . . . Yes, I am so important [to you] that usually you take me and pass me around like a sugar bowl . . . so that everyone can help himself."[13]

Poor Paula, too, was Emma's pretty doll. She would dress her, comb her hair, almost as if to deposit her on the mantelpiece. But Carlo wants to be loved for what he is today, not for what he may become tomorrow. "I do not want to live for tomorrow. I do not want to become someone. I want to be little and I want your caresses. Now. Now."[14]

These two plays could be seen as correlative. They are the two well-wrought faces of the same medal. Ferranti's Carlo is the man who lives the everyday hard life of *rettorica,* who struggles against it and often succumbs to it. It is man with his weaknesses and shortcomings in addition to his high ideals. Devetag's Carlo is *il persuaso;* so, of course, he is dead from the beginning, as only in death does real life come into being. He is the positive side of Carlo that can live only with the death of the rhetorical man. It is a metaphysical play that agrees well with Devetag's own metaphysical painting. (Devetag too, in fact, is a writer and a painter.)

Were Michelstaedter here with us today to watch these plays, he might very well find defects in them. Though he might even dislike them, yet he would certainly appreciate the spirit that animates them—the respect for his own beliefs. He would surely be grateful to Devetag and Ferranti for having made him a character that will live his drama forever rather than the subject of the hundredth scholarly piece.

THE POEMS

"Philosophical poetry" Campailla calls it; and there can be no doubting it. This is poetry that carries on and is nurtured by the same philosophical discourse of *La persuasione e la rettorica* and cannot be understood without it.[15] Michelstaedter's best poetry was written in the last year of his life just as he was writing his dissertation. If we keep this in mind we can see how the two, the philosophy and the poetry, carry on a dialogue where they desperately need each other. If the philosophical discourse never reaches *persuasione,* but can only show a path in the distance, poetry will continue the task. If *persuasione* is the moment of absolute truth, authenticity, consistency, evanescent as it is, philosophical discourse, that perforce develops in time, can never achieve it. On the other hand, the poetical image, the metaphor, the symbol can hope to give a form to that miraculous and unrepeatable instant. As Campailla put it:

Perhaps the most genuine representations of *persuasione* in action Michelstaedter found . . . in the powerful fantasy of 'I figli del mare.'

. . . Where reason fails to proceed to the inaccessible peaks of hopeless dreams, the lively intervention of the poetical moment is extremely meaningful.[16]

Michelstaedter remained outside the mainstream of Italian poetry, just as he did with his philosophy. Nothing of Pascoli or of the *Crepuscolari* can be detected in his poetry. Nevertheless he arrived at twentieth-century themes, such as alienation and indifference, probably with some suggestions from his kindred soul, Leopardi. For Carducci he felt a great admiration, but did not share his worldview. D'Annunzio's poetry, like his theater, was too concerned with form at the expense of content. Once again the influence of contemporary sensibility came from the North. Besides Ibsen, mention should be made of Rilke, although Michelstaedter certainly lacked Rilke's control of his sentimental material and his positive view of love. Among Italian poets there was as always Leopardi, but Michelstaedter did not share his mentor's great faith in the power of poetry. Moreover, he retained a tragic inner disposition that not even his art was ever able to overcome.[17] From Leopardi he did not learn a formal but a moral lesson. He learned to look reality straight in the eye and not to let himself be deceived. It was a lesson of courage and individual engagement. It compelled him to follow reason, though painful, to its extreme consequences.

In his short essay "Postille leopardiane di Michelstaedter," Campailla has pointed out Leopardian echoes not only in Michelstaedter's poetry, but also in his prose.[18] It is difficult to know about direct influences on Michelstaedter as very few of his books have survived. Many were thrown out of the windows and burned during the Nazi raid in 1943 that meant deportation and death for Emma and Elda Michelstaedter. Twenty years ago Campailla, searching among the shelves of the only survivor of the family, Carlo's beloved sister Paula, found the text of Leopardi's *Canti* with comments and annotations in the margins (in Greek). This discovery came to prove Campailla's thesis that the great influence on Michelstaedter came from the later Leopardi, the heroic poet, not the idyllic. Not even "L'infinito," in fact, has annotations or comments; they begin with the ode "A Carlo Pepoli," of 1826. Leopardi's poems that undoubtedly had the greatest impact on Michelstaedter's sensibility were "Il Canto notturno" ("The Night Song") and "A se stesso" ("To Himself"). Not only did they receive a larger number of comments, but their ideas are clearly present in his own poems and in his dissertation.

The oxymoron, with images of mortal life and of death which is life, is the core of "Il canto delle crisalidi" and of "Il canto notturno." Life is nothing but a journey to death. "Nasce l'uomo a fatica ed è rischio di morte il nascimento" (Man is born through labor and the risk of death lies in his coming to life), Leopardi wrote (*PP*, 1:81). "Ogni cosa nasce moritura" (everything is born to die), Michelstaedter echoes in "Aprile" (*Poesie*, 65). The appeal to the stars and to their meaning is also present; the senselessness of nature's course is central in both poems. At birth the absurdity of life has already been established. The act of birth necessitates the risk of death. Parents must console their offspring from the day they are born. Leopardi's voice is heard in Carlo's poem dedicated to his sister, where parents too are described as they care for their children, control, and deceive them with the hope of happiness to come (*Poesie*, 71–72).

Under the poem "A se stesso," Michelstaedter wrote in Greek characters the word/name ARGIA: peace, inertia, rest. The word had already appeared at the conclusion of the first section of his dissertation in a sentence that recurs often in his writings and summarizes his philosophical credo: *di'energeías eis argían*, "through activity toward peace." If death is our end, it must be met courageously through action, and not feared. In "A se stesso," ARGIA is the "rest" Leopardi invokes at the beginning. Even the last deception, that of love, which Leopardi hoped would be eternal, has perished. Facing him only "l'infinita vanità del tutto" is left (*PP*, 1:98). To which Michelstaedter in "Aprile" echoes: "l'indifferente tramutar del tutto" (the indifferent changing of everything) (*Poesie*, 66). The "virgineo seno" (virginal breast) of death in "Amore e morte" ("Love and Death," *PP*, 1:97), in which Leopardi waited finally to fall asleep, is the "benevolo porto sicuro" of Michelstaedter (*Poesie*, 66).

In "A se stesso," however, Michelstaedter not only found his own philosophical credo, but also a similar psychological condition. Leopardi wrote the poem in 1833 after the collapse of his hopes in Fanny's love. The name ARGIA written by Carlo under the title makes plausible the hypothesis that he also felt emotionally close to Leopardi. He, too, as we will see, had suffered because of a woman: Argia Cassini.[19]

When reading Michelstaedter's poems one must keep in mind two facts: they were not intended for publication and the majority of them were written during the last year of his life. They represented another individual and solitary attempt by Michelstaedter to reach the path of *persuasione* that, as he repeated over and over, "is not a route for everybody" and that each individual must take by himself for himself. The last group of poems, however, those that have been collected under the name "A Senia" were dedicated to Argia Cassini, the woman he loved, and were given to her, possibly to continue a dialogue—or better a monologue that, in another form, would have risked misunderstanding.

A few of the poems were composed in 1905; they were first published by the poet Biagio Marin in 1962.[20] The first two are love-poems written for a girl named Elsa ("Se camminando vado solitario" ["If Solitary I Walk"] and "Poiché il dolore l'animo m'infranse" ["Since Pain Shattered My Soul"]). Carlo was only eighteen and still under the influence of D'Annunzio. The tone is emphatic, characteristic of the age. The love experience is projected onto nature and the whole universe, which must palpitate with the same feeling. Love is energy, it is fire that lights up the earth and the sky.

"Alba—Il canto del gallo" was also composed in 1905. It is filled with his love of nature and colored with the impetuosity of his youth and intense sensuality. It is a salute to life and to the new day, vibrant with energy and light. The feeling for nature inebriates the poet who bases his faith in the future on his union with the universe. The bright song of Carlo's rooster contrasts sharply with the plaintive notes of Leopardi's, which wakes up men only to remind them of their life of suffering. There, too, the union of man and nature is absolute; both are bound by the same mechanistic laws, but with Leopardi the emphasis is on their senselessness and on destruction.

Giulio Nerini, briefly mentioned in Chapter 1, is a young composer from Gorizia whose knowledge of Michelstaedter has been limited to the reading of some of his poems. Under the powerful spell of this hymn of life, he set it to music, creating a strongly evocative piece where nature seems to wake up from a primordial sleep that is reminiscent of the weird chords at the beginning of Stravinsky's *Rite of Spring*. Nerini used the computer to compose his piece and achieves an effect which goes beyond that of the poem. There is in his music a metaphysical resonance that surpasses the simple natural fullness and sensuality of "Alba—Il canto del gallo" and that moves it closer to the supreme achievement of Michelstaedter's poetry; to "I figli del mare" ("The Children of the Sea"), for example. Nerini has expressed the desire to put to music this poem too and he will probably succeed, for even in the early one he has caught the tragic sensibility of the author of *La persuasione e la rettorica*. Once again *rettorica* has been bested by a creative effort—a result that would have gratified Carlo.

"La scuola è finita" ("School Is Over"), Michelstaedter's goodbye to school days, was constructed in two parts. The first is an enthusiastic salute to life that lies ahead, beyond the constraints imposed upon the schoolboy. Carlo's enthusiasm reaches out to all fields and activities. He is thirsty for knowledge but also for action and pleasure. His young soul is still under the illusion that both his mind and his body can achieve the maximum in the harmonic union with the whole earth:

> In un amplesso solo e poderoso
> vorrei legare a me tutta la terra
> vincere il fato e la fortuna
> ch'erra cieca nel mondo
> (Poesie, 41)

> [In one powerful embrace,
> I want to bind to me the whole earth
> To overcome fate and fortune
> That blindly wanders through the world.]

Carlo's faith in himself is endless, and with his mind and body he challenges the blind fate that rules over the world. But the second half of the poem presents the other face of the coin. Opposition seems already to be the ruling mechanism of his psyche. Fear of the coldness and cruelty of life overcomes him. School then appears to him as the safe shelter from the hostility of the world outside. The solidarity of friends is a secure harbor. The poem, however, ends with a common rhetorical topos, seemingly intended here to undermine itself. It is, in fact, too artificial and emphatic to be sincere. We can hear the echo of Alfieri and maybe even of that rare, rhetorical Leopardi of "La canzone all'Italia":

> Ma non dobbiamo però chinar la fronte.
> Con ferro in pugno verso l'ideale
> ci batterem con animo leale!
> In alto i cuori!
>
> (*Poesie*, 41)

> [But we must not yield,
> With iron hand toward the ideal
> we must fight with a loyal soul.
> Let's lift our hearts!]

Michelstaedter's best poems were written in Gorizia. For him, just as for Leopardi, the familiar ground was the source of greatest inspiration. He was in Florence in 1907, however, when he wrote several poems that originated in love experiences. His mysterious relationship with Nadia Baraden, the Russian divorcée who committed suicide that same year, has already been mentioned. We know from his words about its depth. Here, in its entirety, is a little jewel—perhaps the only one Carlo wrote for Nadia. It has been unjustly ignored by the critics; although I cannot help proposing, for reasons of rhythm, a lengthening of the last line, substituting *sorride* for *ride*.

> Sibila il legno nel camino antico
> e par che tristi rimembranze chiami
> mentre filtra sottil pei suoi forami
> vena di fumo.

> O caminetto antico quanto è triste
> che nella nera bocca tua rimanga
> la legna che non arde e par che pianga
> di desiderio,

> ma dal profondo della sua poltrona
> socchiusi gli occhi, il biondo capo chino

stese le mani al fuoco del camino
Nadia ride.

(*Poesie,* 43)

[The wood hisses in the old fireplace
and seems to call back old memories
while a thin line of smoke
filters through its cracks.

Oh ancient fireplace how sad
(that) in your black mouth remains
the wood that cannot catch fire
and seems to cry with desire.

But from the depth of her couch
with closed eyes and her head reclined
with her hands outstretched to the fire
Nadia laughs.]

The image of fire, as noted earlier, is central in the world of Michelstaedter. In the last year of his life it acquires a metaphysical connotation pivotal to the understanding of his philosophy. Here it appears for the first time, in a less dramatic context, but still significantly. Nadia is sitting before the fire, stretching her hands toward it. The fire is alive and with its "sibilo" brings back memories of past things which are now only smoke. The wood that is unable to catch fire seems to be crying with frustrated desire inside the opened black mouth of the fireplace. In contrast to it is Nadia's mouth, which is lit by laughter. The fire which lights this poem is of a sensual kind, and its power is enhanced by the image of the mouth. Nadia, in fact, is reduced to a smile. Her eyes are half-closed, her head reclined, yet her smile suffices to ignite the fire.

In March 1907 Carlo began a new romance. He wrote two poems to Iolanda De Blasi, one just before Nadia's suicide and the other afterward, in the month of June. The image of the flame is still present and once more is associated with the woman and with her love. In the light of these poems, the one to Nadia acquires a more intimate quality. In the first of the two poems, "A che mi guardi fanciulla" ("Why Are You Looking at Me, Young Maiden?"), written on Easter Sunday, Iolanda's flaming heart is contrasted with the coldness of Carlo's. The first stanza is built on this opposition and the second on a yet more profound one. Iolanda's flame widens and fades away into the love for mankind and the intensity of nature against which the silence of Carlo's soul acquires the irrevocability of a necessary fate.

Campailla, commenting on this poem, says that Michelstaedter here "declares," "does not explain" the negativity of his existential feelings; "the reasons," he continues, he cannot give and perhaps he does not know them.[21] In my view, Michelstaedter writes poems precisely because he does not want to explain; he creates images and metaphors that are self-explanatory. Would he have ignored the reasons for his feelings if he could then so well analyze them in a letter written in the same period? On May 6, 1907, he wrote to Iolanda asking her: "Do you feel you can love me not for my smile, for my joy, . . . but for this struggle that is in my heart? . . ." "I feel that what I want is far and it is not outside myself . . . but inside" (*Ep.,* 209). The poem is not the ideal locus for explanations. Yet Carlo's inner development finds in his poems a most authentic voice.

In "Senti Iolanda" ("Iolanda, Listen"), written in June, even the sun has become sad. The flame is still burning, but it is no longer a bright flame. It is dark, not because its intensity has decreased, but because Carlo feels that what Iolanda can offer him is not enough. For him, love too must be absolute. Cerruti, who first commented on this poem, saw in it the first manifestations of Michelstaedter's neurosis.[22] It is possible, undoubtedly, yet we must keep in mind that neurosis was connected with his need of totality.

The sea, which he had always loved, became the central character of Michelstaedter's later poems. It is a metaphor that, though recurrent in his letters and philosophical writings, finds its proper place in poetry. The sea is life, authentic life, and even a psychoanalytical approach can only confirm its significance. If the sea symbolizes *persuasione,* as we have seen at the beginning of his dissertation, the conquest of the sea coincides with self-possession, with a return to the origin. Ellida Wangel in Ibsen's *The Lady of the Sea* agrees when she says: "So . . . we took the wrong turn and became land animals instead of sea creatures."[23] She can never be happy trapped on land, until she is given the freedom to decide whether to follow the stranger or to remain with her husband. As a creature of the sea, she represents freedom and authenticity, and she will triumph at the end. Although her freedom will take her back to her husband, that is, to the land, she will have followed her own instincts in so deciding and will finally be able to live with a choice which was hers alone (or perhaps the *rettorica* of her life on land, near her husband, had corrupted her to the point that she could no longer make a free choice). Michelstaedter, too, is a creature of the sea and his metamorphosis begins with the first poem of the sea written at Pirano in August 1908—not by coincidence, surely, the same year in which he had discovered Ibsen.

Amico—mi circonda il vasto mare
con mille luci—io guardo all'orizzonte
dove il cielo ed il mare
lor vita fondon infinitamente.—
Ma altrove la natura aneddotizza
la terra spiega le sue lunghe dita
ed il sole racconta a forti tratti
le coste cui il mare rode ai piedi
ed i verdi vigneti su coronano.
E giù: alle coste in seno accende il sole
bianchi paesi intorno ai campanili
e giù nel mare bianche vele erranti
alla ventura.—

A me d'accanto, sullo stesso scoglio
sta la fanciulla e vibra come un'alga,
siccome un'alga all'onda varia e infida
φιλοβαθεία.—
S'avviva al sole il bronzo dei capelli
ed i suoi occhi di colomba tremuli
guardano il mare e guardano la costa
illuminata.—
Ma sotto il velo dell'aria serena
sente il mistero eterno d'ogni cosa
costretta a divenire senza posa
nell'infinito.

Sente nel sol la voce dolorosa
dell'universo,—e l'abisso l'attira
l'agita con un brivido d'orrore
siccome l'onda suol l'alga marina
che le tenaci aggrappa
radici nell'abisso e ride al sole.—

Amico io guardo ancora all'orizzonte
dove il cielo ed il mare
la vita fondon infinitamente.
Guardo e chiedo la vita
la vita della mia forza selvaggia
perch'io plasmi il mio mondo e perché il sole
di me possa narrar l'ombra e le luci—
la vita che mi dia pace sicura
nella pienezza dell'essere.

E gli occhi tremuli della colomba
vedranno nella gioia e nella pace
l'abisso della mia forza selvaggia—
e le onde varie della mia esistenza
l'agiteranno or lievi or tempestose
come l'onda del mar l'alga marina
che le tenaci aggrappa
radici nell'abisso e ride al sole.

(Poesie, 52–53)

[As friend—the vast sea surrounds me
with a thousand lights. I look toward the horizon
where sky and sea
their life infinitely fuse together.
But elsewhere nature anecdotizes
land spreads her long fingers
and sun narrates with strong strokes
the coastlines, their feet eaten away by the sea
and their tops crowned by vineyards.
And down: in the womb of the coastline the sun lights
up white towns around the bell towers

and down over the sea white sails wander
seeking their fortune.

Next to me, on the same cliff
the maiden stands and vibrates like an alga
just like an alga to the changing treacherous wave
filobatheía.—
The bronze of her hair comes to life in the sun
and her trembling eyes (like a dove's)
look to the sea and to the coast
illuminated.—
But under the veil of the serene air
she feels the eternal mystery of everything
forced to come into being without rest
in the infinite.
In the sun she hears the suffering voice
of the universe,—and the abyss attracts and
upsets her with a shiver of horror
just as the wave does to the seaweed
her roots clutching at the abyss while
laughing at the sun.

Still a friend I look toward the horizon
where sky and sea
their life infinitely fuse together.
I look and ask for life
for the life of my savage force
so that I mold my world and so (that) the sun
might narrate my lights and shadows—
the life that will give me secure peace
in the fullness of being.

And the trembling eyes of the dove
will see in the joy and in the peace
the abyss of my wild strength—
and the changing waves of my existence
will agitate her, now gentle, now tempestuous
just as the wave the seaweed

her roots clutching at the abyss, while
laughing at the sun.]

From the first stanza the opposition between land and sea is stated in full force. Whereas the sea merges with the sky, creating life, the verbs Michelstaedter chose to qualify land are taken from the language of *rettorica:* the land "anecdotizes" (he invented the verb) "spiega" which means "explains" as well as "spreads out." Yet this work of *rettorica* is nullified by the "erosion," the eating away by the sea, on which white sails wander seeking their fortune. White sails, symbols of the souls of *persuasi,* will still be passing on the horizon two years later in "Onda per onda" ("Wave after Wave").

Next to Carlo on the same rock in the middle of the sea stands his Ellida *filobatheía* (lover of the depths), a marine creature who shuns the painful life of the land and is, instead, attracted to the watery depths. Who knows whether Montale had this image in mind when he wrote "Falsetto?"[24] We can almost hear her speaking the words of Ibsen's woman of the sea when she talked "of whales and dolphins, and of the seals that would lie out on the skerries in the warm noon sun. And . . . of the gulls and the eagles and every kind of sea birds. . . . I almost felt that I belonged to them."[25] Carlo and his maiden also marry themselves to the sea, renouncing the life of the land.

However, he is still hoping that in nature he will fulfill his ideal of complete self-realization. Once more he is abandoning himself to dreams that will have the "heroic-vitalistic" connotation of Nietzsche's *Zarathustra.*[26] The woman will find in his wild force her peace, her harbor. Already present are the theme of reaching peace through activity, which will recur until the end, and the image of the lamp that burns for excess of energy.

The important letter to Gaetano that narrates the days spent at Pirano in the company of Paula and the Cassini sisters is of this period. There Michelstaedter had identified himself with the sea, realizing, however, that unlike the sea, he possessed the consciousness of his nothingness. The identification with nature cannot suffice. The sea is here still a symbol of unity, harmony. It is seen as it fuses together with the land (line 34). It is still "il gran mare dell'essere" (the great sea of being), as Dante had called it in *Paradiso* (Canto 1, line 113) and Leopardi had repeated ("Amore e morte," line 7), a symbol of life.

Yet the sea will metamorphose into a much more complex entity, and the metaphor will acquire a more profound meaning. At the end of his book on Michelstaedter, Brianese wrote a moving paragraph about the image of the sea in Michelstaedter's work. The movement of Brianese's prose mirrors that of its content and perfectly renders the contradictory essence of the image described:

> And it is precisely the sea—that sea in which the movement of the waves yet seems to be constantly recaptured in the immobility of the sea as a whole, whereby we can rightly indicate the change of the wave and its inexhaustible becoming, but of the sea as such we can only predicate being and immobility—the sea understood as the discordant unity of being and becoming, the harbor that authentic existence must reach.[27]

The essence of life is conflict, Heraclitus had said 2500 years earlier— and, as Vattimo has recently urged, art must represent it.

BEETHOVEN AND CHRIST

From August 1908 when he wrote "Amico—mi circonda il vasto mare" until the end of 1909 Michelstaedter wrote no poems, or none has survived. By then he was reading only selectively, Ibsen, Tolstoy, and above all the Gospels. Music had taken over his life. He had discovered Beethoven. He had caught the Beethoven fever that had produced the Vienna Secession of Klinger, Klimt, and Mahler in 1902. Beethoven had become the hero-god worshiped by all artists, not only by musicians. And the artists of the Secession raised not a metaphorical, but a real temple to their god. In it Klinger sculpted the cult statue, an impressive seated figure of Beethoven, decorated with various colored marbles, gold, precious stones and ivory, and flanked by the eagle symbol of Zeus. Klimt printed an allegorical frieze in the fresco technique. For Mahler,

Beethoven and Wagner were the only two gods of music. To his beautiful young wife Alma (who after Mahler's death was to become Kokoschka's great love) Mahler wrote, "Now I stick to Beethoven—there are only he and Richard—and after them, nobody."[28] The young Austrian philosopher Otto Weininger was also under the spell. A year after the Secession and soon after the publication of his *Sex and Character,* he rented a room in the house where Beethoven had died; there he shot himself in the heart. He was twenty-three years old.[29]

In Florence, Michelstaedter and Gaetano Chiavacci had become friends with the young musician Giannotto Bastianelli who played Beethoven on the piano for them, evening after evening. Carlo had finally found, in this music, the perfect voice of *persuasione,* free from *rettorica,* wholly authentic and pure.

Two letters written by Bastianelli to Carlo tell a great deal about their friendship and also about Carlo's appreciation of Beethoven. In the first one, of unknown date, Giannotto openly accuses him and Gaetano of not yet understanding the composer. He had played the *Eroica* for them and they had claimed the symphony should have ended after the "Marcia funebre." The Scherzo afterward, they insisted, was out of place. They were, naturally—and Carlo in particular—responding to Beethoven's music in a very personal way, blindly following their own feelings. Carlo's pessimistic disposition could not but be disturbed by the musical sequence. To him the symphony was over with the "Marcia funebre." At the end of the letter Bastianelli tries, though briefly, to explain to his friend the profound meaning of the piece. But what he says about Beethoven sheds light on Michelstaedter. "You lack the heroism," Giannotto writes, "not to be satisfied with suffering in the *Eroica.* But then," he continued,

how can you understand that if Beethoven in the *Eroica* discovers heroism, the immense heroism of the romantics, in the *Ninth* he overcomes it and arrives at such a universal understanding of human things, that, in my opinion, no modern philosophy has been able to portray or develop?

Giannotto concludes his letter with an amusing and provocative remark:

And to make you still angrier, what is "La Ginestra" ["The Broom"] and the whole of Leopardi's production compared to this gigantic and impassable Beethoven? I no longer remember where I read that if a god were forced to recount all his life, he would say it all in two words. Well, Beethoven has done it and his two words are the *Eroica* and the *Ninth*.[30]

But Carlo learned his lesson fast. His friend was to become extremely fond of him and later wrote to him, implicitly comparing him with Beethoven, "When I think of your suffering which is so pure, I believe it is not useless to create. . . . Do not forget me, although I would deserve it, for I am so much inferior to you."[31] Carlo had learned his lesson very well indeed, and Beethoven's music was his teacher.

There is a sequence of letters in the early summer of 1909 where the notes of Beethoven are heard together with the words of Christ. Campailla remarked that the discovery of Beethoven was a religious experience, if by "religious" we mean the experience of truth and *persuasione*. It is Carlo himself who often connects the two experiences, music and religion. He wrote to Paula that the theme of the *andante* of the Ninth Symphony is more eloquent than any word he could ever write her, just as the Gospel according to Matthew would be able to tell her directly and effectively all he had in his mind and soul (*Ep.*, 383): "Beethoven made me yearn with joy and pain. I would like for you to hear this Ninth Symphony; it is more than his other compositions." He tells Paula that after having written his eight symphonies, Beethoven had remained silent for ten years:

The silence of him who has arrived at his last suffering. . . . Man has lost all his individuality, and almost reached universal life. In him everything of the universe suffers. And when, who knows by what mysterious accident, he awakens again to life, it really seems that the whole universe with all its forces awakens, too, from the pain to a last illusionary orgy of free life. (383–84)

Carlo felt envy for Beethoven. He knew he could explain his feelings and ideas much more effectively were he able to write musical chords rather than words.

Only a few days earlier he wrote to his family that he had found in the Gospel "the greatness and the profundity that [he] was searching for—so much superior to the modern philosophies and sciences" (*Ep.,* 381). And in these words we hear a clear echo of Giannotto Bastianelli's letter about Beethoven's music. Carlo was here using the same antirhetorical argument to prove the power of Christ's words as Giannotto had used to point out that of Beethoven's music.

In every letter there is the mention of a piece by Beethoven he had just heard or he was going to hear, as there are references to the life of Christ. In his letter to Rico of June 13, 1909 (mentioned in Chapter 1), Carlo told his friend, "in this period rather than writing my dissertation I have learned to know Christ and Beethoven—and everything else has faded away" (*Ep.,* 398). The word "Calvary" also recurs in the letters written in these months. That *Calvario* was another name for San Valentin is a fact of some significance. In these letters, however, he speaks only of the *Calvario,* making a clear identification between Christ and himself (*Ep.,* 395, 396, 401).

Christ was for Michelstaedter just as Socrates had been, the personification of *persuasione,* of freedom and authenticity in life as in death. The ethical individualism he had learned from Tolstoy and especially Ibsen, with the discovery of Christ acquired the final, ethical element of sacrifice. Michelstaedter's Christ, however, is heretical. There is no heaven after death for his *persuaso.* It is Christ the man Michelstaedter worships, not the son of God: the man who dies to save himself, not the world. The world cannot be saved, each individual must try to find by himself the road to his own salvation. Christ is only a model to imitate and an example to follow. This human nature of Christ makes him the spiritual brother of Socrates, Leopardi, Buddha, and Beethoven.[32]

Rico—the friend who for Carlo was a model of *persuasione,* one of the rare ones who achieved it in his own life—introduced him to Buddha. There was much that Carlo could find appealing in Buddhism. Its antimetaphysical quality, the emphasis placed on the individual, who can and must reach nirvana by himself, the importance given to the present for which alone the wise man must live, and finally the fire symbolism were all characteristics also present in Michelstaedter's philosophy. Yet, the only text on Buddhism we know for certain Michelstaedter read was a German edition of Buddhist maxims and aphorisms, entitled *Indische*

Sprüche. The booklet was found together with a few of his books and reveals many glosses written by him in German in the margin (*Ep.,* 403).[33]

At the end of June 1909 Michelstaedter had left Florence for the last time. His life as a student was over. He was returning to Gorizia with only his dissertation to write, leaving behind his dear friends Gaetano, Vlado, and Giannotto. He was to remain in Gorizia until his death, with a few brief sojourns in Pirano. At home he found his old friends Rico and Nino and, of course, the Cassini sisters.

THE POEMS OF THE LAST YEAR

By leaving Florence, Michelstaedter had tried also to sever the ties that bound him to *rettorica.* Going back home near his beloved San Valentin, the Adriatic Sea, and his Isonzo River was a pilgrimage back to authenticity. Of course there was the dissertation still to write. Yet he could try to transform even that great piece of *rettorica* into a weapon that would undermine itself. He could write an antidissertation. He could build the bomb that would blow up the whole rhetorical apparatus.

In that last year, in fact, his rejection of the life of *rettorica* coincided with his withdrawal from society and his detachment from books. Only Christ, Buddha, and Beethoven remained beside him. He was now far away from Giannotto, and it was Argia who would play his music on the piano.

After more than a year of poetical silence Michelstaedter gives the most essential and antirhetorical form to the contradictory essence of life. The propelling force is once more the antinomy *persuasione-rettorica,* or life-death. "Il canto delle crisalidi" is lapidary.

Vita, morte,
la vita nella morte;
morte, vita,
la morte nella vita.

Noi col filo
col filo della vita

nostra sorte
filammo a questa morte.

E più forte
è il sogno della vita—
se la morte
a vivere ci aita

ma la vita
la vita non è vita
se la morte
la morte è nella vita

e la morte
morte non è finita
se più forte
per lei vive la vita.

Ma se vita
sarà la nostra morte
nella vita
viviam solo la morte

morte, vita,
la morte nella vita;
vita, morte,
la vita nella morte.—
        (*Poesie,* 54–55)

[Life, death
life in death;
death, life,
death in life.

We with the thread
the thread of life
our fate
weaved to this death.

And stronger
is the dream of life—

if death helps us
to live

but life
life is not life
if death
death is in life

and death
death is not over
if stronger
by her lives life.

But if life
will be our death
in life
we live only death

death, life,
death in life,
life, death,
life in death.]

This is the most cerebral of Michelstaedter's poems. It is built on opposition. The final stanza is constructed with the semantic inversion of the terms in the first stanza almost so as to close man's destiny in a circle without exit, and where the two terms are used with opposite meanings in order to point out the contradictoriness and absurdity of existence. The singsong rhythm of the poem transforms it into a folk song whose message is repeated mechanically, without understanding, but whose truth is nevertheless never doubted. The sound, in fact, over-powers its content, obliterates it. The effect is like a cicada's rising and falling buzz.

The chrysalis is a symbol of transformation, of becoming, and becom-ing is passing from life to death. The only consistency that exists is that of inconsistency: meager consolation for the philosopher of *persuasione*. Campailla calls this poem expressionistic, given its almost skeletal essen-tiality. We will have a chance to expand this discussion when talking of Michelstaedter's drawings, yet it is important to keep this aspect of his art in mind, as it seems dictated by an antirhetorical drive and an urge to return to essentials.

The poems of the months, "Dicembre," "Marzo," "Aprile," "Giugno," are inspired by nature, to which Michelstaedter always responded intensely. The sadness of the winter month moves the poet away from nature. The sad drops of rain are metamorphosed into people, "united in society" as grey as the sky above them. Fog and rain are people, boring and slothful. The other three poems and "Nostalgia" written in 1909 are filled with reminiscences of Leopardi. Nature, as she did for Leopardi, helps him to reflect on the unique position of man. Clear echoes of "La quiete dopo la tempesta" ("The Calm after the Storm") resound in "Nostalgia," where even the setting is the same. If nature renews herself in a never-ending cycle, man's seasons, on the contrary, do not come back. The identification of youth and hope at the end is a clear echo of "A Silvia."

Nature is the background against which man measures his difference. Whereas nature smiles again after the storm, man's hopes, which rose again together with the smiling, luminous dawn, are crushed: "le dolci figure del mio sogno / che appena avvicinate dileguaro / tristi, perch'io ver lor fervidamente / mi protendessi / e in me le volessi, me stesso in loro / tutto esaurire" (and the sweet images of my dreams / that vanished as soon as they drew closer / although I stretched myself out to them with all my strength / and wanted them in me and me in them / to be exhausted completely) (*Poesie,* 59). In these six verses even the rhythm reproduces the tension of the content; the first three hendecasyllables end with a *quinario* (a five-syllable verse), "mi protendessi," that leaves the verse in suspension and tension; it is immediately followed by a new hendecasyllable built on a chiastic figure, "e in me le volessi, me stesso in loro," that well renders the image of the fusion of the two elements. The image is suddenly broken by a new *quinario* that establishes its end: "tutto esaurire."

Leopardi is by now only a distant echo and Michelstaedter continues here his own song: "Volere e non voler per più volere / mi trattenne sull'orlo della vita / ad angosciarmi in aspettar mia volta / ed ai giuochi d'amore ed alle imprese / giovanili mi feci disdegnoso" (Wanting and not wanting for wanting too much / held me at the edge of life / in the anguish of waiting for my turn / and I became scornful of the games of love and of youthful deeds) (*Poesie, 59*). There are five hendecasyllables at the center of the poem that represent its heart and core, and diagnose the cause of the poet's *Angst*. The line "Wanting and not wanting for wanting too much" represents the metamorphosis of an entity into its opposite which was epitomized in "Il canto delle crisalidi." One thing turns into its opposite from overabundance, like the flame that burns out, like Carlo being consumed by the intensity of his life. The flame appears here too, immediately after the four lines just mentioned: "A qual pro? Ma alla veglia dolorosa / una fiamma splendeva e la nutriva / una speme più forte" (What for? But at the painful waking / a flame was shining and a stronger hope was nourishing it) (59).

Michelstaedter is here still recalling the hopes of youth and the Leopardian illusions that accompany it.

Ahi, quanto pur m'illuse la mortal
mia vista che di fuor ci finge certo
quanto ci manca sol perché ci manca—
« vuoto il presente, vuoto nel futuro
senza confini ogni presente, placa
il voler tuo affannoso!
non chieder più che non possa natura! ».
Ma il cor vive, e vuole, e chiede e aspetta
pur senza speme, aspetta e giorno ed ora
e giorno ed ora né sa che s'aspetta
e inesorabilmente
passano l'ore lente.
Così è fuggita e fugge giovinezza
ed i miei sogni e la speranza antica
nel mio cupo aspettar ancor ritrovo
insoddisfatti.

Che mi giova o natura luminosa
l'armonia del tuo gioco senza cure?
Ahi, chi il tuo ritmo volle preoccupare
rientrar non può nei tuoi eterni giri
ad ozïare
nel lavoro giocondo ed oblïoso.

È suo destino attender senza speme
né mutamento,
vegliando, il passar de l'ore lente.

(*Poesie,* 59–60)

[Yet how much eluded me
my mortal sight that outside feigns as certain
what we lack just because we lack it—
"empty the present, empty in the limitless future
every present, placate
your anxious will!
Do not ask more than nature can give!"
Yet the heart lives, and wants, and asks and waits
though without hope, waits, and day and hour
and day and hour, nor does he know what it is waiting for
and inexorably pass the slow hours.
So has fled and flees youth
and my dreams and old hope
in my dark waiting still I find
unsatisfied.

What is the use, luminous nature, for
the harmony of your careless game?
Ah, he who wanted to upset your rhythm
cannot reenter your eternal circles
and idle
in the playful and oblivious work.
His destiny is to wait hopelessly
no change,
waking, for the slow passing of hours.]

Among the many echoes of Leopardi that Campailla has pointed out is the use of the verb *finge*. It is the core and the creative force of the "Infinito," but it lacks in Michelstaedter the positive connotation of the creative artistic experience.[34] Michelstaedter does not raise himself above his ontological discourse; to him man creates false images, fakes the existence of that which he needs, precisely because it does not exist. In its contradictoriness, the human essence does not find any solace in the world of fiction. Art to Michelstaedter is the supreme stage on which truth alone must act. The hopes of youth are gone, yet the heart continues to yearn, because that is its life, it "lives, and wants, and asks and waits / though without hope, waits, and day and hour / and day and hour, nor does he know what it is waiting for / and inexorably pass the slow hours." The two short *settenari* (seven syllable verses) after the three hendecasyllables slow down the cadence from the preceding fast beating of the heart. The heart that wants and neither knows nor has what it wants is the poetical translation of the opening line of *La persuasione e la rettorica,* "So che voglio, ma non ho cosa voglia." The only knowledge man has is the knowledge of his wanting. The object of his wanting is ignored; if it were known, human life would cease. The slow passing hours, which at first accompanied rhythmically the beating of the waiting heart, transform themselves at the end into the very object of this waiting. The senselessness of the act thus becomes a tragic agony. At this point the dramatic relief of a Beckett would be welcome, but it does not come.

With nature reawakening even the poet's spirits are lifted, as Michelstaedter never failed to respond to nature's changing moods. In the poem "Marzo" ("March") the month is seen as a young god who amuses himself among the clouds. A god wakes up the earth, which is still in a torpor, and snatched from her the first primroses. Nature begins living again. The new exuberance of nature is placed as a contrasting background to the "timid bourgeois" who loves winter for he can stay locked up in his house, protected under the covers. The frightened bourgeois is threatened by the exuberance of this young god, mischievous and provocative, who forces him out of his warm shelter. Yet the poet concludes, "se t'odiano addormiti / nelle coltri riscaldate / ed i passeri impauriti / nelle siepi denudate, / t'ama il falco su nell'aria / che più agile si libra / nella tua ventata varia / e la sente in ogni fibra / lieto nella tua procella" (But if those who are asleep hate you / under the warm cover / and if in the naked bushes / the naked sparrows hate you, / high in the air the hawk loves you / that more agile hovers in your wind / and feels it in every fiber / happy in your stormy air) (*Poesie,* 62–63).

The hawk that had appeared in *La persuasione e la rettorica* (87) and had returned with his daring flight in Michelstaedter's correspondence, the hawk that with his sudden high soaring so well symbolizes the fleeting life of *persuasione,* whose existence is the instant, reappears here to oppose the mediocrity of mankind. If the bourgeois finds security in his protected dwelling, the hawk renews its strength through winds and storms.

Carlo had written to his friend Enrico: "I felt that I was a hawk defending the purity of the rocks, the air on top of the San Valentin against a flock of crows" (*Ep.,* 360). The hawk is the symbol of strength in itself, of uniqueness. "The flight [of the hawk]," he wrote in his notes, "can be examined in any of its segments, it is always the same and in it, in every part of it, its strength manifests itself to the utmost" (*Opere,* 729). And even when his nihilistic philosophy plunges him into a dark depression and makes him say that "after all a hawk is no more worthy than a crow," because "they both eat in order to live and live in order to eat; and live and eat in order to die," he wants at least to keep the illusion "that the hawk is actually worthier" (*Ep.,* 355). The hawk is strength, courage, speed but it also represents the high, the unreachable, the leap away from matter into the purity of the airy sky.

The image of the hawk was to become central in one of Eugenio Montale's greatest poems. There too, it represents the ideal whose essence consists precisely in its nonexistence, in the fleeting moment of a beat of wings (*di un battito d'ali*). Montale's hawk also appears in a poem built on an opposition ("Spesso il male di vivere" ["Often the Pain of Living"]), like most of his poems. This is the essential opposition of human existence: the opposition between good and evil. He, too, with far superior poetical force, begins with the negative element of the antithesis: evil that constantly surrounds us. Life is evil in all its manifestations. Good appears by contrast in the second stanza. Good is everything that does not exist; the divine, the fantastic, and "il falco alto levato." The movement of the first stanza that goes downward is opposed by the movement upward of the second. To the harsh sounds in the first stanza there is the counterpoint of the liquid flow of the second.[35] "Marzo" was published for the first time by Formiggini in a small book, together with other poems of Michelstaedter's last year and *Il dialogo della salute,* in 1912. Montale could very well have read it and been inspired by it. In any event an image so dear and so relevant to Michelstaedter, a symbol he treasured so much, was to become with just one

stroke by a master one of the most evocative metaphors of modern
poetry:

> Spesso il male di vivere ho incontrato:
> era il rivo strozzato che gorgoglia,
> era l'incartocciarsi della foglia
> riarsa, era il cavallo stramazzato.

> Bene non seppi, fuori del prodigio
> che schiude la divina Indifferenza:
> era la statua nella sonnolenza
> del meriggio, e la nuvola, e il falco alto levato.

> [Often the pain of living have I met:
> it was the choked stream that gurgles,
> it was the curling up of the parched
> leaf, it was the horse fallen off its feet.

> Well-being I have not known, save the prodigy
> that reveals divine Indifference:
> it was the statue in the midday
> somnolence, and the cloud, and the falcon high lifted.][36]

Between the philosophical poetry of Leopardi and that of Montale there
was Michelstaedter's *Angst*.

"Aprile" is one of Michelstaedter's most Leopardian poems. It ends
with an invocation to death that echoes Leopardi's in "Amore e morte."
Yet, here too, Michelstaedter has his own personal message. Elaborating
on the theme graphically rendered in "Il canto delle crisalidi," he invokes
death that is true life, for he is overwhelmed by the nausea of this daily
life that is the real death. Hence the quality of oxymoron in his poetry,
which is strictly dependent on his contradictory ontology, receiving its
final expression in the last line, "si che l'oscurità per me sia spenta." It is a
powerful image that, by calling this life darkness, identifies invoked
death with light:

> Pur tu permani, o morte, e tu m'attendi
> o sano o tristo, ferma ed immutata,

morte benevolo porto sicuro.
Che ai vivi morti quando pur sia vano
quanto la vita il pallido tuo aspetto
e se morir non sia che continuar
la nebbia maledetta
e l'affanno agli schiavi della vita—
—purché alla mia pupilla questa luce
che pur guarda la tenebra si spenga
e più non sappia questo ch'ora soffro
vano tormento senza via né speme,
tu mi sei cara mille volte, o morte,
che il sonno verserai senza risveglio
su quest'occhio che sa di non vedere,
sì che l'oscurità per me sia spenta.

(Poesie, 66)

[Yet you remain, death, waiting for me
in health or sadness, motionless, unchanged,
death, kind safe harbor.
And if to the dead living your pale aspect
is as vain as life
and if to the slaves of life
dying is not but the continuation
of this damned fog
—provided that to my pupil
that looks at darkness
the light be out
and that I no longer know what I endure now
vain torment without path or hope, a
thousand times you are dear to me, death
that will pour over this eye that can no longer see
a sleep without a wakening
so that darkness will for me be forever extinguished.]

By now Michelstaedter was in the last year of his life. But the conflict between real and ideal was still present in all its force. "Risveglio" ("Awakening") opens up with another echo from Leopardi, actually from two of Leopardi's poems ("Il canto notturno" and "Aspasia"), and establishes the opposition right away with a pounding cadence:

> Sta sotto il vento a farsi vellicare
> sta sotto il sole a suggere il calore
> sta sotto il cielo sulla buona terra
> questo ch'io chiamo "io," ma ch'io non sono.
> No, non son questo corpo, queste membra
> prostrate qui fra l'erbe sulla terra . . .
> . . . .
> Io son solo, lontano, io son diverso—
> altro sole, altro vento e più superbo
> volo per altri cieli è la mia vita . . .
> (Poesie, 69)

> [It is under the wind that titillates it
> it is under the sun to suck its warmth
> it is under the sky on the good earth
> this that I call "I," but I is not.
> No, I am not this body, these limbs
> prostrated here on grassy land . . .
> . . . .
> I am alone, distant, I am different—
> other sun, other wind and prouder
> flight through other skies is my life . . .]

Yet the rebellion flares up and dies out in the end. Carlo has not succeeded in rejecting his dependence on nature. He will succeed in his next poem, written for Paula's birthday and dedicated to her. He borrows a *topos* from Leopardi that is older than Lucretius; that of the crying newborn who is consoled by his parents—but this time his mentor is in the shadows. After the long Leopardian first stanza, Michelstaedter takes off on his own, no longer needing anyone else's assistance:

> Paula, non ti so dir dolci parole,
> cose non so che possan esser care,
> poiché il muto dolore a me ha parlato

e m'ha narrato quello che ogni cuore
soffre e non sa—ché a sé non lo confessa.
Ed oltre il vetro della chiara stanza
che le consuete imagini riflette
vedo l'oscurità pur minacciosa
—e sostare non posso nel deserto.
Lasciami andare, Paula, nella notte
a crearmi la luce da me stesso,
lasciami andar oltre il deserto, al mare
perch'io ti porti il dono luminoso
. . . molto più che non credi mi sei cara.

(Poesie, 72)

[Paula, I cannot tell you words that are sweet,
I don't know things that can be dear,
because the mute suffering has spoken to me
and has told me what every heart
suffers and knows not—for it does not confess it to itself.
And beyond the glass of the bright room
that reflects familiar images
I see threatening darkness, yet
—I cannot stop in the desert.
Let me go, Paula, in the night
so that I will create light by myself,
let me go beyond the desert, to the sea
so that I bring to you the luminous gift
. . . much more dear than you think are you to me.]

Truthful, free spirits, Nietzsche had written in his *Zarathustra,* dwell in the desert; they are alone in their search for light; they do not depend on anything.[37]

The sea that Carlo is looking for is the "free sea without shores" ("il libero mare senza sponde") of the poem "Onda per onda," which in these last two months of his life he will struggle to reach with all his strength. "Il dono luminoso" is *persuasione,* is the absolute, is perfection. It is perhaps only a musical and a visual echo that creates an association between this "luminous gift" of Carlo and "il girasole impazzito di luce" of Montale. Yet it is more than a visual and musical similarity that brings these two poems together. Could it be that Montale is asking Carlo for that luminous gift promised to Paula? It is a dialogue between two poets about the gift of poetry. That grace of light for which both were searching and which was denied to Michelstaedter was to descend to Montale. His "sunflower maddened with light" is the homage of a poet to a spirit maddened with light.[38]

In "Onda per onda" the journey has begun; the end is already in sight: the image of the sea will at the end coincide with that of the luminous flame:

Onda per onda batte sullo scoglio
—passan le vele bianche all'orizzonte;
monta rimonta, or dolce or tempestosa
l'agitata marea senza riposo.
Ma onda e sole e vento e vele e scogli,
questa è la terra, quello l'orizzonte
del mar lontano, il mar senza confini.
Non è il libero mare senza sponde,
il mare dove l'onda non arriva,
il mare che da sé genera il vento,
manda la luce e in seno la riprende,
il mar che di sua vita mille vite
suscita e cresce in una sola vita.

Ahi, non c'è mare cui presso o lontano
varia sponda non gravi, e vario vento
non tolga dalla solitaria pace,
mare non è che non sia un dei mari.
Anche il mare è un deserto senza vita,
arido triste fermo affaticato.
Ed il giro dei giorni e delle lune,
il varïar dei venti e delle coste,
il vario giogo sì lo lega e preme
—il mar che non è mare s'anche è mare.
Ritrova il vento l'onda affaticata,
e la mia chiglia solca il vecchio solco.

E se fra il vento e il mare la mia mano
regge il timone e dirizza la vela,

non è più la mia mano che la mano
di quel vento e quell'onda che non posa . . .
Ché senza posa come batte l'onda
ché senza posa come vola il nembo,
sì la travaglia l'anima solitaria
a varcar nuove onde, e senza fine
nuovi confini sotto nuove stelle
fingere all'occhio fisso all'orizzonte,
dove per tramontar pur sorga il sole.
Al mio sole, al mio mar per queste strade
della terra o del mar mi volgo invano,
vana è la pena e vana la speranza,
tutta è la vita arida e deserta,
finché in un punto si raccolga in porto,
di sé stessa in un punto faccia fiamma.

(*Poesie,* 73–74)

[Wave after wave beats over the rock
on the horizon white sails are passing;
the tide that never finds rest
mounts and mounts now sweet, now stormy.
But wave and sun, wind and sails and rocks,
all this is land, and that is the horizon
of the faraway sea, the infinite sea.
It is not the free sea without shores
the sea that waves cannot reach
the sea that by itself generates wind,
the sea that sends the light and takes it back
the sea that out of its one life
kindles and nurtures thousands.

Ah, there is no sea that near or far
a shore does not weigh down, and wind
(does not) remove from solitary peace,
sea there is not that is but one of them.

The sea too is a desert without life,
arid, sad, motionless and weary.
And the circling of days and moons
the varying of winds and coastlines,
the yoke so ties and presses it
—the sea that is no sea although it is.
The weary wave finds the wind again,
and my keel plows the old furrow.
And if between wind and sea my hand
holds on to the rudder and straightens the sail,

it is no more my hand than the sea's
hand and the wave that never rests . . .
For without rest as the wave is beating,
for without rest as the cloud is flying
so it is troubled by the solitary soul
to plow new waves, and endlessly
to set new bounds under new stars
for the eye, fixed to the horizon,
where the sun rises only to set again.
To my sun, my sea through these dirt roads
of land or sea in vain I turn,
vain is the sorrow and vain is the hope,
life is all vain and deserted,
until it gathers into one point
and burns itself into a flame.]

The sea that Carlo is searching for is not the sea before his eyes, with shores and harbors and sails. His is the free sea without shores, that generates the wind, the light, the life within itself. Not the sea in which man usually sails or swims that is as much a desert as the land. The poet's soul needs to overcome all boundaries and create for himself new ones. The verb *fingere* that appears here again has finally acquired the Leopardian connotation of creativity. Yet poetical creativity is not enough for Carlo. The poet's sun, the poet's sea cannot be found on this earth. It will be reached only when he will transform his soul into a flame. "Burning," Montale had said, "this only and nothing else is my meaning."[39] But Montale was able to light his flame in the metaphorical world of poetry. Michelstaedter was not. In him even poetical metaphor was to become flesh.

The coincidence between the theoretical, philosophical work of his dissertation and the synthesizing poetical voice was fully realized. The poem "Onda per onda" ends with the same image as the section on *persuasione*. Even the words are the same, "finché faccia di sé stesso fiamma e giunga a consistere nell'ultimo presente" (*Persuasione,* 88) and "finché in un punto si raccolga in porto, di sé stessa in un punto faccia fiamma" (*Poesie,* 74). Michelstaedter's life is now one with his philosophy and his art. But he will go a step further and realize in his own person that coincidence of opposites that had governed his work and his life, as it governed his philosophy. He will give real life to the central metaphor of his philosophy, the flame to which he had already given a poetical voice. Art will with him become life, and he will fulfill his promise of "living a life like a work of art" (*Opere,* 632).

Michelstaedter in his notes analyzes once more the opposition of life and death and arrives at the identity of *persuasione* and art:

> He who truly wants life, refuses to live in relation to those things that constitute the vain joy and the vain sorrow of others. . . . His life is the refusal of and the struggle against the temptations of illusory satisfactions, and without wasting itself in illusory possessions it affirms shapes and creates itself by itself; this is art. Art is therefore the strongest suffering, the strongest life and gives the strongest joy in the realization of itself. (*Opere,* 705)

Michelstaedter here repudiates the conventional view of an opposition between art and life. He sets himself against a tradition that will outlive him, that of the artist who does not leap into the water, as Montale's Esterina will do, but stays on land and watches. Michelstaedter denies that he who "sees" does not act; he denies the dichotomy between life and contemplation, that writers like Svevo and Musil, for example, made their own. But his refusal is an act of will; the act of practical, not theoretical reason, a desperate attempt to defeat what his own reason had discovered. His final act was to be a proof of it. Michelstaedter could not be satisfied with the "either/or." Although he knew that there was no resolution to this opposition, he wanted to realize that resolution in himself. He could neither choose to be only a man of action—his dream of becoming a sailor did not come true—nor the contemplative artist that steps out of life in order to study and represent it. Art was to become life and life art just as he tried to tell us with the vertiginous rhythm of "Il canto delle crisalidi."

There are a few shorter pieces without a precise date that Campailla placed between "Onda per onda" and "I figli del mare" and before the final great poems. Among them is one, unmentioned in any studies of Michelstaedter, whose theme and rhythm are reminiscent of Belli's masterpiece "Er caffettiere filosofo" ("The Coffee-Man Philosopher"):

Ognuno vede quanto l'altro falla
quando crede passar filo per cruna,
pur spera ognuno d'infilar sua cruna,
né perché più s'avveda dell'inganno
meno ritenta ancora la fortuna.
Ché tale è la sua sorte:
col suo filo sperar vita tramare
e con la speme giungere alla morte.
(Poesie, 75)

Each one can see how wrong the other is,
thinking his thread can go through the needle's eye,
still each one hopes to thread his own
and, though fully aware of the deception, never
slows down the trying of his fortune.
Such is his fate,
to hope of weaving with his thread life
and with his hope to reach his death.

The sameness of men's fate—a race toward death—and the sameness of their self-deception are the themes in both these poems. Of course, it is only an echo, because in the world of the Roman nineteenth-century poet there is no room for the *Übermensch*. There is no hero in the papal states; men are all little coffee beans ending up in the mouth of the grinder.[40] For just a brief moment, however, Michelstaedter too seems to leave his *persuaso* aside and act as the equalizer of the human race.

"The free sea without shores" of "Onda per onda" will become "the fury of the sea" in the last poems. The metaphor of *persuasione* will take over and by opening up in concentric circles will create the music of Michelstaedter's best poems. With them he will embark on his last journey, having abandoned forever the life of the land.

As he steps on the ship for his final journey the sea is smooth, the sails hang inert, the wind is silent over the sea, the sea reflects the sky and the poet concludes: "for now life on board is not work" (*Poesie*, 78). In his extensive monographic study commenting on the poem, Cerruti interpreted the calm and stillness of the sea as the *arghía* Michelstaedter had always longed for.[41] If one keeps in mind, however, that the real journey has yet to start, and if we concentrate on the opening verse that recurs at the end of the first stanza and sets the *Stimmung* of the poem, a different interpretation could be more satisfactory.

The poem begins with the temporal adverb "per ora" ("for the time being"), implying from the start a provisional condition, a condition that will change, that actually must change, because the possibility of the present moment is only a temporary prelude to action. "For now life on board is not work." Work, that is, the real life of the sailor, namely fighting with the sea, holding the ship, raising the sails and struggling with the wind, has not yet begun. Nature is in a phase of inertia, which will need to be overcome if *persuasione* is to be reached.

Per ora a bordo non è lavorare
che inerte pende la vela
e il vento tace sul mare
e il mar è a specchio del cielo
Per ora—a bordo non è lavorare

A sera il sole calerà nel mare
che senza nubi è il cielo
e giù ai confini del mare
l'orizzonte è senza velo
A sera—il sole calerà nel mare

Oggi sul ponte dolce riposare
che senza moto la nave
riposa il riposo del mare
e non si può camminare
Oggi sul ponte dolce riposare

Sola sul dorso del mare
nel mezzo del cerchio lontano
sta sotto il ciel meridiano
la nave a galleggiare
                    (*Poesie*, 78)

[For now on board life is not work
since inert the sail hangs
and silent is the wind over the sea
and the sea mirrors the sky
For now on board life is not work.

In the evening the sun will set in the sea
since cloudless is the sky
and faraway at the limits of the sea
the horizon is without veils
in the evening—the sun will set in the sea.

Today on deck sweet is the rest
since motionless the ship
rests, the same rest as the sea
and it cannot proceed.
Today on deck sweet is the rest.

Alone on the crest of the sea
in the middle of a faraway circle
lies the ship under the midday sky
the ship bobbing up and down.]

The word "mare" appears seven times, and the *are* sound twelve. It creates a slow rocking effect similar to singsong music. Each stanza, in fact, begins and ends with this sound, and the repetition increases its lulling force. Each stanza, with the exception of the last one, opens and closes with the same verse, forming circles that radiate out of the word "mare" placed at the center of each stanza, and of the poem. Thus the sea is the force behind the movement on both the literal and the figurative levels. It is the movement of calm that precedes the storm.

Carlo was at his beloved Pirano, then, once more in the company of Paula and the Cassini sisters. After having been interested in Fulvia for a while, as we know from the famous letter to Gaetano (August 1908), he was by now in love with her younger sister Argia. Her name had become his nemesis—after all, he was still faithful to Heraclitus, for whom the name always reflected the named. Argia played the piano beautifully and he was her devoted audience, just as he had been of his friend, Giannotto Bastianelli, in Florence. By then Carlo was not reading much any more except for the Gospels. He accepted only the simplest of languages, the most direct and authentic, the only language free from *rettorica:* the language of music and that of Christ.

At the end of "I figli del mare" Michelstaedter wrote the date September 2, 1910. As Campailla remarked, this is not a poem that could have been written in a day. Still, the date helps us to place it in a particular moment of his brief life. "I figli del mare" are Itti and Senia, and Senia is the Greek word for stranger; thus, she is the spiritual sister of the Stranger in *The Lady of the Sea.* Ibsen's character represents the power of the life of nature, the sea, but also of the unknown, of darkness, and exercised his power over Ellida even (and more so) in his absence. The name Itti, like Ellida, is a derivation from a Greek word; it means "fish" and "according to the symbology of primitive Christianity, as V. Arangio Ruiz explained, is the 'Savior of himself.'"[42] Itti and Senia are therefore even with their names connected to the symbology of the sea.

If Ibsen was the closest literary influence on Michelstaedter, the Adriatic Sea where he spent that summer month was the real generative force behind this exceptional poetic outburst. In a few days he wrote almost as many verses as he had in the preceding two years. The sea, symbol of life, giver of life, principle of creation, had become also the creative power behind his poetry.

The night of September 2, the last night he spent at the sea, he wrote to his cousin Emilio words that found a place also in his poem. It is a highly metaphorical letter, charged with symbolic resonance that can be better appreciated if we read it as a preface to the verses of "I figli del mare":

> My solitude here is not that of the life in Gorizia that you know—it is not the desert—the voice of the sea is here not the distant voice dreamed of . . . but it is present in all its strength and I am part of its life. The waves beat over the rocks of the deserted coast which ends at Salvore—next to me, safe in the small abandoned harbor is my boat; I write stretched out on a mat in a small hut of stones which must have once been used by the miners that, now having been completely abandoned, I was able to open and take possession of. . . . Tomorrow evening I will leave for Gorizia and I will abandon this life that has been for me a harbor of peace. Tomorrow I start sailing again—with all winds. (*Ep.*, 447)

Dalla pace del mare lontano
dalle verdi trasparenze dell'onde
dalle lucenti grotte profonde
dal silenzio senza richiami—
Itti e Senia dal regno del mare
sul suolo triste sotto il sole avaro
Itti e Senia si risvegliaro
dei mortali a vivere la morte.
Fra le grigie lagune palustri
al vario trasmutar senza riposo
al faticare sordo ansioso
per le umide vie ritorte
alle mille voci d'affanno
ai mille fantasmi di gioia
alla sete alla fame allo spavento
all'inconfessato tormento—
alla cura che pensa il domani
che all'ieri aggrappa le mani
che ognor paventa il presente più forte
al vano terrore della morte
fra i mortali ricurvi alla terra

Itti e Senia i principi del mare
sul suolo triste sotto il sole avaro
Itti e Senia si risvegliaro.—

(*Poesie*, 79)

[From the peace of the faraway sea
from the green transparencies of waves
from the shining deep caves
from the silence without voices
Itti and Senia from the reign of the sea
on the sad soil under a miser sun
Itti and Senia were awakened
to live the death of the mortals.
Among the gray, marshy lands
to the varying restless change
to the deaf and anxious fatigue
through the damp crooked roads
to the thousand voices of anguish
to the thousand ghosts of joy
to thirst, to hunger and fear,
to the unconfessed torment—
to the care that thinks of tomorrow
and to yesterday clutches its hands
that always fears the present above all
to the vain terror of death
among the mortals bent over the land
Itti and Senia, princes of the sea,
on the sad soil under the miser sun
Itti and Senia awakened.]

The poem opens with an image of primordial life from which Itti and Senia, creatures of the sea, are called to the life of man that must be lived on land. Already in the third line the figure of oxymoron appears. The "shining deep caves" are a poetical image of the philosophical discourse of "Il canto delle crisalidi." The deep caves in the sea cannot be but dark, yet this is the darkness of the real life in contrast to that darkness that Michelstaedter wants "spenta," extinguished, in "Aprile," that is, the life on land. From the sea, from its light and from its silence and its peace, Itti and Senia are awakened to the mortal life on land. The four lines at the beginning all start with the preposition "from," each of which generates two in the second part that start with the preposition "to." From peace to torment, from silence to voices of anxiety, from green transparencies of water to marshy damp land, from the reign of the sea to the sad land Itti and Senia are awakened. The contrast between land and sea is underlined by the long list of negative qualifiers that correspond by opposition to the few essential and positive qualifiers of the sea in the first five lines.

Arangio Ruiz called this first stanza "the opening of a legend—sung in the tune of an allegretto."[43] These twenty-four lines, however, have the cadence of drums. From the dramatic crescendo an effect of anxiety and discomfort results. The pounding of the preposition *a,* repeated eight times followed always by negative elements, produces a claustrophobic and maddening effect. It is the life on land.

Ebbero padre ed ebbero madre
e fratelli ed amici e parenti
e conobbero i dolci sentimenti
la pietà e gli affetti e il pudore
e conobbero le parole
che conviene venerare
Itti e Senia i figli del mare
e credettero d'amare.
E lontani dal loro mare
sotto il pallido sole avaro
per il dovere facile ed amaro
impararono a camminare.
Impararono a camminare
per le vie che la siepe rinserra
e stretti alle bisogna della terra
si curvarono a faticare.
Sulle pallide facce il timore
delle piccole cose umane
e le tante speranze vane
e l'ansia che stringe il core.
                    (*Poesie,* 79–80)

[They had a father, they had a mother
and siblings and friends
and they knew (the) sweet feelings,
piety, love and modesty
and they learned the words
that one must worship
Itti and Senia, children of the sea
and they believed they loved.
And far away from their sea
under the pale, miser sun
out of the easy and bitter duty
they learn to walk.
They learn to walk
through roads that the edge encloses
and forced by the needs of the earth
they bend down to toil.
Over their pale faces the fear
of petty human things
and the many vain hopes
and the anxiety that wrenches the heart.]

The metamorphosis of Itti and Senia into creatures of the land is complete. They learn to love and to hate, they learn words, they learn to walk. The line "impararono a camminare" is repeated twice to create an effect of senseless wandering, of continuation of meaningless activity: a self-perpetuating vanity.

Ma nel fondo dell'occhio nero
pur viveva il lontano dolore
e parlava la voce del mistero
per l'ignoto lontano amore.
E una sera alla sponda sonante
quando il sole calava nel mare
e gli uomini cercavano riposo
al lor ozio laborioso
Itti e Senia alla sponda del mare
l'anima solitaria al suono dell'onde

per le sue corde più profonde
intendevano vibrare.
E la vasta voce del mare
al loro cuore soffocato
lontane suscitava ignote voci,
altra patria altra casa un altro altare
un'altra pace nel lontano mare.

                              (*Poesie*, 80)

[But in the depth of the dark eye
the distant pain was still alive
and was speaking the voice of mystery
for the unknown remote love.
And one evening at the sounding shore
when the sun was setting in the sea
and men sought rest
from their laborious idleness
Itti and Senia at the shore of the sea
felt the most profound chords
of their solitary soul vibrate
to the sound of the waves.
And the vast voice of the sea
to the suffocated heart
gave rise from far away to unknown voices,
another land, another home, another altar
another peace in the distant sea.]

The influence on Michelstaedter's philosophical agony of Schopenhauer's *Wille* and Nietzsche's *Wille zur Macht* is evident as is that of the German Romantics and idealists. In his last essay on Michelstaedter, Brianese points out this element, demonstrating the closeness between him and Hölderlin's Hyperion in his striving for the Infinite and the Absolute. Furthermore, the opposition of finite–infinite in Fichte and the necessary unfulfilled aim that corresponds to the never satisfied *Sehnsucht* of the Romantics are also characteristics of Michelstaedter's philosophy.[44] The poem is, in fact, structured by this opposition: finite–infinite. In the stanza quoted above it is the voice of real life—and the voice of the infinite—that is heard, and its sound is born out of the contrast with the life on land, the finite, expressed in the preceding stanza. It is the limit that brings forth the need for the unlimited, as Michelstaedter could also have learned from Leopardi. But, whereas Leopardi will accept the man-made infinite of the poet, and its fictional nature, Michelstaedter will fight for its ontological being.

In the middle of the third stanza the expression "lor ozio laborioso"— another oxymoron—well exemplifies the absurdity of existence. It is the first *ottonario* (a verse of eight syllables) of the stanza after seven longer verses and it brings the rhythm to a halt. From it ensues the *Sehnsucht* for the opposite. The voice of the sea now takes over calling Itti and Senia back to their real home.

Hugo Friedrich, in *Structure of Modern Poetry,* compares oxymoron in twentieth-century poetry to the similar phenomenon of dissonance present in the music of the time.[45] Michelstaedter, in fact, developed the Romantic and idealistic element of the opposition in this direction, denying any possibility of a Hegelian synthesis. The negative moment was the core of his philosophy and the insistence on it proved to him that contradictoriness is the basic element, the essence of man's existence.

The voice of the sea that calls Itti and Senia to their real life creates, by opposition, an ever wider desert of the life on land:

Si sentirono soli ed estrani
nelle tristi dimore dell'uomo
si sentirono più lontani
fra le cose più dolci e care.
E bevendo lo sguardo oscuro
l'uno all'altra dall'occhio nero
videro la fiamma del mistero
per doppia face battere più forte.
Senia disse: « Vorrei morire »
e mirava l'ultimo sole.
Itti tacque, che dalla morte
nuova vita vedeva salire.
E scorrendo l'occhio lontano
sulle sponde che serrano il mare
sulle case tristi ammucchiate

dalle trepide cure avare
« Questo è morte, Senia »—egli disse—
« questa triste nebbia oscura
dove geme la torbida luce
dell'angoscia, della paura. »

(Poesie, 81)

[They felt alone and strangers
in the sad dwellings of man.
They felt more distant
among the sweetest and dearest things
And drinking the dark gaze
from each other's black eyes
they saw the flame of mystery
flickering twice as strong.
Senia said: "I want to die"
while looking at the last sun.
Itti was silent, for from death
he saw new life being born.
And letting his gaze run to the distance
over the shores that locked up the sea
over the sad houses clustered together
by the fearful miserly cares
"This is death, Senia"—he said—
"This sad obscure mist
where the murky light of anguish
and fear moans."]

At the center of the poem and for the first time, Itti, the savior of himself, speaks. Once more he gives voice to the core of Michelstaedter's philosophy. The oxymoron which opposes mortal life to the real life which is the death of "Il canto delle crisalidi" constitutes also the core of this poem. If Senia is overwhelmed by a feeling of nausea toward the life she is living on land, Itti is capable of explaining to her that what she is longing for with her invocation to death is real life, and that the real death instead is the anguish, the fear in the dark mist of the land.

Itti's monologue continues in the following stanza. The new stanza is, in fact, necessary in order to respect the internal structure of the poem. With the voice of death, mist, fear, the poem stops and the negativity brings forth by opposition the positive voice of the following stanza:

> Altra voce dal profondo
> ho sentito risonare
> altra luce e più giocondo
> ho veduto un altro mare.
> Vedo il mar senza confini
> senza sponde faticate
> vedo l'onde illuminate
> che carena non varcò.
> Vedo il sole che non cala
> lento e stanco a sera in mare
> ma la luce sfolgorare
> vedo sopra il vasto mar.
> Senia, il porto non è la terra
> dove a ogni brivido del mare
> corre pavido a riparare
> la stanca vita il pescator.
> Senia, il porto è la furia del mare,
> è la furia del nembo più forte,
> quando libera ride la morte
> a chi libero la sfidò.
> (Poesie, 81–82)

> [Another voice from the depth
> I heard resound
> another light and a more
> joyful sea I saw.
> I see the sea without boundary
> without weary shores
> I see shining waves
> that no keel has ever plowed.
> I see the sun that does not set
> slow and tired at evening in the sea,
> but I see the light

that blazes over the vast sea.
Senia, the harbor is not the land
where at every shudder of the sea
the frightened fisherman runs to shelter
his tired life.
Senia, the harbor is the fury of the sea,
it is the fury of the wilder storm
where death smiles freely
at him who freely challenged her.]

The words Michelstaedter had written in his dissertation and again in his letter to Emilio are here repeated verbatim. They constitute the refrain of this song and will reappear at the end.

In his study of the poem, Brianese sees in the conclusion of this triadic movement sea-land-sea the failure of Michelstaedter's theoretical-existential attempt to achieve authenticity. For Brianese, Michelstaedter, unaware, chooses "the chaos of becoming," and "abandons any demand for a definite absolute truth." If there is no peaceful harbor in which to land, if "the meaning of sailing is given by nothing else than by its very wandering in the fury of the sea; because where it finds rest, there it is the end," then, Brianese concludes, the two possible forms of existence—on land and on sea—are both forms of becoming. Being once more escapes Michelstaedter.[46]

There is a forced attempt in this interpretation to encompass Michelstaedter's philosophy in a Parmenidean frame. But Heraclitus's world was just as present in his mind as the Parmenidean. The need for an immobile absolute is undeniable in Michelstaedter's work, it springs out of a Heraclitean vision of reality, created and ruled by change. The only "authentic" life man can have in the inauthentic life on land is to struggle against it as against the fury of a stormy sea. This is what he means when he calls real life "the fury of the sea." On land man can only struggle with becoming. It is the only honest choice; to combat constantly the *rettorica* of life. Did Michelstaedter intend to show us with his own being that the immobile, absolute state is that of "the soul in the island of the blessed?" Was his death an act of will to reach that island?

The rhythm of this central stanza is more rapid. It must be essential and direct. It consists mostly of eight-syllable lines until we arrive at the philosophical explanation at the end, where the line becomes longer before the short one that brings the stanza to its conclusion. Itti's voice becomes silent and the voice of *rettorica* takes over. The following stanza is the appeal made by *rettorica* for man to return to land. After five stanzas of about twenty lines each, there is one of thirty, as if to underline its rhetorical nature.

Cosí disse nell'ora del vespro
Itti a Senia con voce lontana;
dalla torre batteva la campana
del domestico focolare:
« Ritornate alle case tranquille
alla pace del tetto sicuro,
che cercate un cammino più duro?
che volete dal perfido mare?
Passa la gioia, passa il dolore,
accettate la vostra sorte,
ogni cosa che vive muore
e nessuna cosa vince la morte.
Ritornate alla via consueta
e godete di ciò che v'è dato:
non v'è un fine, non v'è una meta
per chi è preda del passato.
Ritornate al noto giaciglio
alle dolci e care cose
ritornate alle mani amorose
allo sguardo che trema per voi
a coloro che il primo passo
vi mossero e il primo accento,
che vi diedero il nutrimento
che vi crebbe le membra e il cor.
Adattatevi, ritornate,
siate utili a chi vi ama
e spegnete l'infausta brama
che vi trae dal retto sentier.
Passa la gioia, passa il dolore,
accettate la vostra sorte,

ogni cosa che vive muore
nessuna forza vince la morte. »
                    (*Poesie,* 82–83)

[So in the hour of vespers
with a distant voice Itti spoke to Senia;
from the tower tolled the bell
of the domestic hearth:
"Return to your tranquil home
to the peace of your safe roof,
why look for a harder path?
what do you want from the wicked sea?"
Joy passes, so does pain,
accept your fate
everything that lives dies
nothing wins over death.
Return to your life of habits
and enjoy what is given to you:
there is no end, no goal
for those who are prey of the past.
Return to your familiar pallet
to the sweet, dear things
return to the amorous hands
to the glance that trembles for you
to those who helped you
with the first step and utterance
who gave you nourishment
that developed your limbs and your heart.
Adapt yourselves, go back,
be useful to those who love you
and extinguish the ill-omened desire
that pulls you away from the right path.
Joy passes, so does pain
accept your fate
everything that lives dies
no force wins over death."]

This stanza rings with Ibsen's poem "Auf dem Hochgebirge."[47] There, too, is a sound of bells compared to the more alluring sound of the waterfall; water, as Taletes and Empedocles had taught men, is the original element.

The voice of *rettorica* is tempting Senia back to the life on land. The lure is security, shelter versus the danger of the sea, the invitation is to adapt, to conform. In *The Lady of the Sea,* Ibsen, with the voice of Ballested, explains how men "acclimatize themselves," becoming beings of habit, whereas the mermaid, if forced to life on land, dies of it.[48] It is possible that Michelstaedter wrote this stanza with Ballested's words in mind and chose "adattarsi" because it corresponds to Ballested's "acclimatize." The verb must have remained in his mind. He used it in his notes, reflecting on man's ability to adapt himself to his surroundings. In this same discussion he uses once the word "adattarsi" (the same that appears in the poem) and once, recalling Ibsen, "acclimatarsi." Later he wrote it, making it his own, in a letter to Paula where he explained he's getting accustomed ("mi acclimatizzo") to his physical illness (*Ep., 390*).

Campailla pointed out the importance of "acclimatize" for Michelstaedter. "It expressed . . . the central dilemma of his life and work: yield to the allurement of adaptation or refuse compromise up to the end; to be, in short, the offspring of the land or of the sea."[49] That is, the choice was between the life of *rettorica* or the life of *persuasione.*

At the sound of the alluring voice coming from the land, Senia vacillates. Placed at the edge, on the shore, she is torn between the call of the land and the splendor of the distant horizon:

Soffocata nell'onda sonora
con l'anima gonfia di pianto
ascoltava l'eco del canto
nell'oscurità del cor,
e con l'occhio all'orizzonte
dove il ciel si fondeva col mare
si sentiva vacillare
Senia, e disse: « Vorrei morire ».
Ma più forte sullo scoglio
l'onda lontana s'infranse
e nel fondo una nota pianse

pei perduti figli del mare.
« No, la morte non è abbandono »
disse Itti con voce più forte
« ma è il coraggio della morte
onde la luce sorgerà.
Il coraggio di sopportare
tutto il peso del dolore,
il coraggio di navigare
verso il nostro libero mare,
il coraggio di non sostare
nella cura dell'avvenire,
il coraggio di non languire
per godere le cose care.
Nel tuo occhio sotto la pena
arde ancora la fiamma selvaggia,
abbandona la triste spiaggia
e nel mare sarai la sirena.
Se t'affidi senza timore
ben più forte saprò navigare,
se non copri la faccia al dolore
giungeremo al nostro mare.

Senia, il porto è la furia del mare,
è la furia del nembo più forte,
quando libera ride la morte
a chi libero la sfidò »—.

(*Poesie*, 83–84)

[Suffocated by the sonorous wave
With her soul swollen with crying
Senia listened to the echo of the song
in the darkness of her heart,
and with her eyes toward the horizon
where the sky and sea are fused together
she felt herself swaying
and she said: "I want to die."
But stronger the distant wave

broke on the rock
and in the depth a note wept
for the lost children of the sea.
"No, death is not abandonment"
Itti said with a stronger voice
"but it is the courage of death
from which the light will rise.
The courage to bear
the entire weight of pain,
the courage to sail
toward our free sea
the courage not to stop
in the care of the future
the courage not to languish
for the enjoyment of things that are dear.
In your eye under the pain
is still burning the wild flame.
Abandon the sad shore
and of the sea you will be the mermaid.
If you trust without fear
with much more strength I'll be able to sail,
if you don't shelter your face against pain
we will reach our sea.

Senia, the harbor is the fury of the sea,
it is the fury of the wilder storm
when death smiles freely
at him who freely challenged her."]

For the opposition of life–death, the creative force of this poem, this is
the last movement (to develop Campailla's metaphor of the symphony).
After the voice of *rettorica,* it is *persuasione* that sings the final song, and
once more through the mouth of Itti.

Although Michelstaedter had often repeated that each individual must
find the road to *persuasione* by himself, although he admired Christ as
the savior of himself (rather than of struggling humanity) and although
he chose the name Itti for this very reason, he is here trying to save Senia

also. His last poems, in fact, represent the steps of this frustrated attempt. It is long, this song of Orpheus, trying to rescue his Eurydice, and it fails. It will develop over seven poems, beginning with "I figli del mare." There Carlo is not yet Orpheus. He is still Christ who has the courage to die, and knows that the light will be born out of his death. The negation of the flesh, that is, the renunciation of the life on land, of *rettorica,* will give birth to the light of *persuasione.* "Tertium non datur," Michelstaedter had written in his dissertation. Either man chooses the life of *rettorica* or that of *persuasione.* Whichever the choice, the other term of the opposition will, at that very moment, vanish.

In this last stanza, however, the poet seems to interpret Christ's death in line with the Christian tradition—that is, he sees Christ as the Savior of others as well as of himself. And he is not yet totally free and independent. He is, in fact, asking for Senia's help. From her love and trust in him he will gather the strength and courage to undertake the journey. He needs her. He depends on her. But Carlo knows that he who depends on others, on the external world, is still trapped in the net of *rettorica.* Soon he will realize that what he hoped for was only an illusion. In the following poems Christ will become Orpheus and lose his Eurydice forever.[50]

Paula describes the last period in Michelstaedter's life as follows:

Little by little, as he was simplifying his life, his way of feeling, he was reducing his needs. His nourishment had become simpler and simpler. He was freeing himself from that exterior varnish, the temptations from the outside, from all the acquired knowledge, from atavistic influences, it was as if he were forming himself by himself all over again.[51]

He was training himself to live the life of the spirit, almost like a new Buddha. He was working on his dissertation, but he had learned to live with the greatest simplicity. He was feeding himself mainly with fruit, milk, and black coffee and was sleeping on the floor without a mattress. Paula tells us also about his reading, which he had reduced to a minimum.

In one of his papers found on his desk together with the notes of his dissertation there was a page entitled "Bibliography, or God loves the illiterate." Here is the text:

Rather than read, do play or have someone play for you some of Beethoven's music, because your ears could not do you any better service. Eyes are not made to read books. But if you want at any cost to lower them to this service, read: Parmenides, Heraclitus, Empedocles, Simonides, Socrates (in the first Platonic dialogues), Aeschylus and Sophocles, Ecclesiastes, the Gospels according to Matthew, Mark and Luke, Lucretius . . . the Triumphs by Petrarch, and Leopardi's *Canti, The Adventures of Pinocchio* by Collodi, Ibsen's dramas.

No German writer makes Michelstaedter's last reading list. He warns against them. "Read nothing else, especially no German, if you care about your health, for these are contagious, just by looking at them."[52]

In Paula's brief account of the last period, Michelstaedter attempted to reach a state of individual perfection. He strove for self-discipline, for control of a temperament that up to the end would flare into rages; self-discipline to learn how to live without others, to learn not to depend. Even Argia Cassini, who had represented his hope in true love, at the end, had revealed herself as a creature of the land. She was no "lady of the sea" and this final disappointment found voice in his last poems.

Critics have seen in "I figli del mare" the most successful of Michelstaedter's poems, where structure, music, images all work together as a poetical whole. After this he began a philosophical discourse that is, on the surface, with Senia, but is really with himself. "I figli del mare"—the title the poem was given by Chiavacci in his first edition—together with the last seven poems addressed to Senia should be considered part of the same existential journey that had begun in "Onda per onda" and that he had hoped to share with Argia (Senia), his beloved who then was a *filobatheía* (lover of the depths). Carlo may have loved Argia very deeply, even though there appears to have been a crisis in their relationship at the end. The real purpose of these poems, however, is the writer's frustrated attempt to achieve *persuasione*. If at the beginning he thought he could find it in love, he soon realized that love as it is normally intended is also selfish: it is a sign of weakness; it is the manifestation of a need; it is the dependence on the other. The only love that can escape this fate is maternal love. Carlo's famous last letter to his mother, examined in Chapter 1, seems to underline this contrast. It has the same date as the third poem to Senia.

The first poem starts where "I figli del mare" ends. By now Itti has become the narrative "I." The identification has taken place. Carlo's effort now will be to help Argia become Senia. He undertakes his journey to the bottom of the sea, his descent to the origin. This he does with his woman in mind, from whom he derives his strength and for whose salvation, too, the journey will be undertaken:

I

Le cose ch'io vidi nel fondo del mare,
i baratri oscuri, le luci lontane
e grovigli d'alghe e creature strane,
Senia, a te sola lo voglio narrare.

Ché a brevi fiate nel tempo passato
nel fondo del mare mi sono tuffato.
A dare or la patria all'esule sirena,
la patria a me stesso e all'uomo abbattuto
svelare la via del suo regno perduto,
mi voglio tuffare con più forte lena,
ché ogni uom manifeste le tenebre arcane
conosca e vicine le cose lontane.

Ma quel che già vidi nel fondo del mare,
i baratri oscuri, le luci lontane
e grovigli d'alghe e creature strane,
Senia, a te sola lo voglio narrare.
                                    (*Poesie*, 85)

[The things that I saw in the depth of the sea,
the dark abysses, the distant lights
the tangles of algae and the strange creatures
Senia, to you alone I want to recount.

Only with short breaths in the past
I dove in the depth of the sea.
But now with stronger impetus
I want to dive, to give back their home
to the exiled mermaid, to myself, to the prostrate man

so that to every man the inscrutable darkness
will become clear and distant things near.

But what I have already seen in the depth of the sea
the dark abysses, the distant lights
the tangles of algae and the strange creatures
to you alone, Senia, I want to recount.]

The identification between Michelstaedter and Orpheus hinted at in
the first poem is openly stated in the second. The journey is undertaken
for the love of the woman and it is the attempt to possess her that makes
her disappear.

II

Da te lontano, nelle notti insonni,
innanzi agli occhi dove anche io miri,
sempre ho lo slancio della tua persona
come il vento la trae della passione
e la faccia raccolta che la fiamma
nel tempo stesso vela e manifesta.
Ma se l'occhio distolgo dalla strada
arida e sola che percorro oscura
e alla diafana luce lo rivolgo
dell'imagine tua cara e lontana,
invano cerco a me farla vicina,
invano cerco trattenerla, invano
tendo le braccia: nella notte oscura
non anche io l'ho mirata ed è svanita.
E l'occhio stanco e ardente la tenèbra
pur mira densa e inesorata quale
si chiuse innanzi all'antico cantore
che a Euridice si volse ed Euridice
nella notte infernale risospinse.
Spenta ogni luce allora ed ogni via
sbarrata, allor più presso la tenèbra
mi stringe sì che il cuor ignoto orrore
m'invade, non per me se nella notte

solo io soccomba, ma per te, o compagna
forte e sicura—che pel mio piacer,
per la mia debolezza, il mio sostare
non t'abbia risospinta nella stretta
della diuturna sofferenza inerte.

(Poesie, 85–86)

[Far from you in my sleepless nights,
before my eyes wherever I turn them,
always your slender figure soars
just as the wind of passion draws it
and your controlled face that the flame
at the same time shows and hides.
But if I withdraw my gaze
from the deserted, dark road that I walk
and if I turn it to the diaphanous light
of your dear and distant image,
in vain I try to hold it, in vain
I stretch my arms: in the darkness
of night I have not yet admired it but
it has already vanished.
And my tired and feverish eye still looks
at the dense and implacable darkness just as it
thickened before the ancient singer
who turned to Eurydice and Eurydice
pushed back into the infernal night.
With every light extinguished and every road
blocked, darkness presses me closer
so that unknown terror invades me,
not for me if in the night alone I might
succumb, but for you, my strong and confident
companion—you who for my pleasure, my weakness, my halting
might have forced back into the painful
grip of daily inertia.]

The possession of the desired object does not bring about happiness, but rather frustration. The theme that will later be central to Rilke's Duino's

Elegies appears at the core of Michelstaedter's philosophy. It appears once more here, the metaphor of the weight that we encountered at the beginning of *La persuasione e la rettorica*.[53] Its destiny is to hang and its desire for stasis, once satisfied, brings about its end.

Senia is lost. The first half of the third poem is a long series of negations, representing all the beautiful qualities and attributes that Senia no longer has. Michelstaedter again creates his poetry through oppositions, whose force is given by the juxtaposition of the *non* and the positive elements.

III

Non sorridente sotto il sole estivo,
la faccia luminosa e gli occhi chiari
nel doppio raggio del sole e del mare—
non melodiosa in tutta la persona
nel ritmo della danza, o fiduciosa
nell'infuriar dell'onde, come quando
a me che ti chiedevo rispondevi:
« Per me non è mai tempo di tornare,
chi va sicuro non potrà affogare »,
né sbattuta dall'onda musicale
quando senza velami dai tuoi occhi
l'anima fiammeggiava e la tua vita
nelle dita sicure era raccolta—

. . . .
non più cosi ti vidi nel mio sonno,
quando la trama più si fa sottile
e all'anima più pura inverso l'alba
rivela il sogno le cose lontane.

(*Poesie*, 87)

[Not smiling under the summer sun
with luminous face and light clear eyes
in the double ray of sun and sea—
not melodious in all your person
in the rhythm of dance, or trustworthy

in the fury of waves, as when
to me you answered:
"To me never is the time to return,
he who goes secure will not drown,"
neither moved by the musical wave
when without shadows from your eyes
your soul was flaming and your life
in your secure fingers was collected—

. . . .

no longer I saw you in my sleep,
when the weft becomes thinner
and to the soul then purer at dawn
sleep reveals distant realities.]

Senia is no longer "the creature of the sun" for whom he searched
"through the paths of the earth." It is a dream the poet is narrating, a
dream which is a premonition, and Carlo is shaken by it.

Ma ripiegata in piccolo sedile,
come un uccello che ferito a morte
l'ultima vita con l'ali ripara,
d'un velo bianco ti facevi schermo
al freddo e alla vicina fredda morte;
e in faccia era svanito ogni colore,
ogni scintilla spenta, e nelle occhiaie
oscure gli occhi t'eran fatti cavi.
Io ti parlavo e tu non rispondevi,
ma pur col bianco vel t'adoperavi
di riparare l'ultimo calore.
T'ero vicino e tu non mi vedevi,
ma nella morte già eri raccolta
ed alla morte come ad un riposo
stanca le membra e i veli disponevi,
con moto lento, come di chi ascolta
d'una squilla lontana il misterioso
annunzio noto, ch'altri non intende.
                    (*Poesie,* 87–88)

[But bent down on a small seat,
just as a bird that, mortally wounded,
his last life shelters with his wings,
a white veil was sheltering you
from the cold and from the cold death that was near
and from your face every color had vanished,
every spark extinguished, and in the dark sockets
of your eyes the light had sunk.
I spoke to you and you did not answer,
but with the white veil you tried
to protect the last warmth.
I was close and you did not see me
but in death already you were immersed
and tired, you were preparing for death
your limbs and your veils as for a rest,
with slow motion, as he who listens
to the mysterious yet familiar sound
of bells incomprehensible to others.]

Carlo knows that this is not the death they had hoped for together, the death which is real life. Desperately he attempts to call Senia back to life.

Cosí m'eri distolta e la mia vita
invano sanguinava per ridare
a te la vita che s'era partita:
con le mani non ti potea scaldare,
con la voce non ti potea svegliare.
Come da lungi nel plumbeo mare
che si fonde col cielo vela bianca
non più in mare che in cielo navigare
sembra, cosí pur l'anima tua stanca
era già della morte ed era in vita,
t'era fatta la vita sol dolore,
poiché in te la passione era svanita,
ma sulla faccia il pallido terrore
t'era dipinto e t'era chiuso il core.

(*Poesie,* 88)

[So you were taken away from me and my life
in vain was bleeding to give you back
the life that had fled from you:
with my hands I could not warm you,
with my voice I could not awake you.
As from afar in the leaden sky
that mingles together with the sea a white
sail seems to navigate no more on the sea
than on the sky,
so also your tired soul
belonged to death, though still alive,
life had become only sorrow
since in you feeling was extinguished,
but on your face pale terror
was painted and your heart was locked.]

The image of sky and sea fused together appear again here for the third time in his poetry, reflecting Michelstaedter's strong need for unity, for absolute possession (*Poesie, 52, 83*). Structurally, it gives unity to the poem; it is placed in the center and constitutes its core.

Campailla has pointed out the influence of Nietzsche's Zarathustra on Michelstaedter's scorn of death, but also claims that Michelstaedter—he was referring specifically to Itti—"poses himself as the anti-Zarathustra. While, in fact, Zarathustra invites his brothers to remain faithful to the earth . . . Itti points to the sea as the metaphor and the reality of ancient *persuasione*." Campailla says that whereas Zarathustra chose the earth and Christ renounced it for the sky, Michelstaedter did not choose "either the earth that is foreign to him, or the sky which is beyond his reach, but that limbo between earth and sky that is the sea."[54]

In choosing the sea, Michelstaedter expressed a preference for that point in space where the sea fuses with the sky—there is safety, there is the infinite. It is not chance, in fact, that white sails are associated with that distant sea, with the horizon where no more distinction is possible between water and sky. This fusion develops here too in an image characterized by oxymoron. The fusion between sky and sea, which is real life, is used as a simile for Senia's soul, which is now between life and death, where, however, the meanings of the two words are reversed.

Senia, who had been in the past Itti's hope of *persuasione,* is now between unreal life and death.

The final stanza, in fact, is the lament of Itti who thinks back to past hopes and illusions:

> Ahi, non questa sognammo amara morte
> nel suo pallido aspetto pauroso,
> questa che va a picchiar tutte le porte
> e ai morti dalla nascita il riposo
> finge nel tempo eterno e tenebroso,
> ma la giovane morte che sorride
> a chi per la sua cura non la teme,
> la morte che congiunge e non divide
> la compagna e il compagno e non li preme
> con l'oscuro dolore—ma che insieme
> li accoglie nel suo seno, come il porto
> di pace chi ha saputo navigare
> nel mar selvaggio, nel deserto mare,
> che a terra non s'è vòlto per conforto.
>
> (Poesie, 88–89)

> [Ah, not this bitter death we dreamed of
> in its frightening aspect,
> the one that knocks on every door
> and to the dead feigns rest
> in their eternal dark time,
> but the young death that smiles
> to those who do not fear,
> death that does not separate
> but unites man and woman
> and does not press them with dark sorrow—
> but receives them both in her womb,
> as the harbor of peace receives him
> who was able to sail
> in the stormy sea, in the deserted sea,
> and did not turn to land for comfort.]

The identification between beautiful death and real life is complete. Once more it is oxymoron that governs this poem. When death is seen as the "receiving womb" it has metamorphosed just as the chrysalis into its opposite, the life-giving principle. The maternal womb of death will receive the two lovers just as the harbor of peace will receive only the sailor who will have crossed the stormy sea. The sea, the womb, real life all coincide. Man's "beautiful death" is his return to his primordial life.

The dream is over; instead of fear, a new courage has emerged. The dream of Senia/Argia is a warning, and Itti/Carlo is ready for his last attempt to rescue her. At the end of this poem he placed the date: September 10, 1910, the same day he had written his mother his last letter, his spiritual testament, his promise of independence, of action. And with the same enthusiasm he begins the fourth poem of this brief *canzoniere* to Senia. It narrates the beginning of the journey toward that "sea without shores" that has constantly been equated with *persuasione*.

IV

Dato ho la vela al vento e in mezzo all'onde
del mar selvaggio, nella notte oscura,
solo, in fragile nave ho abbandonato
il porto della sicurezza inerte.
Al mare aperto drizzata ho la prora
per navigare, ed alla sorte oscura
la forza del mio braccio ho contrapposta.
Non ho temuto il vento avverso e l'onda
canuta, né la mensa famigliare
e l'usato giaciglio
ho rimpianto o il commercio delle care
e dolci cose. Né deserto e triste
m'è apparso il mar sonante nella notte,
anzi la voce sua come un appello
mi sonò in cor della mia stessa vita;
mi parve dolce cosa naufragare
nel seno ondoso che col ciel confina,
né temuta ho la morte.

(*Poesie*, 89)

[I have given the sail to the wind among the waves
of the stormy sea, in the darkness of night,
alone, in a frail ship I have abandoned
the harbor of safe inertia.
I have directed my prow to the open sea
to sail, and to obscure fate I opposed
the strength of my arm.
Neither have I feared the hostile wind and the white wave
nor have I regretted the familiar things.
Neither deserted nor sad
the sounding sea appeared to me in the night,
but its voice resounded in my heart as a call of life;
shipwreck seemed sweet to me
in the wavy womb that borders the sky,
nor have I feared death.]

For a second time the sea is identified with the womb, thus reinforcing the unity between life and death, between origin and end. The imprint of Leopardi is unmistakable, but superficial. The infinity in which shipwreck is sweet is for Leopardi a man-made creation. It is the creation of the poet. Michelstaedter, on the other hand, once more attempts to give his infinity an ontological status:

Incapable of being satisfied with a purely artistic creation, Michelstaedter has tried, at any price, to make his own biographical reality coincide with that of the demiurge Itti, to the point of deluding himself into thinking that Argia . . . could transfigure herself into Senia.[55]

Just at the boundary between the physical and the metaphorical Senia is waiting for Itti. With him she will start off on the final journey to the open, endless sea.

Alla punta del golfo donde il mare
s'apre libero e vasto senza fine
tu m'attendi sicura e fiduciosa,
le vesti al vento, ritta sullo scoglio.
Costeggiar mi conviene la scogliera

per uscire dal golfo, quindi uniti
navigheremo, poiché a me t'affidi:
sì breve tratto da te mi divide
e dal libero mar sì breve tratto!
—Ma perch'io tenti la bordata e tenda
la vela al vento, pur l'inerte chiglia
non fende l'onda, ch'ora sulle creste
spumanti, or negli abissi, or sur un bordo
or sull'altro la trae senza riposo.
E se l'albero gema, se la scotta
a spezzarsi si tenda, e nella vela
ingolfandosi il vento il mio naviglio
minacci di sommergere, pur sempre
alla stessa distanza io mi ritrovo
dalla punta agognata. Col timone
io m'adopero invano al mare aperto
dirizzare la prora: a chiglia inerte
il timone non giova.

(Poesie, 89–90)

[At the edge of the gulf from where
the free, vast sea opens endlessly
you are waiting, confident and trustful,
you stand on the rock, your veil in the wind.
I must sail along the reef
to leave the gulf, then united
we will sail out, for you trust in me:
such a short stretch divides me from you
and so short a stretch from the free sea!
—But though I try to tack and though
I trim the sails into the wind, still the inert keel
does not plow the wave, that now on the foamy crest
now in the abyss, now on one side,
now on the other drags it without rest.
And though the mast moans, and the sheet
is trimmed to the breaking point, and though the
wind engulfing the sail threatens

to submerge my ship, still always
I find myself at the same distance
from the desired end. With the rudder
in vain I try to direct my prow
to the open sea: nothing can the rudder avail
if the keel is inert.]

The metaphor of the weight that opened *La persuasione e la rettorica* and symbolizes the core of Michelstaedter's philosophy has been replaced by the image of the sailing ship. Its sails are tightened to the point of breaking and the ship pulls with all its force toward the desired end without ever reaching it. That Michelstaedter had his weight in mind can be proven by the page that follows the opening of his dissertation. It is the page with the two metaphors of man's attempts to reach *persuasione:* the mountain and the sea. There is no ship in this description. The narrator is swimming in the sea in a vain attempt to possess it.

The insistence on images of sea and sails cannot but bring to mind another intense seascape: Dino Campana's "Le Cafard," where the language has become as charged and intense as the wind which is filling those sails. The whole scenery vibrates recklessly; Campana's free spirit and his love for the violence of nature and for the irrational will tighten and charge his sails into "l'ultimo schianto crudele!" ("the final cruel tearing").[56] Michelstaedter instead wants possession, control; he cannot submit to irrational forces, both on a linguistic as well as on a philosophical level. Thus his poetry remains caught up in the coldness of his pitiless analysis. His struggle to reach the open sea ends in failure. To the enthusiasm and faith of the opening stanza correspond the disappointment and the defeat of the last one:

Il vento e l'onde intanto lentamente
come un rottame verso la scogliera
mi spingono a rovina senza scampo.
Ch'io debba naufragar senza lottare
fra la miseria dei battuti scogli,
presso al porto esecrato, come un vile,
senza esser giunto al mare, e te lasciando

sola e distrutta dopo il sogno infranto
fra le stesse miserie?

(*Poesie,* 90)

[The wind and the waves meanwhile
slowly push me to a ruin without escape
just as a wreck pushed to the rocky shore.
Must I without fighting be shipwrecked
in the misery of the beaten rocks,
near the hated harbor, as a coward,
without having reached the sea, and leaving you
alone and wrecked after our broken dream
among the same miseries?]

The poem ends with a rhetorical question. The journey to *persuasione* has failed precisely because of Senia. As Carlo had repeated in his theoretical work, that journey must be taken alone, and with no one else's safety in mind, but one's own. Itti, like Christ, can only save himself. And in order to do so, he must be totally independent from the external world and others. Furthermore, man must find in himself the strength to undertake his voyage. He cannot ask for help, nor must he rely on anyone. And this is the hardest task of all. In the fifth poem, in fact, Carlo openly confesses his love for Senia as the source of his strength, as the inspiring flame of his deeds. The poem is clearly an echo of Petrarch's "Solo e pensoso" ("Solitary and Pensive"). The poet shuns human contact because he does not want his love to be known. He feels, in fact, that such contact would contaminate the purity of his love. Its force and power are such that they would make it so apparent in any word uttered or gesture performed. But even away from men, Senia is present in the air, the song of birds and in the murmuring water.

V

Se mi trovo fra gli uomini talvolta,
qualunque cosa io parli, la mia voce
mi par che solo il nome tuo richiami.
Io taccio allora e aspetto trepidando

ch'altri con bocca impura a questa voce
risponda, e del mio bene ascoso mi discorra;
e se pur d'altre cose memorando
mi parlano con voce indifferente,
ma nel loro sorriso, ma negli occhi
mi par d'intravedere ch'altra cosa
vogliono dire, che nel cor profondo
sì mi ferisce. Ché da ogni mio gesto,
ché dal volto mi par ch'altri mi legga
il pensiero di te che sei lontana.
Dal commercio degli uomini rifuggo
allora alla campagna solitaria
o alla mia stanza solitaria e solo
tutto in me mi raccolgo; ma nell'aria,
nel canto degli uccelli e nell'uguale
mormorare dell'acqua, dalle ripe
alte del fiume e pur dalle pareti
della mia ignuda stanza, a piena voce
il tuo nome riecheggia al mio silenzio,
si che palese a ognuno e manifesta
del tutto, al volgo preda senza schermo,
parmi l'anima mia nel suo segreto.
Ed il sogno che nasce palpitante,
la "storia" che non soffre le parole
ma vuol esser vissuta, il più profondo
e caro senso della nostra vita,
che pur uniti e soli sotto il velo
di parole comuni nascondiamo,
d'atti comuni, con gelosa cura
nascondiamo a noi stessi ora del volgo
mi par fatto preda contaminata.

(Poesie, 91–92)

[At times if I find myself among men
if I say anything, my voice
seems only to be calling your name.
Then I keep silent and fearfully wait

that others with impure voice, answer mine,
and speak to me of my hidden love;
and even if they talk to me of other things
with indifferent voices
in their smile, in their eyes I
can see they mean to say something else,
that wounds me through the heart.
For in every gesture, and in every expression
I feel that others read
my thought of you so distant.
Then I flee the contact of men
to the solitary country or
to the solitude of my room and alone
I withdraw into myself; yet in the air,
in the birds' song, in the even murmuring
of the water, from the banks of the river
as from the walls of my naked room, in full voice
your name echoes in my silence,
so that without screen my soul lies open and manifest
to all, with its secret.
And our dream that is born throbbing,
our "story" that cannot bear words,
but wants to be lived, the most profound
and dear meaning of our lives
that though, united, alone under the veil
of common words and actions, with zealous care
we hide from ourselves, now
it has become contaminated prey of others.]

Once again Michelstaedter after the first steps leaves behind his great
models, Petrarch and Leopardi ("La vita solitaria"), and proceeds on his
own. The love between Carlo and Senia has become a story that cannot
bear words, but must be lived. The authenticity of their love cannot be
expressed through *rettorica,* only hidden by it. Words could never do it
justice. Carlo is here striving with all his strength to achieve *persuasione*
through absolute love. And in the following stanza he openly admits that
from this love he has derived the strength to continue his journey.

Nei giorni del dolore e nelle notti
senza riposo, nella valle triste
della sorda fatica e del tormento
senza speranza, nel mio dubitare
cieco, quando l'abisso dell'inerzia,
dell'abbandono m'era aperto ai piedi,
allor fioca scintilla io l'allevava
il mio sogno lontano, ancor ch'io fossi
d'ogni certa speranza privo al tutto;
ma da quello una vena mi fluiva
di forza che nel mezzo delle cose
vane e volgari, delle ottuse cure,
indifferente mi facea e sicuro,
e al dolor mi temprava e ogni timore
del mio stesso soffrir, ogni ricerca
di premi, di riposo, di conforto
ogni viltà dal cuore mi toglieva.
Dal più profondo della mia distretta,
nella mente più oscura quella fiamma
mi era sorta, caduta ogni speranza,
e la risposta al tanto faticare
di richieste alla vita per lei chiara
mi rifulgeva: « Non chieder più nulla,
sappi goder del tuo stesso dolore,
non adattarti per fuggir la morte;
anzi da te la vita nel deserto
fatti—che sia per gli altri nuova vita;
non disperare, ma rinuncia ai vani
aspetti della vita, e nel deserto
sarai tranquillo: dalla tua rinuncia
rifulgerà il tuo atto vittorioso,
ΑΡΓΙΑ sarà il tuo porto ΔΙ'ΕΝΕΡΓΕΙΑΣ ».

(*Poesie*, 92–93)

[In the days of suffering and in the nights
without rest, in the sad valley
of voiceless fatigue and of torment

without hope, in my doubting
blind, when the abyss of inertia,
of abandonment was open at my feet,
then as a feeble spark I nursed
my distant dream, although I
lacked any secure hope;
yet from it a vein of strength was flowing
that in the middle of vain and vulgar affairs
made me indifferent and confident,
and inured me to pain, taking away from my heart
any fear of my own suffering, every search
for prizes, rest, comfort,
every baseness.
From the deepest desperation,
in the darkest corner of my mind that flame
had arisen, once every hope had fallen,
and the answer to my long, fatiguing
requests from life for hope
was shining clear: "Ask no more for anything,
know how to enjoy your very suffering,
do not adapt yourself to escape death,
but by yourself create your life in the desert—
that be new life for others;
do not despair, renounce the vain
appearances of life, and in the desert
you will reach peace: from renunciation
your victorious act will shine,
ARGIA will be your port DI'ENERGEIAS."]

For the first time in his poetry Michelstaedter diagnosed accurately
the nature of his love. What gives him strength, what opens the road to
persuasione to him is not Senia, but his love for her; it is not the woman,
but his dream of her. He is "nursing" his dream although all hopes have
gone. From it, that is, from his personal creation, "the vein of strength" is
flowing. Once again it is the lack, the desire, the negative element, the
hanging weight, that gives him strength. The tension toward *persuasione*
derives from his desire for Senia and the impossibility of his possessing

her. It is in this moment of tension that he sees the light and learns in what direction to go. "In the desert you will reach peace: from renunciation, your victorious act will shine." Through your strength, your energy, your struggle, you will reach peace. "Argia di'energeias," the phrase that had fascinated Carlo once more because of the coincidence between signifier and signified, finds here its perfect place. He had written it in a letter to his friend Gaetano (*Ep., 419*); with it he had closed the chapter of his dissertation on *persuasione*. It was the image placed after that of the flame ("until he will turn himself into a flame and will consist in his last present") (*Persuasione, 89*).

The connection between the two images becomes clearer. In his draft of *La persuasione*, under the epigraph from Sophocles, Michelstaedter had sketched a Florentine lamp with smoke coming out of the small beaks as if the lamp were just about to extinguish itself. The same drawing was found on the edition of the *Indische Sprüche;* but here a sentence in Greek was inscribed to explain it. "The lamp extinguishes itself for lack of oil. I extinguished myself with overflowing abundance."

Here too in the poetical discourse, just as in the philosophical one, the flame has a central position. The distant dream of love, just a feeble spark (in line 42), becomes, after having been nurtured by Carlo, the flame of line 54 which finds strength precisely in the negative element, in the lack, in the dark corner of his mind, once all hopes have disappeared. With a life that has become flame begins the final stanza of the poem:

E sentii la mia vita fiammeggiare
ed il deserto farsi popoloso,
credetti fosse giunto il luminoso
mio giorno nella notte e consumare
quella fiamma mi parve la mia vita.
Ma per più lunga strada il mio destino
mi volse a far cammino: e vivo ancora
mi trovai nel fittizio riposo,
ma a te vicino per più forte andare;
in te concreta vidi la mia fiamma,
in te il mio sogno fatto era vicino
e la mia vita più certa: ogni ritorno,
ogni vile riposo, ogni timore

era morto per me.—Nel mare ondoso,
sulla brulla costiera solitaria,
sotto la forte quercia, a me vicina
io t'ho sentita siccome nel sogno.—
Non Argia ma Senia io t'ho chiamata,
per non sostar nel facile riposo,
e la lingua la fiamma consacrata
con le parole non contaminò.
Pur or mi trovo ancora nella nebbia
e il camminar m'è vano e la fatica
novellamente mi si fa penosa.
Io sento me da me fatto diverso,
se pur vicina ti sento lontana
ancora come un tempo, e la mia fiamma
geme che pur rifulse nella notte
per sua forza, sicura. Nelle tante
piccole e vane cose nuovamente
io mi dissolvo; nell'oscuro giro
della diuturna noia il nostro sogno
parmi tradito e per ignote voci
con parole di scherno messo a nudo,
pesato, misurato, confrontato . . .
Come se ignote mani il focolare
andassero scrutando ingordamente,
e alle ceneri insieme le faville
disperdessero al vento . . .

　　　　　　　　　(*Poesie*, 93–94)

[And I felt my life turning into flame
and the desert filled with life,
I believed my luminous day had arrived
in the night, and that burning flame
seemed to be my life.
But for a longer road my fate
turned me on my journey: and alive
I found myself in a fictitious rest,
yet I stayed near you to sail more strongly,

I saw my flame in you,
in you my made-up dream came close again
and my life more secure; every return,
every cowardly rest, every fear
was dead to me.—In the stormy sea,
on the barren and solitary coast
under the strong oak tree near me
I felt you just as in the dream.
Not Argia, but Senia I called you,
so that I would not stop in easy rest,
and my tongue did not contaminate
with words the consecrated flame.
Still I find myself in the fog
and walking is in vain and the fatigue
again becomes painful.
I feel myself a stranger to myself
I feel you distant even if near,
again like then, and my flame
that once shone in the night
secure in its strength, is now moaning.
Again in the many vain things
I waste myself; in the obscure circle
of daily boredom our dream
has been betrayed, and by unknown voices
stripped of its veils,
weighed, measured, compared. . . .
As if unknown hands were searching
inside the fire greedily,
and to the wind together with the ashes
the sparks were being scattered . . .]

The poem develops with a play of light, an effect of chiaroscuro. And darkness—the negative element—is the propelling force. From darkness, light is born. From absence a presence comes to life. From "renunciation" real possession ensues. The apex of the poem is reached with the identification of Argia with Senia. For the first time the narrative voice, which from the Itti of "I figli del mare" has become the "I" of the poet, openly assimilates the image of Senia to that of Argia, making explicit the desired and hoped-for identification concealed in "I figli del mare." In Carlo's dream Argia has become Senia, "the lady of the sea," the beloved companion in the journey to *persuasione*. But the light does not last; darkness soon takes its place and Senia/Argia is once again lost.

It is not a coincidence that Michelstaedter always uses the word "dream" to characterize his love relationship with Senia/Argia. It is never a reality, the positive rapport, that is. Reality is *rettorica,* it is "dissipating [oneself] in small and vain things," in the "boredom of daily life." Reality is the vulgarization of their love by others, its being "weighed, measured and compared." The sparks of that dream exist only in the imagination.

The intermittence of light and darkness in the poem likely mirrors the ups and downs of Carlo and Argia's relationship. The poem concludes in darkness, doubt, fear, nausea. But Carlo is here still putting himself on trial:

> L'angoscia di non giungere alla vita
> e di perire dell'oscura morte
> te trascinando nell'abisso, Senia,
> mi prende forte sì che dubitoso
> mi son fatto di me, che non sopporto
> le mie stesse parole, e di me stesso
> invincibile nausea m'opprime.
> (Poesie, 94)

> [The anguish of not reaching life
> and of perishing by dark death
> dragging you too, Senia, into the abyss,
> invades me with such violence that doubtful
> I have become of myself, who cannot bear
> my own words, and an unswerving
> nausea of myself oppresses me.]

The nature of human desire is exemplified in the hoped-for identification of Senia with Argia as it is in the metaphor of the weight. It is unsatisfiable. In the last two poems Michelstaedter attributes this impossibility no longer to himself, that is, to his own weakness, but to the

object of desire, as *La persuasione e la rettorica* had well explained. As
Campailla pointed out, Argia is not Virgil's Eurydice, who reproached
her lover for his incontinence, but she is closer to Rilke's "Eurydice
detached from the poet who wants to save her and indifferent to the hope
of coming back to life as she is to the necessity that precipitates her, this
time forever, into death."[57] Although Argia can be seen here as the real
individual who did not live up to the poet-lover's expectation, she must
even more be considered the symbol of desire, the absolute fulfillment of
which can never be achieved. In the last two poems of the *canzoniere* to
Senia, Michelstaedter is very explicit:

VI

Ti son vicino e tu mi sei lontana,
mi guardi e non mi vedi, o s'io ti parlo,
pur amando ascolti, non però m'intendi;
ti sono questo corpo e questi suoni,
ti sono un nome, ti son un dei tanti,
come un altro sarebbe
che per nome e per vista conoscessi.
Io non sono per te « io », la mia vita,
io, questa mia volontà più forte,
il mio sogno, il mio mondo, il mio destino.
Io non sono per te: questo mio amore
disperato e lontano e doloroso
—gli passi accanto e non lo senti amare.
Ma ancor fra gli altri uomini t'aggiri,
con questo parli ed a quello t'affidi,
fra lor vivi e per lor, s'anco a nessuno
dai la tua speme intera e la fiducia.
Ma fra l'oggi e il domani e questo e quello
ti dissolvi, e trapassi senza sole
la tua selvaggia e forte giovinezza,
e la tua speme consumando ignara
sei di te stessa—ed io mi struggo invano.
Mentre mi vince gelosia crudele
non pur di questo giovane e di quello

cui lo sguardo concedi o la parola,
ma d'ogni cosa che ti sia vicina,
ma del sole, dell'aria, ma del pane,
ché di loro ti nutri e a me sei tolta;
gelosia d'ogni giorno, d'ogni istante,
che vivi, che non vivi di me solo,
che l'aria e il pane e il sole, che ogni cosa,
che il mondo intero, che la vita stessa
vorrei esser per te—ma tu l'ignori.
(Poesie, 94–95)

[I am close to you and you are distant
you look at me yet you don't see me, or if I speak to you
you do listen by loving, but do not understand me;
to you I am this body and these sounds,
to you I am a name, one of the many,
as anyone else would be
whom you knew by name or sight.
To you I am not "I," my life,
I, this stronger will of mine,
my dream, my world, my destiny.
I am not for you: this love of mine
desperate and distant and painful
—you pass by it and you don't feel it loving.
Yet still among the others you wander,
with one you speak, in another you trust,
you live among them and for them, though
to no one you give entirely your hope and your trust.
But between today and tomorrow, between one and another
you waste yourself, and burn without sun
your wild and strong youth
and consuming your hope unaware
you are of yourself—and in vain I languish.
While a cruel jealousy overcomes me
not of this or that youth
to whom you give your glance or your word,
but of anything that is near you,

of the sun, of the air, of the bread,
for you feed on them and not on me,
jealous of every day, of every instant,
for you live, and not for me alone,
I who want to be for you the air, the
bread, the sun, everything,
the entire world, life itself—but this you ignore.]

The echo of Leopardi ("La sera del dì di festa" and "A Silvia") has become faint. Michelstaedter's jealousy is existential. His lament is caused by the impossibility of absolute possession. The poem could be read just as the lament of a disappointed lover; yet, the episode prompted Michelstaedter to a profound analysis of love in general, bringing him to the conclusion that perfect love, that is, absolute, unselfish love, does not exist. Maternal love is, perhaps, the only exception. Senia had not lived up to his expectations, but no woman could have. His words are clear. The creature he has in mind does not exist in reality. Indeed Argia is not Senia, just as no other woman could ever be. Two years earlier he had asked Iolanda for absolute love when he wrote: "He who wants to be bound to me must renounce everything, without ambitions, without glories, and devote himself to an intimate dream" (*Ep., 205*). Carlo was still asking for totality. From Argia too he had asked for the same totality. Real love, to him, is to find in the other all that is necessary. Argia must find everything she needs in Carlo; she must not feel other needs. To her Carlo must be air, bread, sun, the whole world, life itself.

The identification between his beloved and Senia does not correspond to any reality. He should have learned from his model, Leopardi, who had sung of this impossibility in "Aspasia" and theorized about it in the dialogue between Tasso and his familiar spirit. Leopardi had sanctioned the superiority of the creature of imagination and had learned to treasure and love it, as Michelstaedter had not. Leopardi knew that the poet's word cannot become flesh. In this lies its power. Yet Michelstaedter up to the end strove for the word to become flesh, for himself to become Christ.

Not even Argia had been able to see Carlo beyond his contingency. He had shouted it out with all his strength in "Risveglio": "No, I am not this body, these limbs, prostrated here on the grassy land . . . I am alone, distant, I am different—other sun, other wind and prouder / flight through other skies is my life" (*Poesie,* 69). Yet not even Argia was able to see the real Carlo and he remained to her "this body . . . these sounds . . . a name."

The last poem to Senia must be read together with the page of *La persuasione* that directly follows the two metaphors of *persuasione,* the mountain and the sea. The poem opens up with a rhetorical question. The battle is lost from the start:

VII

Parlarti? e pria che tolta per la vita
mi sii, del tutto prenderti?—che giova?
che giova, se del tutto io t'ho perduta
quando mia tu non fosti il giorno stesso
che c'incontrammo? Che se pur t'avessi
ora, vincendo, mia per il futuro,
mia per diritto, mia per tuo volere,
mia non saresti più che non sei ora,
mia non saresti più che s'altra mano
ti possedesse. Che pur del mio corpo
sarei geloso come or son d'altrui.
Non più sarei per te la vita intera
ch'ora non sono, se già in me non l'ami:
ma se in me non l'ami, se tua vita
crear non so della mia vita stessa,
che più giova sperar, che più volere,
che mi giova la vita e il mio dolore
e questo amor lontano e disperato?
Fatto sono da me stesso diverso
che contra il fato mi dicevo forte,
poiché ho esperta e ancor vivo ad ogni istante
nella tua indifferenza la mia morte.
Né più mi giova mendicare i giorni
né chieder altro più dal dio nemico,
se non che faccia mia morte finita.

(Poesie, 95–96)

[To speak to you and before you are taken away from me
for life, to take you completely? What's the use?
What's the use, if I lost you completely
when you were not mine the same day
we met? For even if I had you
now, winning, mine for the future,
mine by right, mine by your will,
you would not be mine any more than you are now,
you would not be mine any more than if another hand
possessed you. For even of my body
I would be jealous just as I am now of others.
I would not be for you your entire life any more
than I am not now, if already you do not love that life in me:
but if in me you do not love it, if your life
I cannot create out of my own,
what's the use of hope, why still wanting,
what's the use of my life and of my suffering
and of this distant desperate love?
I have become different from myself
I who had thought of myself as strong against fate,
for still alive I have experienced at any instant
my death in your indifference.
Neither to beg for days helps any more
nor to ask the hostile god for anything else
but that he might put an end to my death.]

In this poem the quest for total possession of the beloved is spelled out together with its necessary failure. Physical possession will not achieve it, as Rilke had also said. The other's innermost being still escapes. The complete fusion of the two lovers is impossible. Thus not even love is the means to *persuasione.*

In *La persuasione e la rettorica,* after describing the vain attempt to possess the sea by him who dives into it, yet remains "alone and different in the middle of the water," Michelstaedter makes an apparently abrupt shift from the image of the sea to love:

Neither if man seeks refuge by his beloved—will he be able to satisfy his hunger: neither kisses nor embraces, nor as many other manifestations as love can invent will ever fuse them together: but they will always remain two, and each one alone and different before the other one. (*Persuasione*, 41)

That fusion that sky and sea had so well and so many times achieved is forbidden to men. *Persuasione* is self-possession, not possession of the other, and man must be alone in order to reach it. In the depths of depression Michelstaedter can only ask for an end to his life, which is nothing but real death.

Chiavacci, in his edition of Michelstaedter's *Opere,* considered "All'Isonzo" ("To the Isonzo River") his last poem. The date Michelstaedter wrote at the bottom of the page is September 22. V. E. Alfieri, on the other hand, considers it to have been written prior to the last two poems to Senia, or at least to the last one.[58] It represents a positive moment in the story of Carlo's love. The sight of Argia is still sufficient to stimulate his courage, to incite him to continue his struggle toward the free sea. The poem "Parlarti?" would then conclude Michelstaedter's poetical production with an appeal to death, thus giving the reader a logical sequence that has its end in his suicide. If, in fact, this is the true order in which the poems were composed, then the crisis with Argia could serve to explain his final act. Yet there is no way to know for certain whether this was the actual sequence of the poems. And what if it were? Would this give us any more right to speculate about the reasons for Michelstaedter's suicide?

Light and darkness constantly alternate in Michelstaedter's writing as they probably did in his psyche. It is our need for answers, explanations, meaningful gestures; our dependence on beginning, middle and end that makes us impose an order upon a series of actions or expressions. It is the "sense of an ending," however tragic, that we must find for our own peace of mind, that makes us interpret and forces us to create systems in which to place all our experiences. We are still caught in the impasse Michelstaedter had denounced and wanted to overcome.[59]

Wherever we decide to place "All'Isonzo," the poem represents all the natural elements, that is, the positive symbology of Michelstaedter's poetical world. The mountain, the wind, the storm, the water as river and as sea, the free sea, symbol of *persuasione* that is reached here by the Isonzo river, they are all present. They also lend themselves to a psychoanalytical interpretation. The wind appears as a fertilizing force capable of impregnating with life the waves of the sea to which the river will go back as its place of origin. The poet is here identifying with his beloved Isonzo river that he had challenged so often, even when the wind, clouds and fog were threatening a storm. The river, impersonated by Carlo, is actually the connecting link between the two metaphors of *persuasione,* the mountain and the sea. Born up on a mountain, the river ends its course in the sea. There it does not die, but "fuses" its water with that of the sea.

> Dalle nevose gole, dai torbidi
> monti lontani con lena rapida,
> con aspro sibilo soffia la raffica,
> rompe la densa greve nebbia,
> stringe le basse grigie nubi
> e le respinge in onde gravide.
>
> Passa radendo sui pioppi tremoli
> —sul nero piano incombe il peso
> della ciclopica lotta dell'etere.
> Ma a lei più forte risponde l'impeto
> selvaggio e giovine del fiume rapido
> cui le corrose ripe trattengono:
> il suo possente muggito al sibilo
> della procella commesce e il vivido
> chiaror del lontano sereno
> riflette livido, nell'onda torbida.
>
> E al mar l'annuncio porta della lotta
> che nebbia e vento nel ciel combattono,
> al mar l'annuncio porta del tumulto
> che in cor m'infuria quando la nausea,
> quando il torpore, il dubbio, l'abbandono
> per la tua vista, Argia, più fervido
> l'ardir combatte e sogna il mare libero.
>
>   (*Poesie,* 97)

[From the snowy gorges, from the cloudy
distant mountains with speedy energy,

with a hard hissing the gust blows,
breaks the thick heavy fog,
squeezes the low grey clouds
and pushes them back in pregnant waves.

It passes skimming over the aspens
—on the black plane the weight of
the cyclopic struggles of the wind hangs.
But to the hissing the young wild impetus
of the fast river answers, held back by eroded banks:
and mingles its powerful murmuring to the hissing
of the storm and reflects livid
the vivid glimmer of the distant
fair sky in the turbid wave.

And it brings to the sea the news of the struggle
that fog and wind are fighting in the sky,
and to the sea it brings the news of the tumult
that rages in my heart, when my daring
made stronger by your sight, Argia,
fights against nausea, torpor, doubt,
abandonment and dreams of the free sea.]

Through poetry Michelstaedter continued the philosophical inquiries of his prose writings, hoping to avoid the traps of *rettorica* he knew so well. Yet the very use of language would make his task futile. If the nature of a scholarly dissertation would bind him to a rhetorical end, he hoped he could avoid that pitfall through the essential language of poetry. His compositions are attempts, obviously revealing a gifted but still inexperienced poetical voice, to convey a metaphysical message—a message of defeat.

Silvio Ramat recognized the peculiar position of Michelstaedter in the tradition of Italian poetry. Developing the long-abandoned line of Petrarch and Leopardi, Michelstaedter connected it with the inspiration that he derived from the philosophy of the North. Ramat calls his poetry "a diary toward the absolute" and sees in Michelstaedter's existential rigor the seed of Italian twentieth-century poetry.[60]

Michelstaedter advocated the dissolution of language, because it was no longer capable of communicating, and pointed to music as the only authentic expressive form. What he had theorized through his philosophical as well as through his poetical writings—for he does theorize even when writing poetry—was being realized by poets like Campana, and musicians like Debussy. If he could not do it himself with his own poetical tools, his philosophical ideas pointed the way for the poets to come.

Carlo had written to Paula that he wished he could express himself through music. Beethoven's Ninth Symphony, he repeated many times, was greater than any philosophical discourse. Music could succeed where words failed. Debussy wrote, "music begins where the word has no longer any power: music is written for that which is unexpressible."[61] If Michelstaedter had not yet acquired the expressive tools for the task, he did nevertheless sense that poetry must give voice to the essence of things, totally stripped of any rhetorical embellishment.

In his original study of Debussy and Montale, speaking of thematic similarity between the two artists, Biasin chooses the sea as an example. The sea is a recurrent image in both the musician's and the poet's works and it is generally a stormy sea. What Biasin says about the sea of Debussy and Montale can well be said for Michelstaedter's: "Often accompanied by the wind, sonorous element that completed its function, the sea is present . . . as a source of inspiration, as the interlocutor, as a descriptive narrative pretext."[62] But in Michelstaedter the sea is something more. It is, as Wagner had said, the best analogy for music. In it man dives to reach inaccessible depths, to approximate the infinite. We cannot but think of Itti's daring dives recounted in his first poem to Senia. Yet Michelstaedter was not able to reach his infinite through poetry, and he was no musician.[63] So he turned to drawing. Finally, by this means, Michelstaedter felt he could arrive at the essence of life.

It was Cerruti who first pointed out the Expressionistic qualities of Michelstaedter's poetry, linking his name with those of Expressionistic painters like Nolde and Kirchner.[64] That was the direction, in fact, in which he was moving. Symbolic images like "mystery," "*Angst*," "fury," "sinister screens," "dark abysses," "turbid lights," "fog," "devouring," "famish," as Folco Portinari acutely observed, are only some of the chromatic tones characteristic of the Expressionistic painters. To Portinari, in fact, Michelstaedter's "poetic Expressionistic solutions that anticipate Campana and Rebora" are even more relevant than his philosophical ideas.[65] But it was not through poetry that his Expressionism was, finally, best realized. His drawings, as we will see, are even closer to the likes of Heckel, Kirchner and Kokoschka than are the symbolic images of his poems.

Chapter 3

THE AUTHENTICITY OF DRAWING

Oh writer, with what letters will you
transcribe with such perfection the entire
configuration that was in the drawing?
—Leonardo[1]

Humor rips the sky apart to reveal the
enormous sea of emptiness; humor is an
expression of the discrepancy between
man and the world . . . is the king of
nonexistence.—Gómez de la Serna[2]

The search for *persuasione* through language failed; linguistic signs are
bound to create *rettorica*. Michelstaedter turned to a new medium: the
graphic sign. He had been drawing since he was in school, showing a re-
markable talent at an early age. Drawing, better than any other medium
of expression, satisfied his need for essentiality; with a sketch he could,
in fact, try to grasp the essence of a subject. After having visited the
Academy in Venice he wrote home, "What interested me above all was
the collection of sketches. Because it seems to me that in the sketch the
soul of the painter can become visible better than in painting" (*Ep.*, 16).
Furthermore, in its economy, in the use of a simple pencil or chalk, the
sketch is an antirhetorical statement. The subject is naked, stripped of
the rhetorical apparatus so common in paintings.

At the time, Michelstaedter was making his own revolutionary contribution to the world of the arts. In those years the group Die Brücke,

192

which formulated the first Expressionist manifesto, was finding a new voice. Michelstaedter's *Procession of Shadows* was sketched between 1903 and 1905, and Die Brücke was founded in 1905. "Love for the essential," as Campailla pointed out, "the naive and the primitive, . . . the rediscovery of the graphic sign are all Expressionistic dimensions, in a radically German cultural *lignée* that goes back to the Gothic artists, like Grünwald and Dürer."[3]

Beside scholastic drawings of high quality, young Carlo had also started to draw caricatures. This is a genre whose historical antecedents must also be sought in the North with artists like Bosch, Brueghel, and, once again, Dürer. The tradition, as Campailla noted, is generally foreign to Italian art with the major exceptions of Leonardo's grotesque figures and Bernini's caricatures.

Carlo was only five years old in 1892 when Edvard Munch scandalized Berlin with an exhibition of his work. The show was closed by public demand, and the event created an uproar among artists protesting the closing and advocating artistic freedom. Like Ibsen, Munch was Norwegian; in Scandinavian art, evil, instinct, and the unconscious had a central role. At the turn of the century the Belgian James Ensor attempted to represent the alienation between man and the world and was questioning "the credibility of the visible."[4] There is little indication in Michelstaedter's *Epistolario* that he was acquainted with either of these artists, or for that matter with the great revolutionary painter who also opened the road to Expressionism, Vincent van Gogh. To speak, then, of a pre-Expressionist Michelstaedter is to point out a sensibility common to artists and intellectuals of the time. The compulsive letter-writer does not mention any of the northern artists or those of *Mitteleuropa,* but neither does he mention contemporary Italian artists. In his letters home only those belonging to the classical Italian tradition are deemed worthy of comment. In Venice he visited the *Esposizione* (*Biennale* of 1905) and wrote home that "the modern painters seem to lack fantasy and paint portraits only" and those not very well (*Ep., 20*).

Paul Vogt defined Expressionism as the art form that tried to voice the basic contradiction of existence, the dichotomy between reason and instinct. He claimed such an art could only come from the North, from a tradition as ancient as that of Gothic art. The Mediterranean artist, by contrast, sought perfection and order through his art and considered form capable of creating harmony even between contrasting elements. The Nordic artist, instead, "opposed the principle of the ratio with [the] principle . . . [of] artistic creation as reflecting the tension of human existence."[5] For Ladislao Mittner, Expressionism was not only an artistic style but a life-style. To him it is one of the hardest "isms" to define precisely because it was characterized by contrast, variety, opposition to rules and models.[6] These loose characteristics are precisely the ones that would have made Expressionism agreeable to Michelstaedter, who refused all "isms" and labels.

Michelstaedter, however, knew nothing about Expressionism, the cultural movement, which was born in the last years of his life. Its literary voice, the journals *Der Sturm* and *Die Aktion,* began publication respectively in 1910 and 1911 and the artistic groups Die Brücke and Die Blaue Reiter were founded respectively in Dresden and in Munich in 1905 and 1911. Yet he shared with the Expressionists the craving for essential expression, for antirhetorical statement, the interest in man's psyche, and the fascination with primitive art.

When Michelstaedter left Gorizia in October 1905 it was not to travel to Vienna where he was enrolled to study mathematics, but to Florence. With his family's permission he undertook a cultural voyage south to see drawings, paintings, buildings, monuments. He already considered himself an artist. In his first letters home, during a stopover in Venice (October 23, 1905) he wrote: "I found that those primitive painters (of the fourteenth and fifteenth centuries, for example Lorenzo Veneziano, Vivarini, and Quirizio da Murano) lack technique, but have more expression than the later ones" (*Ep.,* 15). He had also admired the *Assumption* by Titian, but observed after seeing those early works that "the *Assumption* did not impress me as before. The painting remains a masterpiece, but the figures seem to lack that indefinable expression that moves and 'conquers'" (15). The same characteristics he found in Giotto, another primitive artist whom he greatly admired (22). He insists on the "marvelous technique" of the great masters like Tintoretto and Veronese, but finds them all lacking "the true ideal expression that elevates a painting to the level of a work of art" (13). Tintoretto, in his view, prints beautiful "color photographs" (16).

What Michelstaedter admired most about the great artists Raphael, Michelangelo, and Leonardo were their drawings; Leonardo's were of course the greatest, because they revealed "the restlessness of his mind, his continual searching and the constant tension toward an unreachable ideal" (*Ep.*, 16). Carlo, before such examples, is compelled to copy a sketch by Leonardo. What he is insistently searching for in all works of art is the expression of an inner reality; he is constantly looking for authenticity, for *persuasione*. From Florence he writes to Paula and describes to her all he had done and seen in his first days in the city. He feels compelled to note his disappointment with Botticelli whose "man-nered" (*manierata*) style takes away strength from the idea. Even of Raphael, Titian, Dürer, Van Dyck, and Rubens, he writes, "if you with an effort strip away the surface of the painting [the perfect reproduction of nature] and try to dig deep down in it to find the idea, *the expression,* that which, after all, gives meaning to the work of art, you will find it only in rare cases" (*Ep.*, 36). The constant exception of course is again Leonardo and the primitives like Lorenzo Monaco, Filippino Lippi, and Memmi.

Besides visiting museums, Michelstaedter drew constantly. In line with his Expressionist taste he preferred pencil, pen, or chalk to brushes for the production of his favorite genres: the sketch and the caricature, which in the words of Campailla "give back the results of an inner vision and not the exterior facade of things."[7] Michelstaedter indeed felt that only with drawing, that is, with brief, scarce strokes of the pencil, could he hope to grasp the secret of a personality; only thus could he avoid the risk of *rettorica* to which writing so easily succumbed.

If we keep in mind that this philosopher and poet, as he is best known today, considered himself above all a painter, and went to Florence to learn this art, his artistic production immediately acquires an existential meaning. Was Michelstaedter's pictorial language more advanced than his prose and poetry? Campailla believes that it was and finds a reason for this in his being "un uomo di frontiera" who learned written Italian as a second language—a similar condition as Italo Svevo's. Michelstaed-ter's conviction of the inadequacy of language, however, cannot be ex-clusively explained with his own feeling of inadequacy, as Campailla suggests, since he had learned Italian as a second language. Such a rea-son in fact is not sufficient, just as the ignorance of Latin was not enough to explain Leonardo's own struggle against language. His famous rhetori-cal question, quoted even by Calvino ("O scrittore con quali lettere scri-

verai tu con tal perfezione la intera figurazione qual fa qui il disegno?"—
"Oh writer, with what letters will you transcribe with such perfection the
entire configuration that was in the drawing?") is not addressed simply to
Leonardo the writer, but to all writers. It is a dispute over two forms of
expression, and to Leonardo as to Michelstaedter the graphic sign was
far superior to the word.[8]

Although Michelstaedter studied classical languages, philosophy, and
history during the first year in Florence, while preparing for his courses
at the University of Vienna, he never stopped drawing and painting. He
drew everywhere, at cafés, in the classroom, on any piece of paper, even
directly on coffee tables; at any moment he might feel the need to fix an
expression, a movement of the soul that otherwise would extinguish
itself with the same rapidity with which it had been born. It was his
constant search for *persuasione,* his antirhetorical fervor, that can explain this urge to draw, his obsessive need for truth beyond the appearances that were so much a part of his person. His ethical interest brought
him to portraiture, and that too was to be realized through sketching.
A portrait is much more effective if done without the subject's knowing.
He is caught in that brief moment when his essence comes to light
in a fleeting expression. It was this that Michelstaedter tried to fix on
paper.

His letters to his family are decorated with sketches. He started as
soon as he left home, on the train where he drew "the magnificent young
lady with glasses" and the "nice family" of father, mother, and two little
ones (*Ep.,* 10, 11). Even after having started to attend classes at the
Istituto Superiore, he continued his artistic practice. "I always draw," he
writes home on November 9, 1905, "according to my habit, and I have
already drawn all the types at home and those in the two little restau-
rants. . . . Yesterday evening at the *trattoria* I copy an old priest, . . . the
drawing afterwards went around the room and conquered all hearts.
They thought I was a professional painter, or at least a student, and asked
me where I studied" (60). His pride verging on vanity is justifiable as his
surviving sketches testify.

His talent, surprisingly, was untutored. He never took regular classes
in either drawing or painting. In the same letter he also mentioned having
met a young man who studied at the Scuola libera del nudo, to which he
introduced Carlo. In the letter he expressed his intention of going to the

school on a regular basis to copy statues in order to learn to draw the human body. He had had no experience with the entire figure, and hoped eventually to take the entrance exam and enroll in the school; he never took the exam, however, and was never admitted. Was it fear of failing? Or (more likely) lack of time? We do not know for sure but we do know, however, that his pride was involved. He rejected the idea of taking the exam at an early date, and concluded: "I will take the exam in February with a greater chance of succeeding. Do not talk to anyone about this, though, because were I to fail the exam I would be upset if others knew about it" (*Ep.*, 61).

Very diligently he began to go to the Academy to copy statues whenever he had free time from his regular classes. And even when in class, he always managed to draw a portrait or caricature of the professor who happened to be lecturing. The following year, although his studies demanded more time, he continued to go there or to a gallery every day (*Ep.*, 86). Drawing was, in fact, as much a part of his daily life as reading, studying, or walking. In a letter to his mother, after telling her all about his term papers and all the texts he was reading he adds: "And now I draw and paint like crazy and I feel great" (151).

In March 1907 the students of the Institute published a single issue of a satirical journal called *Gaudeamus igitur,* to which Carlo contributed most of the caricatures of professors and students. The journal, of which there is a single surviving copy (in the Fondo Michelstaedter in Gorizia), is a jewel of satire. There are many brief pieces written in a rhetorical, pompous style with Latin inflections and syntax that accompany caricatures of members of the Institute, a beautiful long poem called "The Young Ladies" that is an imitation, in the same meter, rhythm, and with many of the same verses of Foscolo's "Sepolcri." The Young Ladies, rather than the tombs of great men, are here the source of poetical inspiration. It is a clever piece that shows a perfect knowledge of the classical masterpiece, and a good poetical ear; it reveals the understandable boredom that such a long, archeological poem, albeit with its undeniable virtues, must have provoked in the class. The issue ends with an amusing interview with the librarian of the Institute to whom the students are very grateful. Not only had he obtained for them a beautiful, comfortable reading room, he had made it accessible to both ladies and gentlemen. The poor man, put on the spot by such candid remarks, could not but show his fear and embarrassment as he considered what might happen in the room with the advent of spring.

Most of the pages are filled with caricatures, each with a satirical caption. Though they are without signatures, Michelstaedter's hand as we have seen it in many drawings of his *Taccuini* (*Notebooks*) is clearly recognizable. In fact, they repeat in several cases drawings that appeared first in his notebooks. He might well have been the author of all of them. The professor, as the embodiment of *rettorica,* is a recurrent theme in Carlo's drawings, so much so that Campailla will give the name *Retoriché* (written in Greek) to one of his most effective.

Michelstaedter's large production of caricatures has been unjustly ignored by most of the critics; they thought it inconsistent with the seriousness of his dissertation and final gesture. This was, clearly, a superficial judgment. Michelstaedter was equally serious as philosopher and caricaturist. With grotesque deformation, he was launching his challenge against the logic and the harmonious order of the world. Humorous in a Pirandellian way, his caricatures rendered concrete the "feeling of the contrary" that forces the artist to represent a naked reality, stripped of the rhetoric of appearances. Philosophically the choice of the caricature marked the phase of negativity, of the destruction of beautiful appearances. A revolutionary moment, a cry of protest, but also a cry of *Angst,* like the famous one by Munch.

MICHELSTAEDTER AND PIRANDELLO

Many scholars have commented on the Expressionist qualities of Pirandello's work. Graziella Corsinovi's *Pirandello e l'Espressionismo* deals with this at length. In it Corsinovi shows how the Expressionist narrative was the necessary consequence of a belief in "the mendacity of words, the inadequacy of language to express that unknowable truth that constantly escaped any definition." That truth, she continued, can be only "suggested and evoked"; for this purpose, "it must rely on different expressive means, in particular figurative ones."[9] Corsinovi was here talking of Pirandello's narrative, so close in its way to Expressionist painting. She could just as well have been commenting on Michelstaedter's ideas about language and on his preference for drawing.

Together with their strong polemic against rhetoric, against fixed rules, Expressionist artists carried out an equally strong attack on compartmentalization of knowledge and art. They all tried different artistic media. Many distinguished themselves almost equally well in various art forms. Schönberg was both an exceptional musician and a playwright; the Austrian Kokoschka, a painter and playwright; Kandinsky and Klee, painters and poets. Pirandello and Michelstaedter were both writers and painters, with, moreover, a profound love for music and its great expressive capabilities. They resorted to these activities, however, with different purposes and, naturally, with different results.

In order to relax the tension of his excited mind, Michelstaedter took long climbs on the San Valentin or swims in the Isonzo River, whereas Pirandello painted. Yet they had in common the background: nature. Michelstaedter rarely painted nature; he left very few landscapes. It is interesting, however, that of the few landscapes he did produce, one, *Marina,* is in line with the style of *Macchiaioli* and similar to the *Marina di Porto Empedocle* painted by Pirandello. Michelstaedter's unpublished piece is a watercolor. Although the style of both is similar, the effect is not. Pirandello painted six boats, four with people aboard, probably fishermen as they are preparing for a fishing trip. The two figures in the foreground wear rolled-up trousers, and one is holding a fish basket. The scene is obviously naturalistic. Michelstaedter's is not; there is only one boat with one man in an inclined position just as is the mast. Even here two figures are in the foreground, but they are women wearing long dresses. The scene is surrealistic. One could almost think of Charon having left off two passengers at the shore of the river Styx after their final journey.[10]

Painting and drawing were for Michelstaedter a search for the expression of his authentic voice. Man's innermost nature, his essence, was the object of his search. For Pirandello, painting was merely a hobby. As Michelstaedter resorted to mountain climbing to find the stability, order, and peace that only nature could give him, so Pirandello found this refuge in the exercise of his graphic skills. It was a release from the tormented search into the depths of the human soul that was his, as it was Michelstaedter's, compulsive labor. The results of Pirandello's brushwork are strangely bland and conventional landscapes for the most part, but the long list of grotesque characters in his stories, novels, and plays are the equivalent in words of an Expressionist drawing or a caricature. Although his creativity, in contrast to Michelstaedter's, could only find an outlet in words, the impulse to draw was present and it influenced his art profoundly.

Antonio Alessio rightly pointed out the pictorial quality of Pirandello's narrative, underlining the fact that it is filled with lively portraits and that one of Pirandello's basic characteristics was that of writing through images.[11] Most of Pirandello's characters are grotesque. They are individuals whose essence, or inner being, has been shattered, who are one, one hundred, one hundred thousand, whose fragmentation is represented exteriorly, through the deformation of features. Confronting the crisis of the world and of the self, Pirandello turns to writing; Michelstaedter to drawing. Pirandello sketches his characters with his narrative style; Michelstaedter with his stylus.

At the origin of Michelstaedter's characters is the same "sentimento del contrario" essence of humor, explicated by Pirandello in his famous essay written in 1908. In his analysis of humor Pirandello had at his disposal some psychological tools that Michelstaedter lacked.[12] Yet many of the latter's caricatures embody the very spirit of Pirandello's humor. Had he read Pirandello's essay? We have no way of knowing. It is, therefore, all the more interesting to be able to establish a parallel between the theory and Michelstaedter's graphic art—even more exciting, to try to connect some of Pirandello's characters with Michelstaedter's caricatures.

In his essay on caricature entitled "The Rationale of Deformation," Rudolf Arnheim, following a common trend, degrades caricature in the artistic hierarchy. "Its 'weakness,' he claims, "is inevitable because caricature is always 'illustrations.'"[13] Commenting on the similarity between caricature and Expressionist art, Arnheim points out that their profound difference lies in their different statements. Caricature "character[izes] particular individuals or species"; its result is comic, whereas Expressionist art deals "with the nature of perceived existence as a whole," and often creates a tragic effect.[14] What concerns us, however, is the end of his essay, where, examining the work of Honoré Daumier, master of caricature, he sees a shift in tone and overall effect. His caricatures, in fact, are not all comic; many, on the contrary, create a moving impression like some of the *types parisiens*. In a particularly striking one the ridiculous features of the woman's and man's faces are undermined by the tenderness and emotions they express while admiring the moon. Here in fact the basic definition of caricature as a portrait where "the prominent features of an individual are stressed by exaggeration for the purpose of immediate recognition and spontaneous amusement" is clearly inadequate. After realizing, therefore, that in Daumier "the deformation of the human norm acquires a deeper meaning" Arnheim asks: "But is this really caricature?"[15] The "depth of meaning" of so many of Daumier's works elevates them to the level of true art.

Daumier here seems to be creating the "sentimento del contrario" that Pirandello describes in detail in his essay "On Humor" and that so many of his characters represent so well. Daumier's noses raised in contemplation of the moon bring immediately to mind the pure and naive gaze of Ciaula upon his discovery of the moon.[16] At the core of humor there is the essential contrast or opposition between exterior and interior, between what appears outside to the eyes of the beholder and what instead is hidden deep down in the soul. Pirandello makes a specific distinction between "l'avvertimento del contrario," which produces a comic effect, and "il sentimento del contrario," which produces humor. When Marmeladoff in *Crime and Punishment,* after narrating the details of his miserable life, is ridiculed in the tavern and shouts out that what he is saying is not laughable for he feels everything he is saying, he is a humorous character. Those around him, instead, who laugh at his story, stop themselves at the surface of his words; thus to them the effect is comic.[17]

Pirandello devoted some affectionate and enlightening pages to Don Quixote, for him the humorous character par excellence. Can it be pure coincidence that Don Quixote and his inseparable Sancho Panza are one of Honoré Daumier's favorite subjects? Among his representations of the famous pair is an inspired sketch of Don Quixote on horseback and Sancho Panza on his donkey seen from behind as they are starting on their journey of fantasies and dreams. In one of his two paintings, dated 1864, the two knights are resting under a tree. While Sancho is fast asleep Don Quixote rests with his head leaning back against the tree, lost in dreams and adventures. In the background, Sancho's donkey is spread out on the ground asleep, while the white stallion of Don Quixote stands as a light in the night, in unison with the adventurous spirit of his master.[18] Cervantes had created the perfect humorous character whose deeds and adventures are undoubtedly ridiculous but whose soul is truly tragic. Daumier and Pirandello, as did Miguel de Unamuno, used him as a role-model, and left their own indelible marks on him.

The close relationship between caricaturists and Expressionist artists was recognized by the latter, who hailed Daumier as their spiritual ancestor, "for in and with Daumier the tradition of physiognomic experiment began to be emancipated from that of humor." These words of Ernst Gombrich sum up the development, but need to be qualified. The humor he is talking about is closer to the comic than to Pirandello's notion. "Without this breaking down of Daumier's barriers between caricature and great art," continues Gombrich, "a master such as Munch could never have evolved his intensely tragic, distorted physiognomies, nor could the Belgian Ensor in the same period have created his idiom of terrifying masks which so excited German Expressionists."[19]

Sketches were to become popular among Expressionist artists, precisely because of their antirhetorical nature. Life is often ugly, dull and painful; the beautiful exterior facade, a pitiful illusion. Their sketches were an undisguised polemic against a tradition of idealization; their goal, to express the essence of life, that which lies behind the harmonious, pleasant varnish of the surface. "The importance is to strip the eye and the hand, . . . to undermine the presumptions of rhetoric in order to find again the rhythm of intensity. . . . Not the true, not the apparent, but the authentic!"[20] So speaks Flaminio Gualdoni of the four founders of Die Brücke and his words could be applied to Michelstaedter's art, too. His most revealing works are, in fact, sketches. Sketch thus accomplishes a twofold purpose. On the formal level, it opposes all ornate and rhetorical styles, with the simplicity of its structure and technical means, chalk, pencil, charcoal or pen—the same simplicity used by Pirandello in his spare prose to counter D'Annunzio's flowery and sonorous style. On its philosophical level, the sketch, because of the rapidity with which it can be done, could better than any other technique grasp the essential elements of a subject. With the few strokes at his disposal the artist had to eliminate the inessential and concentrate on the unique elements of his subject.

The pursuit of a beautiful style, the preoccupation with form, was seen as a "hindrance of the full expression of 'inner reality.'" With such a statement Franz Marc was carrying out the same antirhetorical discourse as was Carlo Michelstaedter.[21] If it is true that "the Expressionists sought . . . a negation of the concept of style and a diminution of its importance on the grounds of its 'insincerity' and its 'dishonesty,'" then Michelstaedter may be considered an Expressionist too. In 1975 Campailla published a very limited edition of *Opera grafica* with Campestrini Press in Gorizia. This attractive book, with many of Michelstaedter's art works, quickly sold out and unfortunately was not reprinted. Those without access to this book can find a dozen or so of his works reproduced in the earlier biography or they can consult the originals of Michelstaedter's graphic art in Gorizia's public library.

In his essay "Tra pittura e narrativa nella novella pirandelliana," Alessio "suggests the possibility of a true relation between figurative art and [Pirandello's] narrative."[22] Pirandello's expertise at painting is well known. Besides being a painter, he was also an art critic and wrote many articles and reviews of exhibits. It is understandable, then, how Pirandello's approach to narration, as Alessio argues, could be similar to that of an artist to painting. The scholar points out this characteristic by examining descriptions of characters as well as of scenery in many of Pirandello's short stories. It is no coincidence that Pirandello, who painted so many landscapes, left nature out of his narrative, as Michelstaedter left it out of his paintings. "Nature is dull (stupid)," Pirandello once said to Rosso di San Secondo.[23] This is why he painted landscapes, he continued, and this is also why he found little interest in nature when searching for the meaning of life—in his writings.

Far from a general supposed insensibility to the problem of style, there is in Pirandello an anguished attempt to "reabsorb" style in the "immediacy of expression" as the critic De Castris, quoted by Alessio, has put it.[24] Pirandello's antirhetorical credo was well expressed in his famous speech in honor of Giovanni Verga. There he argues for a "style of things" against D'Annunzio's "style of words." His open attack on *rettorica* finds in the Expressionist technique its proper narrative means. And *rettorica* for Michelstaedter was not only a category dealing with style and the organization of discourse, but a label including all systematic knowledge, science, philosophy, that presumed to provide the definitive answers to a quest for meaning. We find the same polemic in Pirandello, whose many characters are real personifications of such *rettorica*. There are numerous drawings—some could be called caricatures, though "grotesques" is probably a better qualifier for them—that are not necessarily portraits or precise caricatures of specific people, but which become personifications of *rettorica*. They translate on a graphic level the creations of Pirandello's prose. The character that personifies *rettorica* in both has certain basic characteristics. For example, he has a large head, often bald, clearly disproportionate in relation to a body that is always short, often stout, to which the head is immediately attached without the need for a neck. He often has a moustache, but above all his eyes are puffed up with lids so swollen that they can rarely have been opened.

The individual who has overworked his brain to the point of needing a larger head to contain it, whose body, therefore, suffers at the expense of the head, and is often crooked, atrophied (like the splendid caricature of Avvocato D'Andrea in *La patente*), cannot see real life around him any longer. He has lost all contact with it. His eyes closed, he becomes incapable of knowing anything. Thus all his knowledge transforms itself into its opposite: total ignorance and an inability to live.

Michelstaedter left a series of characters who symbolize *rettorica*. From the figure sitting at his desk with a moustache to whom Campailla gave the name *Retoriché* to the masterpiece *Homo Sapiens,* they share many traits with Pirandello's characters.[25] The sketch *Retoriché* (similar to one in the above-mentioned *Gaudeamus igitur*) represents a professor behind his desk who reads from his notes and who, benumbed by his own *rettorica,* is about to fall asleep (Fig. 1). The eyes, in fact, are totally closed. If we think that Michelstaedter, continuing an ancient tradition, gave enormous importance to the eyes of the persuaded, which he always represents as enormous, profound, wide-opened in an ethereal expression, the symbolism of the spiritual limitations of the rhetorician is obvious. The torpor of *rettorica* is a spiritual death. The hands that hold the paper are skeletal; they are the hands of a corpse, almost as if signifying the cause-effect rapport between *rettorica* and death. The head, almost bald, is out of proportion with the body, which can be detected under the black jacket as a skeleton. The moustache completely covers up the mouth in order to make any possible sound confused and senseless.

Similar eyes belong also to *Homo Sapiens* (Fig. 2); they are equally puffed up and closed. The silhouette is small and squat, the enormous, bald head is directly attached to the body without the support of a neck. Another enormous, very Austrian moustache frames a thick nose that

Figure 1, top. Carlo Michel-
staedter. *Retoriché* (1905–7).
Black and color pencil. Courtesy
of the Gorizia Civic Library.
Figure 2, bottom. Carlo
Michelstaedter. *Homo Sapiens*
(n.d.). Watercolor and pencil.
Courtesy of the Gorizia Civic
Library.

resembles a penis (the moustache, in fact, underlines this similarity).[26] As in the case of *Retoriché* the mouth is blotted by the moustache. It could also be absent. No articulate sound can be uttered by such a character. The small, stumpy figure is standing at attention and is only partially covered by an Egyptian-like uniform—a *trapezium* over the pubic area and two breast-straps—that leave visible a clumsy and ridiculous nakedness, perhaps in order to underline the eternal imbecility of the human species. Here too the eyes are swollen and closed in a torpor characteristic of military *rettorica*. They are similar to those of the professor just examined. The big pointed head (the oval shape of some of Pirandello's characters) probably suggested to Campailla the title *Homo sapiens*. By creating such contrast between the image and its label, Campailla has effectively illustrated Michelstaedter's constant attack on the emptiness and absurdity of names.

Turning briefly to Pirandello's novellas, we note just a few of his characters who are rendered in a similarly Expressionist style with similar characteristics. Romualdo Reda, for example, in "Dal naso al cielo" ("From the Nose to the Sky") symbolizes the *rettorica* of science. This is how Pirandello describes him: "Very small in stature, almost without neck, with that flat face, leatherlike, . . . with those eyelids puffed up like two bags, that hid his eyelashes." This is the appearance of the famous chemist Romualdo Reda who has remarkably been elected senator.[27] And here is the portrait of the ironically named Cedobonis ("I yield to good men"), "doctor in medicine, professor of philosophy in a high school and of pedagogy in a girls' school"—a perfect example of the accumulation of knowledge. "A native *Calabrese,* stout, black, bald, with an enormous, oval-shaped head, without neck, just like a mule, with a leather-like face, in which enormous and ebony black eyebrows and moustache stood out."[28]

Both Michelstaedter and Pirandello represent their characters using certain physical traits as indicators of a similar spiritual essence. Reda and Cedobonis, like Michelstaedter's professors, are in fact knowledgeable individuals. They are real scientists and philosophers. The grotesque expressive form they are given by their creators is prompted by a common mistrust in such knowledge. Concerned with books and formulas, they have lost the sense of life, as well as their physical shapes. It is always the body that suffers through the overworking of the brain, and here the body is used to symbolize the life of instincts, the only real life. In "La signora Speranza" ("Lady Hope") Pirandello continues the description of Cedobonis, making obvious the correlation between his physical appearance and his spiritual being. "Resigned victim of his abundant scientific, philosophic and pedagogical doctrine, he was reduced to live almost automatically, with his filing cabinet brain, where thoughts—precise, adjusted, weighed—were placed according to various categories, in perfect order."[29] The strict relationship between mind and body is spelled out in what follows. "Perhaps his robust and vigorous body would have gladly lent itself to violent exercise, and to life without so many rules and reins; but Cedobonis had attached to it a filing cabinet . . . and did not allow it any movement, any expansion not in accord with the dicta of science, philosophy and pedagogy."[30]

Students of Michelstaedter have had problems in reconciling the tragic philosopher of *persuasione* with the caricaturist. After his death, his close friends Arangio Ruiz and Chiavacci published only a few of his serious drawings, thereby demonstrating their own lack of comprehension. How could the committed philosopher produce humorous drawings, except as a diversion? Campailla tackled this issue by pointing to two episodes in Michelstaedter's life.[31]

The first occurred during his inaugural year of study in Florence in the austere Marucelliana Library. There he sat one day completely absorbed, so at least it seemed, in his reading, in the silence of this shrine of knowledge and wisdom, next to other absorbed readers. Suddenly, he proceeded to unwrap a sandwich and to chew on it, accompanying this irreverent act with outrageous laughter. Though Campailla finds in this episode an element of infantilism, the psychological mechanism that must have triggered it seems very similar to one well diagnosed by Pirandello in "Non è una cosa seria" ("It Is Nothing Serious"). Perazzetti is considered mad by society only because he often let his vivid fantasy take over and burst out in irrepressible laughter. At times Perazzetti cannot help it; his devilish fantasy literally overcomes any rational attempt at control.

Perazzetti's fantasy, Pirandello tells us, would often produce "the most extravagant images," "comical aspects which could not be expressed." It would "unveil before him certain strange, hidden analogies, present him with such grotesque and funny contrasts, that laughter would burst out without any possibility of control."[32] In what seat of the human psyche did this strange process take place? It occurred in what Pirandello called "the cave of the beast." Inside all of us, deep down, hidden by the mask with which we cover ourselves, there is an aboriginal beast which, once tickled, comes out with all its force.

Perazzetti was an individual who could neither control the beast of his own psyche, nor could he forget the presence of the beast in others. So when he looked at men he often could not help seeing, instead of the artificial, pompous facade, the beast who ruminates and defecates. And the more the individual was pompous and filled with himself, the more all these base images of bodily functions would take over his imagination. Then he would burst into frenzied spells of laughter. When in the company of simple people, in fact, this phenomenon would seldom occur. It was the force of the contrast between exterior and interior that triggered the mechanism.

Michelstaedter, sitting in the library in the temple of wisdom and knowledge, surrounded by people so engaged and absorbed in their pompous roles of scholars and repositories of knowledge, suddenly felt just like Perazzetti. Perhaps all those heavy antique chairs transformed themselves before his eyes into many commodes on which naked scholars wearing only spectacles continued their profound meditations. Once more it is Pirandello who comes to mind with his description of the humorist: "He [the humorist] sees the world not exactly in the nude but, so to speak, in shirtsleeves. He sees a king in shirtsleeves, a king who makes such a great impression when we see him composed in the majesty of his throne with his crown, scepter and mantle."[33] Who knows how Michelstaedter saw the serious scholars around him that day at the Marucelliana Library?

Campailla tells us of a similar, perhaps even more serious, episode recorded in a letter from Florence, dated September 30, 1907, when Carlo was twenty years old. One day he went to pay a visit to some friends of the family, and on his arrival he found out that many misfortunes had just befallen them. After sitting, seriously, through such a tragic list of events he could control himself no longer and burst into laughter. The episode was analyzed with psychoanalytical tools by Campailla, with reference to Freud and Kris. He explained it as the coming to the surface of aggression which, after having been rejected by the superego, is sublimated to the pleasure principle, and "frees itself in a tendentious comic expression."[34] Freud in 1905 showed that at the root of the tendency to caricature is the impulse to aggression, and Campailla used this discovery to interpret Michelstaedter's love for caricatures. No one doubts the soundness of such an interpretation, and probably even Pirandello and Michelstaedter would have agreed with it. Yet, Pirandello's own analysis in "Non è una cosa seria" goes beyond the question of motivation and develops into a philosophical discourse about the relativity of everything, the impossibility of finding truths or ultimate answers. It therefore undermines the very results of psychoanalysis.

In his "Psicologia del comico nei disegni di Michelstaedter" Campailla continued and developed psychological analysis of his drawings. Although he, surprisingly, never mentions Pirandello, he clearly agrees with his concept of humor. The aggressiveness that psychoanalysis has discovered "is in the first place . . . the emotional result of a disproportion felt between ourselves and the reality that surrounds us, or between the interpretation that others give of us, and the one we ourselves formulate and that we alone believe reliable."[35] The latter statement seems to have been taken out of the core of Pirandello's philosophy. It is the theme of *One, No One, and a Hundred Thousand*. It is Moscarda's tragedy, his obsession that will bring him to "suicide"—a social suicide, so to speak, in his decision to remove his own being from social intercourse with men. To his wife Dida, in fact Vitangelo Moscarda is her own creation. He is not Vitangelo, but Gengé, as she calls him. "A very stupid Gengé . . . who . . . without knowing anything, hid in his heart a burning affection for Maria Rosa." And Moscarda well knows that "If Dida . . . attributed that secret fondness to her Gengé, it hardly matters whether it was true to me. . . . Gengé's reality did not belong to me, but to my wife, Dida, who had given it to me." Pirandello's philosophical conclusion is that

> Superficially, we call [the many, unsuspected realities others attribute to us] false assumptions, wrong judgments, gratuitous attributions. But everything that can be imagined about us is really possible, even if it is not true for us. The others don't care whether or not it's true for us. It is true for them.[36]

Pirandello concludes that it can even happen that others force you to recognize that the reality they give you is truer than the one you give yourself. Of course this is Moscarda who has arrived at such a discovery after a long time spent observing and analyzing himself and others. Not everybody can reach such a high level of consciousness, fortunately, as life at such a level is no longer possible.

What level of consciousness did Michelstaedter reach in his brief life? No one can say, yet his rebellion against social rules, against philosophical systems, dogmas, whether religious or political, were founded in a relativism that is very close to Pirandello's more elaborate and conscious philosophy.

If caricature reveals an aggressive will, it also is prompted by an ethical need. The physical ugliness that the caricature depicts is clearly the expression of a spiritual ugliness that the observer, here the artist, condemns. Those who recognized in Michelstaedter's caricatures a playful vein were far from the truth. The misunderstanding of his caricatures precludes a balanced assessment of Michelstaedter, the philosopher of *persuasione*. With very few exceptions, in fact, there is no light, kindhearted touch in his drawings, but a severe, moralistic judgment passed on a society he profoundly despised, the *koinonía kakón* (community of cowards) of *La persuasione e la rettorica*.

There are pages in Pirandello's essay *L'umorismo* that can be considered an Expressionist manifesto. Let there be no doubt that Pirandello places the humorist in a privileged place among the artists. Traditional art in general "abstracts and concentrates, that is, it catches and represents the essential and characteristic ideality of both men and things." "Art, like all ideal or illusory constructions, . . . tends to fix life," thus it creates an artificial, untrue reality. To the humorist the artist's activity "oversimplifies nature and tends to make life too reasonable or at least too coherent."[37] Pirandello is here developing a discourse similar to that of artists like Munch or Ensor; he is attacking artistic idealization and proposing a new type of artist, the humorist, who is closer to Expressionism. "For the humorist, causes in real life are never as logical and as well ordered as they are in our common works of art, in which, basically, everything is arranged, organized according to the writer's proposed objective." There is neither order nor coherence in most human actions. Inside of us there are "four or five different souls: the instinctive, the moral, the emotional, the social—constantly fighting among themselves."[38] The type of action the subject will perform depends on which of them takes over at a given moment. But we are so naive as to think that that particular moment is the expression of our true essence which instead we ignore, because it never manifests itself in full. If an epic or dramatic poet composes a character, the humorist will do the opposite. He will decompose it. The humorist knows no heroes. What he wants to grasp is "bare life, nature without order, . . . bristling with contradictions," so distant "from the ideal contrivances of ordinary artistic conceptions, in which all the elements are visibly held together in close interaction and collaboration."[39]

While Pirandello was writing these words, in Germany, Nolde, Heckel, and Schmidt-Rottluff were painting their tortured self-portraits.[40] Even more interesting and certainly less well known was the young Viennese painter Richard Gerstl. In a few years he had gone from the late Symbolist tradition, through the *Sezession* style of Klimt, and had arrived at an Expressionist technique that was concerned with new aspects of the human psyche that Freud was concurrently investigating. He had probably lived through too much too intensely, in too short a time, just as Michelstaedter was doing. Two years older, he took his life two years before Michelstaedter, in 1908, the same year that Pirandello's essay appeared.

DRAWINGS AND CARICATURES

Some of Michelstaedter's earlier drawings—studies of eyes, of noses and portraits, like the fine profile of a child done when he was only fourteen—have survived. The eyes, from the start, were his favorite subject and the one that most intrigued him. Windows of the soul, they can never lie. Thus the characters who personify *rettorica* will have their eyes closed and those symbolizing *persuasione* will have theirs wide-open, often in a mystical gaze.

By 1905 Michelstaedter had already made many caricatures and sketches. All the notables in Gorizia went down before Carlo's sharp pencil. By the time he left for Florence he had filled several notebooks with portraits of schoolfriends, professors, acquaintances. Few can now

Figure 3. Carlo Michelstaedter. *Processione d'ombre* (1903–5). Black pencil. Courtesy of the Gorizia Civic Library.

be identified, as he very seldom recorded the name of his model. One exception is the sketch of the distinguished fellow-citizen Graziadio Isaia Ascoli with his white flowing beard.

Probably in 1903 he drew *Processione d'ombre* (*Procession of Shadows,* Fig. 3), a little jewel of Expressionist technique. Six dark silhouettes in profile are walking on what might seem the rounded shape of the earth, one after the other, with no contact. They are all alone in the world; their bodies are somewhat curved as if under a heavy burden, some are even crooked. Campailla rightly called them "shadows"; no feature is visible, their faces are totally black, but their shapes show all their frailty. In the foreground barely recognizable, is the Castle of Gorizia, a black spot that gives a final Kafkaesque touch of alienation to the ghostlike scene. The castle, in fact, can be perceived as a prison to which the sad souls, now on a brief recreational walk, are soon to return.

The stylization of *Processione d'ombre* achieves its peak and perfection in two of the most Expressionist of Michelstaedter's sketches, *L'uomo nudo* (*The Naked Man*) and *Demone* (*Demon*) (Figs. 4, 5). Ferocious in their essentiality, they reveal an exclusive concentration on the

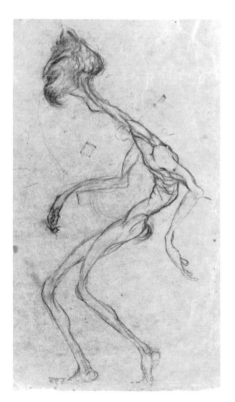

Figure 4, top. Carlo Michelstaedter. *L'uomo nudo* (1903?). Black pencil. Courtesy of the Gorizia Civic Library. *Figure 5, bottom.* Carlo Michelstaedter. *Demone* (1903?). Watercolor and pencil. Courtesy of the Gorizia Civic Library.

body. The faces, in fact, barely decipherable, disclose demonic traits. They are scribbles, underlining their corruptibility, vanity, and ugliness. The extremely long arms and the arched body emphasize a kinship with primates. The human face has disappeared; the eyes, vehicle of the soul, do not exist. We are in front of weak, corruptible, and corrupted matter. Both figures have devilish traits. Actually the naked man is closer to a devil than is the figure called "demon." In the former, in fact, small horns and a tail can be detected. The beard and the long aquiline nose are even more accentuated than in the latter.

There is a strong resemblance between these figures and Paul Klee's etching *Two Gentlemen Meet, Each Suspecting the Other of Having the Higher Position.*[41] Klee drew it in 1903. Because no direct influence is possible, the similarity reveals a shared sensibility and view of the world. Klee's figures can be described as more nearly caricatures than Michelstaedter's. There is interaction between the two gentlemen, and their falsely humble gesture is clearly ridiculed by their nakedness and the exaggeration of their pose. In Michelstaedter's, the humor, if it can be detected, is extremely serious, and nearer to Pirandello's conception. Man, the highest creation in the scale of beings, the creature closest to God, is nothing but corruptible matter. The power of the image is created by the force of the contrast between exterior and interior.

Klee began his work using grotesque distortion, characteristic of the Expressionist groups of Dresden and Berlin, but he abandoned it in an attempt to achieve an expressive form "that involved rather than shocked his viewers."[42] Michelstaedter, who was drawing mainly for himself and was not too concerned with a public, had no specific man in mind when he made these two drawings. He was trying to fix on paper the essential elements of mankind. Under the burdens of life these figures are also curved, almost incapable of walking any more. No clothing, no camouflage hides the inner nothingness of man. His spiritual weakness has been given a form that shocks the viewer, who sees in it the horrendous portrait of himself. Stripped from exterior embellishment the man of *rettorica* is shown in all his naked ugliness.

On the opposite end of the spectrum is *il persuaso,* who strives for authenticity, who does not accept the false lure of *rettorica,* but pursues truth in every moment of his life, who "possesses everything in himself" and does not "hang" like the weight in dependence on others (*Persua-*

sione, 41). On the same page where the *Demon* appears, Campailla published *Figura volante* (*Flying Figure, Op. gr.,* 119), perhaps drawn in the same period with a similar technique but with quite different results. The naked figure who is flying, detached from earth, is arched upward, almost imitating the outline of what could represent the sun, the moon, or earth itself. The head is seen in profile; a long chin and nose can be detected, the right arm and hand are outstretched to emphasize the arch that the right leg and foot are to complete. It could be a trapeze artist fixed in that instant of flight between one hold and the next one; yet the figure could also represent *il persuaso* "teso come un arco verso il destino," (stretched or drawn like a bow toward destiny) (*Opere,* 648). The Italian verb *tendere* has the threefold meaning of stretching, drawing, and aiming. Likewise, the noun *arco* means arch and curve as well as bow. Brianese, who gave his book on Michelstaedter the title *L'arco e il destino,* made this correlation between the drawing of the flying figure and the sentence Michelstaedter wrote when talking of Corrado Brando in D'Annunzio's *Più che l'amore.* "He is the hero called to the highest ideals who sacrifices himself to them . . . whose individuality is *tesa come un arco verso il destino*" (*Opere,* 648). Brianese also made a connection between the image of the bow in Michelstaedter and Zen philosophy, where the archer in the action of drawing the bow personifies the paradox of the maximum of power with the total absence of action.[43]

The drawn bow of Michelstaedter's metaphor, finally, is not only represented in the *Flying Figure,* but even more in the curve of the hyperbola in *La persuasione e la rettorica.* "Hyperbolic is the road to *persuasione,*" wrote Michelstaedter, "for just as the hyperbola approaches the asymptote ad infinitum" without ever reaching it, "so the man who by living wants only his life, approaches the straight line of justice ad infinitum" (*Persuasione,* 78). The geometrical image of the hyperbola better than any other can express the paradox of life, and the negative essence of *persuasione,* that can never exist in actuality, but only in potentiality. In the *Flying Figure,* Michelstaedter has anthropomorphized the hyperbola, giving physical form to *il persuaso.* The *Flying Figure* constitutes the complement to the *Procession of Shadows* where the curve is downward, representing the earth weighed down with human bodies. The earth has disappeared, the body is arched upward, weightless and luminous. "Art does not render the visible, but renders visible," Paul Klee said, giving voice to a general trend of the time.[44] It would seem that Michelstaedter, without being aware of the artistic revolution taking place at the time, "advocated the opinion that what was really worthy of a picture was the communication from within"[45] and not the reproduction of external reality.

Campailla, in his search for direct sources or models for Michel-staedter's art, came up with no specific name. Carlo never mentions any artist of his time. We know, for example, of the friendship with the Bolaffio family—he writes of their coming to visit him in Florence—but Vittorio Bolaffio, just as the Slovene Luigi Spazzapan (who also lived in Gorizia) would become known as painters only after Michelstaedter's death (*Ep.*, 94).

Although some of the outstanding Italian painters in those years were Michelstaedter's age or a little older, their works were not well known until the second decade of the century. The *Manifesto* of the Futurist painters was published on February 11, 1910, by Balla, Boccioni, Carrà, Russolo, and Severini. Like Marinetti with his article (published a year earlier) in *Le Figaro,* they attacked all past tradition, and advocated total freedom of expression. This drastic act followed a period of artistic stagnation. Since the *Macchiaioli* in the late 1860s Italy had not pro-duced any outstanding artist.

Michelstaedter never even mentioned the French Impressionists. As for Futurism, he cited it only once, and then with evident scorn (he had in mind literary Futurism, which preceded the pictorial manifestation of the movement). In his polemic against words and labels that pretend to camouflage a lack of content, this is what he wrote regarding the Futurist artists: "[If] I write all the foolish things that wine and vices suggest to me—I am not stupid and impotent, I am an original artist; in fact I am a 'Futurist'" (*Opere,* 702).

The general silence in regard to contemporary painters extended as well to the caricaturists. Between the nineteenth and the twentieth cen-turies, caricature reached the peak of its fame. It had become an important feature of many newspapers and magazines. Among the most popular creations were *Capitan Fracassa, Don Chisciotte, Guerin Meschino,* and *Travaso delle idee.*[46] Meanwhile in France the weekly *L'Assiette au Beurre* (1901–12) had become very famous for its political satire. Michelstaedter could also have been acquainted with the German *Simplicissimus* and *Fliegende Blätter* to which distinguished artists, such as Kollwitz, Kubin, Steinlen, Grosz, and Pascin, contributed. There is no way of knowing, however, whether or not he read any of them. He certainly had no exposure to local caricatures: during the whole of his life, none was published in Gorizia.

In a letter home Carlo expressed his desire to contribute sketches and caricatures to the Florentine opposition journal *Cyrano*. Nothing came of it and the frustrated artist had to content himself two years later with the college publication *Gaudeamus igitur*.[47] Some of his caricatures and sketches display similarities with the late nineteenth-century tradition of Daumier, Claude Monet, or Toulouse-Lautrec. The *Tipi goriziani I* (*Types from Gorizia, Op. gr.*, 43), for example, reminds us of Monet's *Cinq Personages (Five Characters)*.[48] Yet most of his drawings have Expressionist qualities, and with few exceptions they cannot be labeled caricatures. Few, in fact, could be considered funny or present exaggerated features.

In most of the portraits dramatic effect is obtained through deformation, rather than exaggeration. What is implied by this distinction? Although deformation can often be a consequence of an exaggerated treatment of a feature, not all deformations are the result of such a process. There are, for example, two powerful drawings of an old man's head where the slight deformation of certain facial features creates a dramatic effect. *Uomo con baffi a spazzola* (*Man with a Bushy Moustache*, Fig. 6, watercolor and pencil) stares at us in a disturbing, upsetting way; his wide-open eyes are placed far from each other, almost on his temples. Thus the power of the gaze reaches out of the natural trajectory, making escape from it impossible. The flat, wide nose seems to pull up the corner of the mouth which is covered by a bushy moustache hinting at a smile that in its ambiguity could be that of a drunkard or a madman. There is a sense of discomfort, but also one of sadness. We feel we are witnessing the tragic decay produced by time and the approach of death. The face, in fact, is covered with wrinkles that cut deep into the skin, creating an effect of physical suffering. Oskar Kokoschka's portrait *Vater Hirsch* (*Papa Hirsch*) has a less humble sitter than Michelstaedter's *Uomo con baffi a spazzola*, but it too represents the corruption of the human body (Fig. 7).[49] Papa Hirsch's features once might have been

Figure 6, top. Carlo Michelstaedter. *Uomo con baffi a spazzola* (n.d.). Watercolor and pencil. Courtesy of the Gorizia Civic Library.
Figure 7, bottom. Oskar Kokoschka. *Vater Hirsch* (1907). Oil on canvas. Courtesy of Neue Galerie der Stadt Linz, Austria.

nobler and more refined; time, however, has exacted its due, as with the peasant drawn by Michelstaedter. Shortly they will look just alike; death the equalizer is fast approaching.

Schizzo incompiuto (*Unfinished Sketch*), the head of an old man, is also a work in watercolor and pencil (*Op. gr.*, 109), whose power emanates from the rough sketching, the sense of precariousness. He, too, wears a hat. His face, eaten up by the salty air and by the sun, is shriveled; his mouth has disappeared under a big moustache; and his eyes are closed. He could be a sailor. The weathered face, the product of an intensely lived life, is certainly not the face of the man of *rettorica*. It is probably that of one of the sailors who one day asked Michelstaedter to join them on their life at sea. With them he felt always at ease, for they were as authentic as nature.

The most moving of old faces is one, previously unpublished, of a man wearing a large hat that covers his forehead completely (Fig. 8). His face is made up of wrinkles that cut deep wounds into it. His eyelids are heavy and can barely be open. The weight of the years is felt in each line. In contrast to the previous two sketches, this is the parabola of human life in descent; the head represents the final step before the end. Michelstaedter's character portrays not only the drama of decay and death but also the awareness of it: this is his profoundly moving quality.[50]

The tragedy of decay is also the central theme of Fig. 9, *Alla stazione* (*At the Station*), where the old woman's face almost disappears inside the enormous skeletal hands that are wrapped around it, like death's sickle. The fancy hat emphasizes by contrast the tragedy of that painful face. It is the type of contrast Pirandello described in *On Humor* when speaking of the aged woman who makes herself up in order to hide her age. The woman whose spectacle is considered comic by the superficial observer, if examined in depth will reveal her inner tragedy; she is aware of her decay, and her camouflage is an attempt to regain the love of her man. This awareness is what transforms the aged woman into a humorous character.

Pirandello's category of humor could well be applied to another woman's head. A watercolor and pencil sketch, *Fascino* (*Fascination*, Fig. 10) represents an extremely ugly face in profile. Her posture, smile and hairdo reveal a vanity, an aspiration to a certain beauty. Campailla calls her languid attitude ridiculous. It shows how unaware she is of her ugliness.

Figure 8, above. Carlo Michelstaedter. *Testa di vecchio* (n.d.). Black pencil. Courtesy of the Gorizia Civic Library. *Figure 9, below.* Carlo Michelstaedter. *Alla stazione* (n.d.). Black pencil. Courtesy of the Gorizia Civic Library.

Figure 10. Carlo Michelstaedter. *Fascino* (n.d.). Watercolor and pencil.
Courtesy of the Gorizia Civic Library.

The effect she can also produce, however, is that of pity and compassion. Profound sadness can be sensed in her gaze, a sadness that undermines the provocation of her ugly smile. Maybe she knows, after all, that no lover will ever come, that the offer will remain forever spurned.

Compassion is totally absent from the watercolor of the priest. Michelstaedter could not have been more ferocious. Campailla's title, *Santità* (*Holiness*), once more emphasizes the contrast between exterior and interior (*Op. gr.,* 108). The character is a priest whose holy role is underlined by the enormous halo dwarfing the rest of the figure. Once more a large head directly attached to the body emphasizes the clumsiness and puppetlike quality of the subject. The extremely unpleasant features of the face reveal an ugliness more spiritual than physical. The eyes are narrow and close together in a staring gaze. The mouth is bent downward in a grimace filled with bitterness. The drawing suggests wickedness, and its power resides in the contrast between it and the character that represents such evil. The minister of God, who should be the living embodiment of divine goodness, has the face of evil incarnate. This is an extreme example of *rettorica*.

In 1905 the group Die Brücke was formed in Dresden by four architectural students: Ernst Ludwig Kirchner, Erich Heckel, Fritz Bleyl and Karl Schmidt-Rottluff. Kirchner cut the text of the manifesto in wood and ended it with the following words: "Everyone who with directness and authenticity conveys what drives him to creation, belongs to us."[51] The group was to wait two years to have its first exhibit in a Dresden gallery. The first genuinely revolutionary exhibit by Die Brücke took place in 1910; it is thus unlikely that Michelstaedter saw their works, although he would gladly have signed their manifesto. "Directness" and "authenticity" were among the most important words in his vocabulary.

Several portraits of males call to mind Heckel's painting and etching techniques. All German Expressionists in their search for essentiality tried their hand at woodcut and etching. They all admired the early German examples of it and studied with devotion Cranach, Benam, and Dürer. The geometrical treatment of the surface with sharp lines and corners, emphasizing the harshness of the faces, is characteristic of woodcut and etching, and Expressionist artists carried this quality over in their paintings. It is also present in several of Michelstaedter's drawings.

The harsh face of *Conferenziere K* (*Lecturer K*, Fig. 11), the furtive *Assenza* (*Absence, Op. gr.*, 65) the enigmatic *Volto* (*Face*, Fig. 12), and the almost Cubist self-portrait (Fig. 13) all present this geometrical treatment of the surface. The bone from the side of the forehead comes down to join the cheekbone in one single line that extends down to the chin. Michelstaedter's drawings call to mind Heckel's self-portrait of 1917 (Fig. 14) and the portrait of his brother of 1923 (Fig. 15).[52] Although in the *Conferenziere* this treatment is broken up, producing the effect of a cracked surface, the face must represent the negativity of *rettorica,* while *Volto* instead is closer to Heckel's portraits. The high forehead, the deep gaze, the beautifully arched eyebrows, present in all of them, give to their expressions an air of spiritual nobility. *La grande caricatura* (Fig. 16) (watercolor and pencil) is close to Heckel's portrait of a man of 1919.[53] These characteristics are even more emphatic and the faces have become emaciated, almost ascetic (that of Heckel) and extremely idealized (that of Michelstaedter). The latter can also call to mind the dreamlike face of the knight Don Quixote. Hollowed cheeks, pointed chin, enormous, wide forehead—balding at the temples—both faces are filled with spiritual life whose depth is unreachable.

The spiky faces and figures become an exaggerated trait of E. L. Kirchner's work. One of Michelstaedter's drawings especially, *Uomo con pizzo* (*Man with Pointed Beard*), is very close to Kirchner's angular faces (Fig. 17). It was not included by Campailla in his *Opera grafica* and has never been published. It could very well represent another of his famous professors or lecturers, as it shows obvious similarities with them. The shape of the head, the nose, the chin with the pointed beard could even have inspired Kirchner as he painted the triangular face of Alfred Döblin in 1912 (Fig. 18).[54]

Kirchner's famous Berlin street scenes well exemplify the alienation of the bourgeoisie, the reification of the individual, his own devastating loneliness in the critical years just preceding the First World War. Speaking of the artists of the Munich Secession, Kirchner wrote: "Why do the nice gentlemen of the Secession not paint life? They don't see it, they cannot see it, because it moves, and if they represent it in their studios, it becomes a pose and not life."[55] He never ceased trying to grasp it in his drawings and paintings, just like Michelstaedter.

Once enrolled at the Institute in Florence, Carlo's study schedule

Figure 11, top left. Carlo Michelstædter. *Conferenziere K* (1905–7). Watercolor and pencil. Courtesy of the Gorizia Civic Library.

Figure 12, top right. Carlo Michelstaedter. *Volto* (n.d.). Watercolor and pencil. Courtesy of the Gorizia Civic Library.

Figure 13, left. Carlo Michelstaedter. Self-portrait (n.d.). Black pencil. Courtesy of the Gorizia Civic Library.

Figure 14, top left. Erich
Heckel. Self-portrait (1917).
Woodcut. Courtesy of Granvil
and Marcia Specks.
Figure 15, right. Erich Heckel.
Portrait of the artist's brother
(1923). Watercolor, gouache, and
black crayon. Courtesy of the
Association Fund, Busch-
Reisinger Museum, Harvard
University.
Figure 16, top right. Carlo Michel-
staedter. *La grande caricatura*
(1908?). Watercolor and pencil.
Courtesy of the Gorizia Civic
Library.

Figure 17, right. Carlo Michel-
staedter. *Uomo con pizzo* (n.d.).
Black pencil. Courtesy of the
Gorizia Civic Library.
Figure 18, below. Ernst Ludwig
Kirchner. Portrait of Alfred
Döblin (1912). Oil on canvas.
Courtesy of the Reinisches
Bildarchiv, Museen der Stadt
Köln.

became very demanding. Yet he never stopped drawing. Even after two years in Florence with increasing work for his exams he wrote home: "With regard to painting, although I have not pursued regular studies, as I could not, lately I have cultivated it more and better, especially sketching, which is more worthwhile than anything else and I hope I will be able to do something with it, by devoting a whole month of continuous study, immediately after my exams" (*Ep., 222*).

In Florence, he found his best human subjects for his sketching at the Institute. Lecturers, professors, often boring and pompous, were an easy target. They were the very embodiment of *rettorica,* of empty words; they were the defenders of a world that had been reduced to a glittering empty shell. Yet Carlo did not stop within the walls of the Institute. In another letter home written only two months after the one cited above he told his family: "Today I drew for the entire morning a beautiful and interesting face, and it did me a lot of good. I hope I can erase the awful shame of the horrible portrait of the little Guarnieri" (*Ep., 291*). He had been probably commissioned to do a traditionally attractive oil portrait of a child and he had been working on it every morning, with obvious personal dissatisfaction. Oil painting was a too rich and decorative medium of expression. Drawing was always more congenial to him.

Of the 138 items published by Campailla—and a good number have still not been published—more than one hundred are drawings done with pencil or ink. About thirty are watercolor and pencil and only eight are oil paintings. This is, of course, the best proof of his preference for drawing and for simplicity. Even color was felt to be a means of false embellishment. His watercolors, in fact, use very pale tints. Colors are used very sparingly just as aids and often only for the background, never as the primary means of expression, which always remains the line traced with a black pencil. That simplicity and essentiality Michelstaedter was striving for had been advocated as the essence of caricature as early as 1676 by an illustrious member of Louis XIV's Academy, André Felibien. Probably with the masterpieces of Gian Lorenzo Bernini in mind, Felibien had defined caricature as "a likeness done in a few strokes."[56]

Kris, who with Gombrich wrote an essay on the principles of caricature, offers a philosophical interpretation of such emphasis on simplicity and essentiality. "In these simplifications," he writes, "the abbreviated style itself acquires its own meaning—'Look here,' the artist seems to say, 'that is all the great man consists of.'"[57]

Although Michelstaedter's caricatures are not so stylistically reductive as those of Bernini, there is in them a similar effort to get to the core of the subject and to do away with accessories that are only false constructions themselves. Caricature, thus, achieved a paradoxical result, that of being truer to life than the subject. This is clearly what Michelstaedter was striving for: that authentic expression he had never captured in all his linguistic attempts. He used this technique of simplicity not only in his caricatures but in all his sketches. Few are funny and even in those cases, the laughter soon becomes sour.

Some of the *Tipi in viaggio o nei luoghi di cura* (*Travelers and Visitors at a Spa*) are simply funny—for example, the fat man (*Op. gr.*, 50). This is one of the very few full figures drawn by Michelstaedter. It reminds us vaguely of that brevity of stroke that Bernini manifested to such a powerful degree. Already, one of the *Types* (*Op. gr.*, 52) is closer to Heckel's painful faces than to a comic caricature. The same brevity of stroke can be seen in *Heronda* (*Op. gr.*, 66) and in *Compagno di scuola* (*Schoolmate, Op. gr.*, 38), but it is lost in *La botte di ferro* (*The Iron Barrel*), where the insistence on the lines is overwhelming (Fig. 19).

Campailla, who named *La botte di ferro,* had in mind those pages of *La persuasione e la rettorica* where Michelstaedter imagines a conversation with the happy bourgeois after an abundant meal. "You see?" the fat gentleman tells the pessimist Carlo, "You see? Life has its beautiful sides too. One must know how to live it . . . to enjoy what our times offer us . . . to know how to grab . . . this pleasure or that one with wise measure." The fat man represents the compartmentalized individual whose life is organized, as Pirandello so often repeated, like a filing cabinet. In one drawer science, in another one, art, and then there is the big drawer for business and the other quite large one for the family. Each activity must go in the right drawer at the right moment. Everything is taken care of. Nothing can upset the organized life of "il grosso signore," not even death. He has taken care of that too, with a splendid life insurance; and how proud he is! He is in an iron barrel, "as one says" (139–40). Michelstaedter, who identifies such a gentleman with the bourgeois "dreamed of by Hegel" (140) draws his portrait with black and color pencils. In contrast to those mentioned before, the fat man's drawing is loaded with heavy lines. His essence consists only in his flesh, in his heavy appearance, in sheer matter. There is no space left for any breath of soul. The drawing consists of a large flat face with a bald head attached, as usual, directly to the chest, which can be perceived—only the upper part is visible—as enormous.

The *Iron Barrel* becomes Grosz's *Ehrenmann* (*The Man of Honor*) (Fig. 20) and degenerates into so many caricatures that testify to the corruption and collapse of the bourgeoisie.[58] The little hair that the Iron Barrel and the Man of Honor still had on their heads disappears altogether; the facial expressions become harder. It is harder to camouflage their profound impotence with a rough veneer. There are other characters in Michelstaedter's graphic work who could be considered forerunners of Grosz's. His *Teste di gomma* (*Rubber Heads*) (Fig. 21), for example, or *Homo Ridens* (*Op. gr.,* 14), bears similarities to Grosz's portrait of Max Hermann-Neisse (Fig. 22) and *Köpfe* (*Heads*).[59] Some of Michelstaedter's boring professors and lecturers will degenerate into the characters of *O alte Burschenherrlichkeit* (*Oh, the Joys of Student Days!*) and some of his fellow students or *Tipi goriziani* (*Op. gr.,* 38, 43) will deteriorate into Grosz's *Nachwuchs* (*The Younger Generation*).[60] The decay of society that Michelstaedter had diagnosed did happen, and Grosz's repulsive characters were its byproducts.

CARICATURES OF FATHER

Among Michelstaedter's caricatures there are three—two watercolors and one sketch—that require special comment. They represent his father and are particularly ferocious. One of the watercolors and the sketch are almost alike. Alberto Michelstaedter is caught in flight as he is ascending to heaven to be received by the open arms of the Holy Father (Fig. 23). His hands are joined in prayer; his face, turned up to God. The ferocity of the image lies in the legs, which are those of a woman and are exposed by the opening of the robe during the ascent. This ridiculous effect is underlined by the contrast between the legs and the pious, almost ascetic expression on Alberto's face. The watercolor is a completed painting, whereas the sketch is rough and unfinished. The sketch, previously unpublished, could have been a first draft and it presents a feature absent

Figure 19, top. Carlo Michelstaedter. *La botte di ferro* (1905–7). Black and color pencil. Courtesy of the Gorizia Civic Library. *Figure 20, bottom.* George Grosz. *Ehrenmann* (1921). Pencil. Copyright by the Estate of George Grosz/ VAGA, New York, 1991.

Figure 21. Carlo Michelstaedter. *Teste di gomma* (n.d.). Black pencil. Courtesy of the Gorizia Civic Library.

Figure 22. George Grosz. Portrait of the poet Max Hermann-Neisse (1927). Oil on canvas. Courtesy of the Museum of Modern Art, New York.

Figure 23. Carlo Michelstaedter. *Assunzione 2* (n.d.). Watercolor and pencil. Courtesy of the Gorizia Civic Library.

Figure 24. Carlo Michelstaedter. *Assunzione 1* (1903–5). Black pencil. Courtesy of the Gorizia Civic Library.

from the more complete watercolor: a soft, long mane of hair that flows over Alberto's shoulders (Fig. 24). Carlo, who decided not to include it in the watercolor, might have thought that such an insistence on feminine features would undermine the satirical effect. In the watercolor Alberto's hair is nicely shaved; his face is as austere as the one we know from photographs, so that the contrast between it and the legs is extremely powerful.

A representation like this is the psychoanalytical critic's dream, especially when juxtaposed with the one where Alberto is portrayed with the body of a sphinx against the background of a desert complete with palms and pyramids (Fig. 25). The story of Oedipus immediately comes to mind and causes us to wonder, as Campailla did, if Carlo could have heard about Freud's theories. If he had, it is curious that Freud's name appears nowhere in his papers. Sophocles, on the other hand, was his acknowledged master.

His close relationship with his mother and his strong devotion to her have already been explored. Beside the letters, we also have the answers to the questionnaire used in the family game mentioned in Chapter 1. To the question "Which ideal would you want in your wife?" Carlo had answered, "that she be like my mother."[61] More than once he had expressed his concern about his mother's physical and mental well-being, to the point that he had to stop confiding in her for fear of worrying her too much. He even had to hide his own feelings, to pretend to be what he was not, and this was to him the most excruciating experience: not to be himself with his mother. In many letters he had lamented the scarcity of her correspondence; in others he had poured out to her his intense and total love. In his relationship with Iolanda he was looking for the same total love he knew only his mother could give him.

On the other hand, the letters written exclusively to his father were scant, businesslike, often with bourgeois clichés, and were clearly written in order to please him. The letter Alberto wrote to his son on the occasion of his leaving for Florence gives us a typical portrait of a father, a figure that must embody solid moral values and be concerned with imparting them to his offspring. Although all these elements furnish the grounds for a psychoanalytical interpretation of Carlo's caricatures (and it is tempting to draw the obvious conclusions that buried in his subconscious was a desire to sleep with his mother and kill his father),

Figure 25. Carlo Michelstaedter. *Padre-sfinge* (n.d.). Watercolor and pencil. Courtesy of the Gorizia Civic Library.

extreme caution should be exercised. Freudian analysis can help in the study of this relationship, but I believe an undisciplined and exclusive use of it can lead to error.

After all, Alberto Michelstaedter was not the ogre that one might have expected him to be. He showed a great deal of tolerance and understanding toward his son. The fact is, he did not object to, but actually approved of Carlo's studying in Florence. Such paternal behavior was hardly typical of authoritarian, repressive fathers.[62] Furthermore, the letters Carlo wrote home, to all the members of his family—father included—reveal a good deal of easiness and bluntness. Although he might have frequently hidden from them his deep depression and his pessimistic views, he was always outspoken. Even his language was free from formality and often turned coarse. In several instances Carlo even addressed his "carissimi" with profanity, used, naturally, as a form of endearment. If he felt so comfortable as to call his family *stronzetti* (little turds), the pressure of authority in the household could not have been so very heavy (*Ep.*, 46).

With these qualifications in mind, Campailla's psychoanalytical reading of the caricatures is valid. Yet it is not necessary, it seems to me, to accept entirely the parallel Campailla drew between Michelstaedter's life and that of authors like Kafka or Proust "who lived their entire human experience with a dramatic incapacity to emerge from the realm of familiar impressions." They were able to free themselves only on the artistic level, exploiting images created by their distorting imaginations.[63] It should, in fact, not be forgotten that Michelstaedter died at age twenty-three. The symbolism of these caricatures seems clear and the imagery so obvious that Carlo must have been perfectly aware of what he was doing. Was he consciously psychoanalyzing himself?

In his brilliant study of psychoanalysis and caricature Ernst Kris, who follows Freud, writes that "the comic originates in the conflict between instinctual trends and the superego's repudiation of them," and that "its position [is] midway between pleasure and displeasure."[64] The instinct of aggression that is at the origin of caricature is sublimated in the artistic process. Caricature, therefore, can be seen as a therapeutic art form; it is the healer of the very illness that is at its origin. For Kris, the caricaturist teaches us to see the victim portrayed "with different eyes."[65] The artist is able to draw out of his subject aspects of his nature that escape the superficial observation of the viewer. In support of his thesis he uses

Philipon's clever transformation of Louis Philippe's head into a *poire* (pear). Philipon is ridiculing a particular individual, the king of France, and all those who know him can experience this transformation.

What Michelstaedter undertakes, however, is slightly different. Although Alberto Michelstaedter is easily recognizable in the *Assunzione (Ascent)*, his transformation is not, for it does not derive from his physical characteristics. Carlo does not exaggerate any of his father's existing features. Instead he gives a physical appearance, a tangible shape, to his subconscious. The authority of the father figure, reinforced by the presence of God, the father figure par excellence, is a camouflage of human weakness. Such weakness Carlo chose to represent with feminine attributes. Alberto thus loses his own individual connotations and becomes the symbol of fatherhood as such. This reading is supported by the watercolor of the father-sphinx. Alberto lends his face to the representation of the universal father figure as it is perceived by the universal son.

OIL PAINTINGS AND FAMILY PORTRAITS

Although sketching with pencil was Michelstaedter's favorite form of expression, he did try his hand at oil painting. At the end of 1905 or beginning of 1906 he did an original portrait of his new friend Vladimiro Arangio Ruiz, whom he had met in Florence (Fig. 26). He talks about "Vlado" (as he was called by friends) in a letter written to Paula on May 17, 1906, where he also mentions this portrait. Campailla called it *Rivelazione (Revelation)*, and sees it as the "Expressionist image of the seer who does not stop at the surface of things, but wants to grasp their essence."[66] It could also be called *Persuasione* for it is an obvious attempt to give a face to *il persuaso*. The body (only the chest) is practically nonexistent, poorly drawn, almost rachitic. To this shriveled-up chest a powerful head is attached. It is drawn with an Expressionist technique, where sharp lines emphasize the angularity of the face. The focal point is the eyes, which here are opened wide in a piercing gaze almost too powerful to bear. Their stare strips the beholder of all his defenses and cuts, without compassion, to the soul. The forehead is enormous and luminous, receiving light from the charging power of the eyes below. Over the wide and high forehead a thick mane of hair opens up to crown this

Figure 26. Carlo Michelstaedter. *Rivelazione* (n.d.). Oil on cardboard.
Courtesy of the Gorizia Civic Library.

magnetic personality. The almost total absence of the lips, the pointed mouth that continues the sharp line of the already pointed nose, creates a beak that calls to mind a bird of prey. In looking at the face one cannot but think of the image of the hawk, dear to Michelstaedter and recurrent in all his writings. The presence of such a mouth emphasizes the piercing quality of the eyes. All the features in this face are working together to the same effect, to assure its identification as *persuasione*.

In 1906 Carlo had met Nadia Baraden. In the poem he had written for her, "Sibila il legno" (examined in Chapter 2), Nadia was represented as a blonde head, a smile and two hands outstretched toward the fireplace. The poem created an image of light out of darkness: Nadia's luminous hair, her smile, and the fire contributed to Carlo's success in creating the same effect when he painted her portrait, probably at the beginning of 1907 (Fig. 27). But the luminous effect is much more powerful; Nadia's eyes, which in the poem were closed, are here wide-open. The light of Nadia's soul seems to radiate from her beautiful eyes, which are endowed with a profound spiritual power. Her hair scintillates as delicate strokes of gold illuminate it. Even the white, high-collared blouse shimmers.

Between this painting and Kokoschka's portrait of Tilla Durieux[67] (Fig. 28) there is a more than casual affinity. Both artists treat the pictorial surface with broken strokes rather than with a fluid, continuous motion of the brush. It is the light especially that makes them so much alike. Tilla's luminous eyes, however, are charged with a magnetic force that no longer emanates out of a pure soul, as in the case of Nadia, but out of a tormented psyche. Her gaze shows the traits of madness. The spirited eyes painted by Kokoschka will undergo yet another transformation and acquire a sickly, eerie quality in the portrait of the Marquis of Montesquieu.[68]

With this Viennese painter, who was also a writer, Michelstaedter had much more in common than with the German artists of Die Brücke. Besides being culturally closer to him Kokoschka too was an individualist who did not follow a school and did not wish to belong to a group. Like Michelstaedter, he was extremely interested in the psychology of his subjects. This appears clearly in the portraits he painted between 1907 and 1910, the same years of Michelstaedter's own philosophical and artistic production. Beside the portrait of Father Hirsch, of Tilla Durieux,

Figure 27, left. Carlo Michelstaedter. *Ritratto di Nadia* (1906–7). Oil on canvas. Courtesy of the Gorizia Civic Library.
Figure 28, below. Oskar Kokoschka. Portrait of Tilla Durieux (1910). Oil on canvas. Courtesy of the Reinisches Bildarchiv, Museen der Stadt Köln.

and of the Marquis de Montesquieu already mentioned, Kokoschka in those years painted oil portraits of Karl Kraus, Adolf Loos, Ludwig von Janikowsky, Peter Altenberg and Peter Baum, all of which show his concern with the lesser known aspects of the human psyche.[69] It is through the eyes and the hands that Kokoschka tries to express them, ghostlike hands and eyes that give an eerie quality to all his portraits.

The writer and archeologist Albert Ehrenstein, one of Kokoschka's intimate friends, said that in his portraits Kokoschka would strip naked the moral skeleton of his model.[70] A few years later the artist made one of him. Kokoschka himself, speaking about his models, who were often prominent figures in society or in the cultural world, said that what he was after was the moment in which they would surrender their defense mechanism, the reins that held back their intimate self, and unleash it. The painter thus has a role similar to that of a psychologist. On his canvas he reveals to his sitter "his emotional and intellectual disequilibrium."[71]

As with Michelstaedter, in Kokoschka's early portraits, and most of all in his *Marquis de Montesquieu,* color is not so important as the line that traces in visible form the invisible elements of the psyche. "As Van Gogh had done in his portrait of Dr. Gachet the line upon and even below the painted surface [was] unraveling . . . the secrets of spiritual physiognomy."[72] The light touch used in the treatment of the oil colors in *Le Marquis de Montesquieu,* done during 1909–10, is so delicate as to give the impression of a watercolor. Michelstaedter had used the technique of pencil and watercolor in several of his portraits, in an attempt to achieve the same effect. The line was his basic expressive means always. Even in his best oil portraits, that of his mother, the line remains the most powerful creator of emotional nuances. He succeeded in expressing the torment of the soul with his pencil, far more effectively than with the richness of oil colors. His oil paintings with a few notable exceptions are conservative in style and conception. He painted two oil portraits of his oldest sister Elda, a beautiful head of an old bearded man and a self-portrait. They are all of fine quality, elegant and harmonious, an example of classicism and tradition which are absent from his drawings.

In Michelstaedter's self-portrait, which Campailla called *Autoritratto su fondo fiamma* (*Self-portrait on a flaming background, Op. gr.,* 123), the dramatic use of the color, the refined, almost affected elegance, reveal an aestheticism reminiscent of D'Annunzio—the fiery red in the back-

ground seems almost an echo of his *Il fuoco*. Michelstaedter's soul with
all his torment is already there, but it is harder to detect. The beauty of
form hides it in part. We must study the eyes if we want to find it. On
stylistic grounds Campailla attributes it to the same period as Nadia's
portrait. Were the two portraits made to face each other? Nadia is
smiling at Carlo almost as if she were uttering the words of the dialogue
he wrote two years after her death. She is in control of the situation; she
has a peaceful conscience. Carlo has not, and in the exchange it is she
who puts him on trial and rebuts all his statements.

In the dialogue Carlo insists that he still loves Nadia and she tells him
that he has never loved anyone, but "in everyone [he loved] only himself"
(*Dialoghi,* 98). Nadia's accusation is much more profound than that of
unrequited love. It is Carlo's being that is on trial here. He does not know
unselfish love. He cannot love without being loved. His own love depends
on that of others. He is not self-sufficient, autonomous. He needs others;
he depends on others. He is not immune from those faults of which he
accuses other men. "Poor Carlo!" Nadia exclaims. "You have nothing
and you give nothing, but you will always ask, and be more and more
miserable because you *are* not and you cannot love, but you ask for love
in order to delude yourself that you are someone. But nobody can love
him who is not." To which Carlo has only one reply: "Nadia, I will kill
myself!" (*Dialoghi,* 98).

Nadia's luminous eyes pierce Carlo's soul and, as Kokoschka had said,
bring out "his emotional and intellectual disequilibrium." Carlo's self-
portrait is still controlled; the formal decor holds back the storm that is
building up inside. Only Nadia can see it. And Carlo knows she is right;
his eyes are filled with a sense of tragedy. What Nadia has seen, Michelstaedter will be able to represent in his later self-portraits for which he
will abandon the false *rettorica* of colors. These unmerciful self-portraits
will be his last gift of love to someone who for that love had, probably,
died.

"It is significant," Campailla wrote, "that among [Michelstaedter's] oil
portraits the most beautiful and profound" is the portrait of his mother,
"for it is true that the best things are born out of understanding and
love."[73] And one could add that the portrait of Emma Michelstaedter is
undoubtedly also the most moving of Carlo's entire production. Emma

is the mother figure, the symbol of that unselfish love he had looked for in all the women he encountered; of that love neither Nadia, nor Iolanda, nor, at the end, even Argia could give him.

All the power with which Carlo's words were charged in that famous last letter to his mother is concentrated in this portrait (Fig. 29). Here he succeeds in grasping the dramatic essence of Emma's soul and renders it by a contrast. Her face, treated with an uneven, tormented stroke, reveals an internal drama; at the same time it emanates and inspires a profound calm. The eyes are not looking at us, but are perhaps staring at the only object of love; that object which is the cause of happiness, but also of suffering; and of deep suffering precisely because of profound happiness. This contrast appears on the surface in the shape of a sub-dued, barely hinted-at smile. The portrait of Carlo's mother becomes the portrait of all mothers, the classical icon of pietà and symbol of a universal and eternal suffering, whose intensity is strengthened precisely by the powerful submission that controls it.

Pietà has been treated by many artists, from Michelangelo's early example of classical beauty and composure, to the shocking and macabre composition Kokoschka drew for the poster of his own play *Murderer, Hope of Women* that was presented at the Summer Theater of the Kunst-schau in Vienna in 1908.[74] In Kokoschka's work the body of the son in bloody red is almost dismembered. The face, half-covered by the right forearm of the mother that seems to crush him rather than lift him—as her other arm is doing—is a painful mask from which all trace of humanity has disappeared. The most terrifying part, however, is the mother's face, almost reduced to a skull, a mask of death. The shocking effect the image provokes is also caused by the ambiguity of its meaning. Is it the symbol of the greatest human suffering, that of a mother before her dead son? Or is it rather the mother's possessive love that suffocates and kills the son? The contrasting action expressed by the two arms of the mother supports the second hypothesis. It is the same overpowering love that saves and kills, as the tragic faces confirm.

Michelstaedter's oil painting of his mother radiates a beauty and composure that place it at an enormous distance from Kokoschka's *Pietà*. Yet he drew—not painted—another portrait of his mother where beauty, if not composure, has disappeared (Fig. 30). It calls to mind the intense drama of one of Käthe Kollwitz's late self-portraits, drawn years

Figure 29, top left. Carlo Michelstaedter. *Ritratto della madre* (n.d.). Oil on canvas. Courtesy of the Gorizia Civic Library.
Figure 30, top right. Carlo Michelstaedter. *Interpretazione della madre* (1907). Watercolor and pencil. courtesy of the Gorizia Civic Library.
Figure 31, left. Käthe Kollwitz. Self-portrait (1935). Lithograph. No. 82-1967, Kupferstich-kabinett, SMPK, Berlin. Courtesy of the Kupferstichkabinett.

after the death of her beloved son Peter in 1914 (Fig. 31). Campailla significantly calls this portrait of Emma *Interpretazione della madre*. It is made with light watercolor and heavy pencil. The surface is almost tormented by the accumulation of black lines that cut into the face, neck, shoulders. Even the elegant high-collared shirt of the oil painting is absent. The shoulders, roughly sketched, seem bare. No clothing is there to camouflage the painful humanity of Emma. We are in the presence of her soul, her essence. The inner turmoil, created by the most intense love that is also the greatest terror, is sculpted over her face. Her hair, which is unkempt, is in sharp contrast to the neatness and elegance of the oil painting. It is certainly one of Michelstaedter's more successful Expressionist works—one in which, to use Klee's aphorism, the invisible has become visible and the exterior no longer exists.[75]

SELF-PORTRAITS

Eight self-portraits of Michelstaedter remain, all made probably in the last three years of his life. They range in style from classical to Expressionist. We have already mentioned the oil self-portrait, probably made in early 1907 together with the portrait of Nadia. Also in a classical tradition of beauty and harmony is the drawing in pencil called *Autoritratto con cravatta*. Although no date accompanies it, the conservative style makes it quite safe to attribute an early date to it. The expression is serious and intense, but perfectly controlled. The lines of the eyes, nose, and mouth are smooth; they form the noble features of what can be perceived as a noble soul.

In May 1907, probably shortly after the *Autoritratto con cravatta* (*Op. gr.,* 99), he painted another self-portrait that shows a change in both style and content (*Op. gr.,* 104). Although the face is still beautiful, the inner harmony has been broken. The line, in fact, no longer has an important role. Chiaroscuro is here the expressive means. Even where the line is still present, as in the tracing of the nose, mouth, and eyes, it is no longer fluid and continuous as in the preceding work but broken and irregular. This is clearest in the right ear, which is practically indistinguishable from the sideburn. The concentration is on the soul of the subject. For this purpose even clothes have disappeared. His chest, roughly sketched, is naked. Attention is focused on the eyes. They are of one who seems to be in a state of hallucination. The almost prophetic expression reminds us of Vlado's. The frowning eyebrows reveal the mental state of one struggling to arrive at the unattainable *persuasione*. The inner turmoil is stylistically rendered by the chiaroscuro, the broken line, the disappearance of any exterior embellishment. A beautiful touch is the out-of-place curl hanging over the middle of his forehead. The hair, for the first time unkempt, expresses on the surface the internal state of agitation.

The successive self-portraits show a clear development away from old tradition and toward a representation that is less and less concerned with exterior beauty and more and more with the inner world of the individual. In line with the Expressionist tradition the tormented psyche becomes the main object of the artist's work.

Between 1908 and 1909, as we have seen, Michelstaedter grew disgusted with books, this museum of *rettorica,* where words and sentences, like cold stones, are placed next to each other in great abundance but are completely devoid of any life and meaning. He remained interested in the works of Tolstoy, Ibsen, some of Plato, and his last discovery, the Gospels, where the emphasis is on man's life, not on his words.

Only religious texts remain from Michelstaedter's library: a French translation of the Gospel according to John, an edition of Psalms and of the New Testament. An anthology of Indian maxims has also been found. It was Rico Mreule, one of Carlo's best friends, who introduced him to the thought of Schopenhauer as well as to the Buddhist doctrine. This shift took place toward the end of Carlo's academic life, and it was very significant. Enough of philosophical and scientific texts that were only shells without life: he now wanted living truth, truth that compels action, not words. Christ, like Socrates, was a model to imitate, not a divinity to worship.

In his interpretation of the figure of Christ, Michelstaedter was very close to Nietzsche's and to Buddhist doctrine. When Nietzsche in the *Antichrist* attacks the concept of redemption through Christ, he is using the same argument as Michelstaedter's. Only Christian practice, only a life similar to the one lived by him who died on the Cross is Christian, said Nietzsche. Michelstaedter echoes: "Christ saved himself because out of his own mortal life he was able to create the divine . . . but nobody is saved by him who does not follow his life: but to follow is not to imitate" (*Persuasione,* 103–4).[76] Thus for both philosophers Christ died not to redeem men, but to show to them how one must live. "Precisely this practice is his legacy to mankind."[77] With such a belief, Michelstaedter and Nietzsche were sharing one of the basic principles of Buddhist doctrine.

There is another Buddhist principle that Michelstaedter shared in full: "Do not seek Buddha outside," which means "do not seek Buddha at all, whether inside or outside, for as long as one seeks Buddha, the true Buddha cannot self-awake."[78] Seeking Buddha is to lack something, it means to have one's own self determined by external dependence. It means not to be autonomous, self-sufficient, in full possession of oneself. Michelstaedter repeated this maxim over and over in his dissertation, but perhaps succeeded in expressing it with greatest effectiveness in some of his notes included in his *Scritti vari.* "Only when you no longer want, you will have what you seek, because that which you want is the absolute being, and all your will is nothing but contingency: it is not in itself. Only when you no longer ask for knowledge will you know, for your asking darkens your life" (*Opere,* 781).

There is no doubt that toward the end of his life Michelstaedter became almost religious, mystic, but his "religion" was entirely human. Neither god, nor heaven, nor hell, nor dogma had any part in it. Rather than "religion" one should perhaps speak of ethics. His concern was with man's perfect realization of his own potential. It is a manmade achievement that ends with the end of his life; it is a moral imperative that is its own reward.

Buddhism offered much that Michelstaedter could share, but its direct influence is difficult to judge. Buddha's name is only mentioned a few times in his writings, with no further elaboration, and always together with a few other *persuasi,* such as Socrates and Christ.[79] For all we know, he knew only the *Indian Maxims* mentioned before. But he could have learned more about Buddhism from Schopenhauer, who had discovered great wisdom in Eastern thought. The specific source of this influence, however, is actually of little interest to us. What matters is that his sensibility, his intellectual and ethical concern brought him very close to Eastern thought.

Buddhism inspired Michelstaedter not only in his writings but in one

Figure 32. Carlo Michelstaedter. Self-portrait (1908). Watercolor and pencil. Courtesy of the Gorizia Civic Library.

of his self-portraits (Fig. 32). As noted earlier, he very seldom drew the entire body, and never in portraits. Reasons can be found: for example, his discomfort in dealing with human anatomy, possibly because of his bourgeois upbringing. Campailla noted that even in his few nude figures—all males—he never drew the genitals. Be that as it may, at the end of his life Carlo's concern with ethics grew stronger, and we know from his sister that he lived the last months in a very simple manner that seemed close to the asceticism of a monk.

The pencil and watercolor self-portrait in question is, in fact, one of the very few works that has the date and place—Florence, June 1908—written in Michelstaedter's own hand. Although his features are recognizable, they have undergone a deformation that will be present in all the subsequent self-portraits. He appears older, the facial features are hard, and what little of the body was present in the earlier drawings has disappeared. No chest, no neck have been drawn. There is only a head severed from its body, placed against a black background. Despite the chiaroscuro treatment of the face, it is the light, not the shadows, that makes the stronger impression. The dark zone, in fact, is delimited by the black eyebrows that are drawn almost as a borderline between the lower dark part and the light forehead. The luminous effect is enhanced by the total lack of hair; he is here completely bald. It is the head of a Buddhist monk, no longer concerned with the materiality of the body, but completely concentrated and absorbed in the attempt to reach nirvana. But it is also a mask devoid of any trace of humanity.[80]

The year 1908, in which Michelstaedter did this self-portrait, marked the end, as we have noted earlier, of the brief career of the artist Richard Gerstl. He was twenty-five years old when he took his own life. He too executed many self-portraits, even more than did Michelstaedter. In the last year of his life Gerstl's preoccupation with self became a mania. Within the space of a month he drew at least four self-portraits. The faces he painted convey the strong impression that this young artist was trying to do on paper what Freud was attempting through an analysis, to cut open with his pencil the most secluded parts of his psyche in order to bring to the surface its unknown, mysterious traits and fix them on paper.

Between the spirited eyes and the tragic expression of Gerstl's last portraits and Michelstaedter's there is a strong kinship. Yet, while Michelstaedter's hallucinated glance reveals an effort to maintain control over his tormented soul, Gerstl seems to be totally aware of his own mental unbalance, as if he were trying very hard to grasp the internal disease, in order to understand it and cope with it. The self-portraits are all so similar, yet different since they do reveal a change of emotions, a passing from one state of mind to another.[81] Common to all, however, is *Angst*.

Is it a coincidence that Gerstl painted an oil portrait of his entire figure on a blue background? Naked from the waist up, with a towel wrapped around his hips, the figure is extremely stylized. The emaciated body, the erratic posture, the immobile fixed gaze and the shaved head are reminiscent of Japanese art and Klimt. Yet the immediate impression this figure evokes is of a Buddhist monk who has finally succeeded in detaching himself from matter. It is, indeed, Gerstl's only self-portrait whose exterior projects a sense of inner equilibrium. The struggle against the forces of evil seems here to have been won.[82]

Richard Gerstl was a great influence on Arnold Schönberg who, immediately after Gerstl's suicide—Gerstl killed himself after Schönberg's wife decided to leave him and return to her husband—began to paint with increasing fervor. Schönberg, too, left portraits and self-portraits whose main feature is the eyes. In 1910, the year of Michelstaedter's suicide, Schönberg painted a self-portrait with oil on wood. As in the bold self-portrait of Michelstaedter, only the eyes are emphatically drawn.[83] The lower part of the face, in fact, almost vanishes into a fading blot of red that lacks any contour. Here, too, the enormous forehead and the boldness of the head are luminous, charged with light from the power of the eyes below. Here too the dark eyebrows trace a border, to divide into Manichean extremes, the dark and light parts. The importance of the eyes reaches its climax in Schönberg's two oil paintings of 1910: *Gaze* and *The Red Glance,* where the frightful power of the eyes has obliterated every other feature.[84]

Both of Michelstaedter's last self-portraits dating to 1910 are lost, though fortunately photographic reproductions have survived. The opposition between darkness and light is a salient feature of both. His head (*Op. gr.,* 136) is drawn in the middle of a black background so that it seems almost to come out of or to be engulfed in a vortex of light. Whereas the right side of the face is sunk in the darkness of the background, the left receives light from the vortex. It is a mask, similar to the portrait examined before, but a more human mask, that is torn between light and darkness, good and evil in a never-ending struggle. The treatment of the surface, the chiaroscuro effect that shines light on the eyes and only the left side of the face, together with the upward direction of the gaze call to mind the self-portrait made one year later by another Expressionist artist: Max Beckmann, only three years his senior.[85] Below it, Michelstaedter inscribed the same phrase of Heraclitus that had already appeared in *La persuasione e rettorica* (54) and synthesizes the spirit of *il persuaso:* "In the night man lights his own lamp." He must fight his battle alone.

Campailla calls the vortex of light "a mystic halo," thus underlining the parallel between Christ and Michelstaedter (*Op. gr.,* 36). It is, of course, the Christ that he believed in and strove to imitate, the Christ, savior of himself, who in the darkness of life was able to create his own light—a light, however, that brightens only the path of him who has created it.

Writing to Gaetano on April 25, he reiterated his moral credo. "What are you worried about? What do you fear? No one can take anything away from us. Life is not worth our tears. But let us continue to move ahead, and try to be self-sufficient in everything; there is nothing that is too hard, no situation that is unbearable" (*Ep.*, 438). Nothing can happen to him who has everything in himself, who depends on nobody and nothing; he can be his own savior. These are the words Carlo also wrote in his last letter to his mother in the hope of convincing her that she needed not to worry about his being different from other youths who depend on others. "I know," he writes, "that I cannot expect anything from anybody; so I have nothing to fear from life, nothing can change me, nothing can stop me" (*Ep.*, 451).

Through his tormented struggle Michelstaedter had aged dramatically. In his last self-portrait (Fig. 33), he is almost unrecognizable. Commenting on it, Campailla speaks of "an unbelievable acceleration of his spiritual parabola" (*Op. gr.*, 34). It is enough to place this portrait next to the oil painting done in 1907 to realize the incredible evolution not only of his artistic technique but also of his spiritual self. The broken line of this portrait seems once more to cut deep into the skin with a technique similar to that of Expressionist woodcut or etching. The eyes, the darkest features of the face, for the first time are not staring at us. The head, in fact, is barely turned to the right side. Here is a face hardened by internal suffering that has cancelled the beauty of the features of the older portraits. Michelstaedter is barely recognizable. The outline of his nose and mouth has changed and his chin protrudes. His nose, always drawn before with a straight line, has become aquiline. This, together with the angularity of the other features, mouth and chin in particular, and with the presence of so much black, contribute to the impression that one is looking at a large hawk, a hawk that has finally realized that "after all a crow is just as worthy as a hawk. In one way or in another they both eat in order to live and live and eat in order to die" (*Ep.*, 355).

Michelstaedter's last self-portrait is strongly reminiscent of a sketch of Karl Kraus drawn in India ink by Kokoschka in 1909 (Fig. 34). Although

Figure 33. Carlo Michelstaedter. Self-portrait
(1910). Black pencil.
Courtesy of the Gorizia
Civic Library.

Figure 34. Oskar
Kokoschka. Portrait of
Karl Kraus (1909). India
ink. Reprinted from *Der
Sturm*, 1910.

the two men did not have similar features, the two drawings have a stylistic quality that reveals a closeness in spirit. The roughness of the line is even more accentuated in Kokoschka by the use of the pen. The effect he creates is, therefore, even more devastating. The shabbiness of their clothes is a strong antirhetorical statement. The battle against hypocrisy, against beautiful veneers of words, that Carlo had fought within himself and in his small circle of family and friends, Kraus had waged throughout the entire bourgeois population of Austria in the fiery pages of his journal, *Die Fackel* (*The Torch*).

Kraus's battle was linguistic. He began by attacking the very language of the bourgeoisie in order to point out the discrepancy between words and content. His principal enemy was *rettorica,* the corruption of language. A master of words, he was fully aware, before Wittgenstein, of the strict connection between thought and verbal expression. To Kraus the health of the world resided in the genuine, that is, demystifying use of the word; a "word that by remaining faithful to its original content, denounces the misuse of it."[86] Only through the redemption of language could man hope to save himself. In this portrait, however, Kokoschka gives us a Kraus who has nothing of the fire that was ignited in his journal. It is the face of a suffering, crushed man whose eyes—eyes like those of Michelstaedter that do not face us—are filled with sadness and resignation. It seems as if the artist, who as a seer can reach the most secret places of the human soul, had seen how costly the war that Kraus was fighting against the world was, and had portrayed all the scars.

A new generation of artists rebelled against the status quo and the hypocrisy of their times and demanded change. A drastically different reality called for a drastically different graphic style. Schönberg's discovery of atonality was prompted by his brutally frank realization that contemporary society, as well as his personal world, was collapsing. In painting, artists like Kokoschka and Schiele expressed on their canvasses, through the breakdown of the figures, the end of an era and, implicitly the birth of a new one, while writers like Trakl, Musil, Kraus, Svevo, and Michelstaedter recorded it in their pages.

Michelstaedter's last painting was probably not a portrait, but a landscape (*Op. gr.,* 141), perhaps the only one he ever did; in any event, the only one left. Hills under a cloudy sky; a ray of sun pierces through the grey masses of clouds: they justify the optimistic title *E sotto avverso*

Figure 35. Carlo Michelstaedter. "The lamp goes out for lack of oil. I extinguished myself with overflowing abundance" (1910?); translated from Greek. Black and color pencil. Courtesy of the Gorizia Civic Library.

cielo luce più chiara (*And Under Hostile Sky a Clearer Light*). Here the opposition between light and darkness and good and evil has moved outdoors. The strength of the light is such as to overcome the darkness of evil. The painting was going to be a gift for his mother on her birthday. It synthesized the core of his last, long letter. In the darkness of life Carlo was pure light that would overcome the evil of matter. The gift was never given. On his mother's birthday Michelstaedter shot himself in the temple with the gun that he had taken from the study of Rico Mreule, after his friend had courageously left for America.

The one portrait of Rico by Michelstaedter (*Op. gr.,* 131) is shocking to look at now, a posteriori. This young man who had introduced his friend to the thought of Schopenhauer and Buddha, who was one of the few living examples of *persuasione,* is represented with a tragic expression. It is the only portrait of a *persuaso* whose eyes are lowered and half-closed. The features are strong, the forehead high and luminous, yet the eyes and the mouth express only sadness. Did Rico foresee the tragic end of his friend? Did he hold himself responsible? Did Carlo?

Two last drawings are in their strange way self-portraits. They represent his faithful oil lamp that had lighted so many of his evenings of writing. He had even made the shade for it with his own hands. It was especially dear to him. He drew it once on a page of the first draft of his dissertation. The lamp is burning; two lively flames emerge (*Op. gr.,* 137).[87] He drew the lamp again on the first page of the final copy of *La persuasione e la rettorica* (Fig. 35). This time, however, no flames are coming out, only two streaks of smoke. Michelstaedter himself explains to us the symbolism of his lamp. In the margin of a page of the *Indische Sprüche,* in fact, he repeated the drawing, but this time he had followed it with a gloss in Greek: "The lamp goes out for lack of oil. I extinguished myself with overflowing abundance" (*Op. gr.,* 140). With incredible courage Michelstaedter had succeeded in portraying his own death.

Epilogue

"LA VITA NELLA MORTE"

I spoke my word and my word is tearing
me apart! Thus my eternal lot wants it;
as a proclaimer I perish.—Friedrich Nietzsche[1]

The opposition between life and death had been constantly in Michelstaedter's thoughts. The paradoxical essence of man, who lives only for the future, for what is not, who hurries to his death, whose desire to live is coupled with his impulse toward death, was also being studied by Freud in those years. In *Beyond the Pleasure Principle* Freud discussed two sets of opposite impulses in man. The sexual impulse drives man towards the continuation of life; death impels him back to an original, inanimate state.[2]

Michelstaedter gave form to this paradox of human life in the poem "Il canto delle crisalidi," examined in Chapter 2. Life and death are strictly intertwined to the point that one transforms itself into the other. It was a theme that haunted more than one artist in that period. In 1910, the year Michelstaedter killed himself, Max Klinger made a dramatic painting called *Dead Mother.*[3] A naked baby is sitting on the chest of a dead mother. His eyes are frightened; his gaze seems to ask for an explanation, for help. Behind him is the darkness of night. Life, that sprang out of death, will soon return to it. Schiele, working contemporaneously, left many drawings and paintings representing mother and child. In all of them death is present in the face of the mother figure. Once she has given life she is already dead. The color, the shadows, the expressions painted on the faces of all his mothers show the traits of death. She is the principle of both beginning and end. Origin and end coincide. Man tends to return to his mother's womb.[4]

That Michelstaedter felt the connection between life and death intensely is evident from his identification of the true life with the sea, "the free sea without shores." To Paula, in that last year of his life, he had written: "Let me go beyond the desert, to the sea," and to the sea was his final poetical journey. Even the myth of Orpheus, revived in his poetry, takes place on the sea. Michelstaedter had decided to live his life at sea after finishing his dissertation. To return to the beginning, to the place of origin, was his urge. In his last letter to his mother he had stated, very dramatically, that the thread of his life passed through her hands. She had given him birth, she alone had been capable of pulling him back to life when he felt like abandoning it. At the end it would be she who, like Atropos (Fate), will cut the thin thread that still held Carlo to this earth.

Serious study of suicide began at the turn of the century. In 1897 Emile Durkheim published *Le Suicide,* inaugurating the sociological approach to the issue. According to Durkheim the cause of suicide could be found in the relationship between man and society. In April 1910 the Vienna Psychoanalytic Society held the first symposium on suicide. Among the participants were Adler and Freud. The causes of suicide were now to be sought inside the human mind. In 1917 Freud published his essay *Mourning and Melancholia.* From the theory of suicide as displaced hostility that had come out of the Vienna Conference, he began to develop his own theory of the death instinct. To those two approaches to suicide a third has been added in more recent times: the philosophical approach. Writers like Camus and philosophers like Wittgenstein realized that man's first task in life is to cope with the absurdity of his existence, and with the irrational forces that rule the world. Suicide to them became a deeply philosophical existential issue; one every man must face and resolve for himself.[5]

In the medical world, quite naturally, the leading approach is the psychological, and today there is a tendency to regard suicide as a "mental health problem."[6] Thus the debate never ends between those who consider it a mental illness and those who do not. The former continue to believe in the presence of a pathological state in the suicidal person; the latter, instead, claim that many suicides are committed by people in perfect control of their minds. The main problem here, of course, is raised by the definition of mental illness. It is by now rather widely accepted that the borderline between sanity and insanity is rather thin. Madness, as Pirandello repeated many times—and many scientists agree—can be triggered in all of us. As long as we control our instincts society does not become aware of such a presence, but each of us knows that often the struggle to restrain them is extremely difficult and at times futile. Freud called it the id, Pirandello the beast that is in all of us. It is the instincts that by their very nature cannot follow logic or behave according to reason, and if not controlled provoke pathological actions. The capacity to control these inner forces is called sanity; the failure, insanity.

The debate between followers of the two approaches, though interesting, is pointless in the case of the individual with no medical history who succeeds in committing suicide and is no longer here to undergo physical and mental tests that would declare him sane or insane. Furthermore the complexity of the phenomenon should make anyone who undertakes the study of suicide extremely cautious. As Joost Meerloo said, in such a complex act "there is never only one cause. . . . There is a constellation of obvious and more hidden motivations." Thus "in the investigation of suicide, just as in the clinical practice of psychiatry, both intuition and logical deduction are equally necessary."[7]

The most honest approach is, therefore, to keep in mind, as Edwin S. Shneidman has said, that "it is unlikely that any one theory will ever explain phenomena as varied and as complicated as human self-destructive behaviors."[8] If such an honest position gives us freedom of movement in this field of study, it also requires us to be open to all these various approaches. We must accept that our investigation will never yield a final answer. We can only work with hypotheses, which no matter how attractive, must remain in the final analysis just that: working hypotheses.

In Michelstaedter's case, many have wished to see a philosophical suicide. It is undoubtedly an attractive hypothesis; yet it is a deliberate choice determined by the unconscious rejection of the other hypothesis: that of mental illness. There is still a rather widespread tendency, at times even a compulsion, in those who admire the work of a suicidal artist, to justify the final act in philosophical terms, as if a suicide committed for nonphilosophical reasons would detract from the value of the artist's work. A philosophical suicide, such as Socrates', enhances the philosopher's credibility. Needless to say such behavior still reveals a widespread discomfort when dealing with mental disturbances—a discomfort we do not experience when considering physical ones. Unconsciously some of us still apply a moral label to the mentally ill. If insanity must be, then let it at least be the noble madness of the genius, of the visionary, of one who has discovered the absurdity of life, the cruelty of truth. So the advocates of philosophical motives would speculate, but speculation it remains.

Only two weeks after Michelstaedter's death the writer Giovanni Papini, himself a follower of Schopenhauer's pessimism, wrote an article in *Il resto del Carlino* entitled "A metaphysical suicide." For Papini, Michelstaedter had killed himself "in order to accept . . . to the end the consequences of his ideas." His name was placed near those of the Cyrenaic philosopher Hegesias, Filippo Mainländer, and Otto Weininger. Papini had not read a single line of Michelstaedter; he was merely fascinated with his final gesture.[9]

Two years later, after the publication of a volume with some of Michelstaedter's writings, Emilio Cecchi wrote in *La Tribuna* that the young philosopher "had made of himself such a daring model of philosophical stoicism" that he had transformed himself into a myth. As a consequence "he could no longer bear that his own physical being would not coincide with the being of his myth."[10]

Twelve years after his death his close friend Vladimiro Arangio Ruiz developed an interpretation along a more philosophical line. In speaking of Carlo's suicide Arangio Ruiz used the very words Carlo himself had written in his autobiographical pages: that he had died "for overwhelming abundance of life." He emphasized the great demands Carlo had made upon himself, that he had elevated his own being to a height and expected from himself a perfection that cannot exist in human life. He was made of the same stuff of which heroes and saints are made.[11] In this view emphasis was also placed on Carlo's youth, when idealism reigns uncompromised. Accordingly Silvio Benco pointed out that often young philosophers search for coherence and honesty to the point of choosing death in order not to compromise. To them "truth is everything; and they kill themselves in the name of truth."[12]

It was his other faithful friend Gaetano Chiavacci, the recipient of so many dramatic letters, who confirmed that Carlo's idealistic death was consistent with his idealistic life. He rejected, however, Papini's formula of the metaphysical suicide, pointing out that Carlo was, philosophically, against it. Chiavacci demonstrated his respect and devotion to his friend's memory when he wrote that he lived in full, in his own person, the existential demand that thought and life, ideals and action coincide. He was simply repeating his friend's categorical imperative. Although this line of interpretation has been broadly called that of "philosophical suicide," a narrower classification is necessary. If someone kills himself because he cannot achieve what he had set out to achieve, if his ideal was too high and failure was a necessary consequence, suicide should in this case be called a moral act. The word *philosophical* is too broad and lends itself to different types of interpretation. To the contemporary scholars who attribute it to Michelstaedter, the expression "philosophical suicide" has a theoretical rather than ethical connotation. Some of these scholars are trying to explain Michelstaedter's suicide as the logical, final piece in his nihilistic philosophical system. Suicide, that is, had to follow the last words that concluded *La persuasione e la rettorica;* it is the supreme enactment of the coincidence between theory and practice, knowing and being. Such an interpretation would give us a coherent, systematic picture of Carlo Michelstaedter the man and the philosopher, a picture where every piece finds its logical place. Here we are still prey to the systematic fallacy that mocks postmodernists. If we follow Michelstaedter's philosophy to the end we must agree with such an interpretation—that is, if we want to see his suicide as a philosophical statement. Here I am only trying to say that what is generally considered to be a result of a certain reading, must instead be taken as a priori, a premise from which to depart. In short, we must want to read in his suicide a philosophical statement in order to find it. We must want to make Michelstaedter's life and theory coincide, just as he wanted to. There is no doubt that this coincidence was *his* goal. Yet, when we impose such a reading on Michelstaedter's suicide, we are enmeshed in the systematic fallacy. We want him to have ended his life coherently, logically. According to Harrison, he killed himself in order to enact *persuasione,* because, as Brianese well saw, the identification of authentic life with no-life is "the only plausible and non-contradictory explanation that the text allows."[13]

> To be persuaded means to abandon *rettorica* completely: suicide is an attempt at such abandonment. But "the persuaded," insofar as he wills

to exist authentically, is doomed to be defeated. Because what he wants implies, in order to be achieved, the extinction of the will: the extinction of life, the annulment of being. "The persuaded" dies in order to live authentically.[14]

Brianese's reasoning is perfectly coherent, perhaps *too* coherent. But the question remains: why should we expect such coherence between text and life from Michelstaedter when we know that he failed so many times in the simplest situations? Up to the end, as Paula, who loved him (thus protecting him) and admired him (thus minimizing his defects) testified, he was often overcome by rage, and would let out violent outbursts he could not control and for which he felt afterwards deeply guilty.[15] How can we be so sure he did not kill himself because he realized he was so far from the *persuasione* that he so warmly espoused? As he had said in the *Il dialogo della salute,* he felt so disgusted with himself because he could talk so intelligently and wisely about *persuasione* but was not able to live it. The examination of his letters (in Chapter 1) revealed many admissions of his inconsistencies; of his "feeding himself with words," of not being able to transform words into deeds and of so often letting his temperament take over.

When in the last page of his dissertation he talks about the danger of *rettorica* in pedagogy, teaching youngsters how to write about great individuals, like Socrates or Christ, but not bothering to teach them to live as they lived, Michelstaedter is also talking about himself. He could well see that despite his knowledge of and admiration for Socrates and Christ, he was incapable of living as they had; he was fully aware that for him, too, practice was one thing and theory another.

In examining now the passages where Michelstaedter speaks openly of suicide we begin with a page from his notes:

A youngster educated in a religious boarding school turns, by reaction, toward everything he knows goes against the so-called human laws and develops his brain in speculations about man's psyche and the mystery of nature. He sees too much and in his saddened soul the source of feelings dries out. He feels this and suffers. He wants, therefore, to launch himself into the midst of life in order to excite the paralyzed fibers of his soul with stronger sensations. And he does this.

But he cannot regain the lost spontaneity and realizes that all his enthusiasms are fictitious and that he has not changed. And with the cruel, habitual sincerity toward himself he examines his own inner being, analyzes it, and then with calm and with a reasoned resolution he kills himself, thus giving back to the mother earth the energies that in himself were fighting a useless battle. (*Opere,* 630)

By developing Jung's and Freud's theory of regression, Joost Meerloo sees in suicide a dual impulse. On the one hand it represents the attempt to return to a pure primitive form of life by regressing to nature; on the other hand it represents a "progressive and even heroic form" of overcoming the self in the attempt to reach for "eternal values."[16] The page by Michelstaedter just quoted could very well fit into the "regressive" aspect of Meerloo's theory, whereas his insistence on "the beautiful death" and on "making himself into flame" could satisfy the "progressive" view. Both aspects are in fact present in Michelstaedter's speculation on self-inflicted death.

Among Michelstaedter's notes there is a quote in German from the last scene of act 4 of Ibsen's *Hedda Gabler*. It is Hedda speaking: "I know that Ejlert Lövborg had the courage to live his life according to his own mind . . . that he had the strength and the will to break away from the banquet of life—so young" (*Opere,* 678). This sentence, part of which he borrowed for his *Il dialogo della salute* and placed in Nino's mouth, must have haunted him. We know that in Ibsen's story Hedda will soon be disappointed in her wishful thinking as she will be told that Ejlert Lövborg did not even have the courage to shoot himself in the temple. Yet the quote in itself states a powerful truth in which Michelstaedter certainly believed if he added to it the exclamation "To die at the right time!" (678). It was the preaching of Nietzsche's Zarathustra. "He who has accomplished his task dies as a victor"; "I exalt my death: the free death that comes to me because I want it."[17]

Perhaps Michelstaedter felt that he had given of himself all he could, that he had nothing more to accomplish or to say. Those who knew him said that he had lived in a few months many years of his life. He had aged precociously, as his last self-portraits show; he had lived all his intense life as a meteor. He had "extinguished himself with overwhelming abundance." As Hedda had wished for Ejlert (and will accomplish herself), Michelstaedter had the courage to end his life with a shot in the temple.

In his *Epistolario* there are many instances, as we have already seen, where Michelstaedter analyzes himself pitilessly, bringing into the open the precariousness and sickness of his psyche. Specifically about suicide, however, he writes only twice. On September 2, 1909, from the deepest yet lucid depression Carlo wrote to his dear Rico that his friend's words had made him realize even more than before the tragic truth of his own life, his total failure:

> That truth tells me: "you have failed, all your hope is in vain and whatever you do or say is only a useless and dishonest ὀρέγειν [trying]" I say and I repeat it to myself. . . . I have felt in myself the brutal ὁρμή [impulse] without either foundation or form and I searched in the world for the νοῦς [the clarifying principle] of my life while considering every action as indifferent and provisional. I have not lived with a strong faith, but with confidence in myself and in the future, and skeptical of all present things. I laughed at everything. (407)

But Carlo has now realized the precariousness of that self-confidence and the brutality of the force that keeps him alive: "Only one reaction is now left to me: to leave, to destroy this body that wants to live." It is once more Rico with his coherent behavior who, by contrast, makes Carlo aware of his own weakness and instability. The letter in fact ends with these words: "You, on the contrary, are always the same; and even if you now live less, nevertheless you still live in the same way. And to realize this difference between us puts me immediately in contact with the sad story of my life and of life in general" (*Ep.*, 408). It is Rico, then, who offers Carlo the immediate pretext for his self-destruction. And it is with Rico's pistol that he will accomplish it.

By the end of 1909 Michelstaedter had arrived at a very rigorous moral position. He reiterated his strong categorical imperative in a letter to his uncle Giovanni Luzzatto written shortly after that to Rico. Carlo's uncle is here depicted as a model of rectitude and goodness. The example of Giovanni's life will stimulate him to live accordingly. "And with the same intensity with which I feel hungry or tired, I now feel the necessity to be at my place with active dignity—or not to be any longer. And as long as I breathe this air and nourish my body the word you asked me for and that I gave you, will not be an idle word" (409). Luzzatto who lived

in New York had come to see his family in Gorizia after the death of
Gino. His presence must have rekindled the painful memory. We do not
know what promises Carlo had made to him. Giovanni might have told
Carlo that with Gino's disappearance it was he who had now the respon-
sibility to be his parents' spiritual support, and that he counted on him
for this. He was the only son left and it is likely that such a request would
be made to him rather than to one of his sisters. It is speculation, of
course; yet we can be sure about how traumatized Michelstaedter must
have been by the news of his brother's death by suicide; Nadia's death
had been only two years before. It must have been a great shock to his
already tormented psyche.

Suicide is again discussed in a letter to Gaetano written two months
later. As we know from a previous letter (July 18, 1908) the two friends
had often spoken of this subject. This time it is approached openly and
directly because Carlo is not speaking of his own urge, but of Gaetano's.
He can therefore be more detached, objective, and wise. Gaetano is in a
depressed state and Carlo is trying to help him by explaining to him the
irrationality inherent in the act of suicide. "He who in order to flee from
pain thinks of death does not measure its implications, just as he was
unable to measure the implications of life. He deludes himself that his
reasoning is sound by falsely attributing a consciousness to death; the
consciousness of the end of suffering" (418–19).

The idea of suicide must have dwelt in Michelstaedter's mind for a
long time, as he returned to the same argument and with the same words
in *Il dialogo della salute*. The discussion here is between Rico and Nino.
After having reached the Leopardian conclusion that "to be born is
man's misfortune," Nino remarks: "It is better then to leave the banquet
[of life] early and by one's own will" (*Dialoghi,* 74).[18] To which Rico replied with the same example Carlo had given to Gaetano in his letter. He
reproaches his friend for acting as the child who shouts "If you don't let
me be the king I will play no more—while all your being wants nothing
more than to play" (74). Rico then proceeds to use with Nino the same
argument Carlo had used with Gaetano, in order to show him the absurdity of resorting to suicide in the hope of being able to witness the disappearance of one's suffering, as if death were a conscious state: "[Man]
becomes aware of his own life only when he cannot satisfy certain needs;
in death this awareness sees happiness as absence of needs. But happiness

without consciousness does not exist. Thus he attributes to death the consciousness of the absence of needs" (76–77). In the next pages suicide is analyzed in detail with a surgeon's scalpel. The insistence on this topic is a proof of Michelstaedter's fixation with it. Suicide had been on his mind at least since Nadia's and he could not stop examining it in the hope of discovering its inner rationale.

To Nino, who still justifies suicide because it brings about the end of consciousness, Rico replies:

> Your invocation of death is only your fear of death. In your invocation it is your weakness that speaks, asking for pity and for a shelter from pain. . . . You are asking for sleep, oblivion, not for death. If life is a burden, he has the courage of death who carries life until it crushes him, so that his death will be a vital act. The man who willingly departs from his life, in whatever way, has not the courage of death, but a fear of it. (*Dialoghi,* 79–80)

He who voluntarily gives up life, seeks comfort, and rest. If one really sees the vanity of existence, one must not pity oneself but feel scorn. "Man does not ask for death but dies and in it he lives, for he does not ask to be, but is" (81). Schopenhauer had said that with suicide man does not destroy his will to live, but only to suffer.[19]

Michelstaedter's analysis of the suicide-wish found a depth close to that reached by Freud in 1917 with his *Mourning and Melancholia.* To Nino, in fact, who can no longer reply, Rico yet more mercilessly continues:

> I will kill myself, you think. And then you add, almost unintelligible even to yourself: "and then they will see." And what will they see? They will see how I give no value to all their things, how superior I am, they will understand how, when I became angry, I was mortally, divinely sad. (*Dialoghi,* 82)

Carlo is here describing "the interplay between murderous impulses and suicidal drives" as he foresees Nino's fantasies "in which suicide [would] represent the ultimate act of revenge aimed at a disappointing object, or at a real or imagined persecutor."[20] Without being fully aware of it, Michelstaedter, it would seem, was approximating Freudian analysis.

How could Carlo describe these symptoms so well and in such detail to Nino? He knew them because he had detected them in himself; because he was feeling the very things he was warning Nino against, because he, too, was at the verge of suicide. And before Nino's appalled silence Carlo began all over again, but this time, it is he who is the object of psychoanalysis.

In choosing suicide man is not acting as a *persuaso*. In fact he still depends on and allows himself to be guided by external considerations; he is not yet self-sufficient. This is the main reason why suicide is condemned. Yet suicide is not only dismissed on a logical level but also for humane reasons. It is in the letter to Gaetano that this reason is expressed and not in the *Il dialogo della salute,* where Michelstaedter remains faithful to a strictly philosophical discourse. In the letter, he speaks words very like those uttered by the philosopher Plotinus in one of the most famous of Leopardi's *Operette morali.* When the reason of logic has exhausted its argument, it is the reason of sentiment that takes the floor. "If life is nothing more to you," he writes to Gaetano, "what motive gives you the right to an act that by ending it [life], is so terribly unjust toward those who would truly give their lives for your good?" (*Ep.,* 419). "Let it be reasonable to kill oneself," Plotinus had said, "and against reason to continue to live: certainly the former is a cruel and inhumane act. And one should not choose to be a monster according to reason rather than to be a human being according to nature." And why shouldn't we have any consideration for those who love us? asks Plotinus. "He who kills himself has no care for or thought of others; he does not ask but for his own usefulness; he throws, so to speak, behind his back all his loved ones and the whole human species."[21]

The letter to Gaetano ends with the same words as *Il dialogo della salute.* To Gaetano and Emilio, but above all to himself, Michelstaedter continues repeating the words of *persuasione* that he is trying so hard to enact. "Nothing to expect, nothing to fear, nothing to ask—to give everything, not to go, but to persist. There is no prize, no rest. Life is all a hard task" (*Dialoghi,* 85). This is the moral imperative that Carlo repeats to Gaetano, the only one that will lead us "through action to peace" (*Ep.,* 419), the beautiful death that is the real life.

The dialogue was written in 1910, Michelstaedter's most intense but also loneliest year. It was the year he spent away from his friends, with Rico traveling to America; Vlado, Gaetano, and Giannotto in Florence; and Nino in Vienna. It was the year of his "working for death" as he described his making the handles for the urn of his brother's ashes. The ashes of Gino had arrived from the United States, making his suicide dramatically tangible to the whole family. Carlo had closely followed and helped with the work on his tomb.

But above all it was the year of *La persuasione e la rettorica,* where he left "many drops of [his] uncontaminated blood" (*Ep., 443*). He who had been constantly fighting against *rettorica* was now forced to write a rhetorical piece; a dissertation, the epitome of *rettorica.* Michelstaedter, however, did not write a traditional dissertation. His work became a piece of powerful rhetoric against dissertations, against intellectual theories, elaborate systems, that pretend to have the final answers for everything. The work that had started as a scholarly research project changed in the process of being written. At the end it questioned its very nature, its existence. And Michelstaedter accomplished this goal through the very use of rhetoric, by creating a work that is at the same time the triumph and the fall of *rettorica.* What other end but silence could follow it?

According to this logic, Michelstaedter's suicide could be interpreted as the ultimate, coherent gesture of an idealist who, having realized that language is rhetorical by its very nature, that words are the most deceitful tools man possesses, renounced language altogether. He renounced language in the name of an authenticity that man as the living being endowed with speech cannot possess. He renounced the only possible life granted to man: the life of *rettorica.*

If the use of language is doomed to become *rettorica,* if words are destined to lose touch with their original contents, *persuasione* will be achieved only through silence. "Language," wrote Michelstaedter at the end of his dissertation, "will arrive at the limits of its absolute *persuasiveness*—that which the prophet achieves through a miracle. It will arrive at silence when every act will have its absolute effectiveness" (*Persuasione, 173*). *Rettorica,* thus, can be defeated only through silence. The real *persuaso* does not need words. "The more vain a man is," Rico said in *Il dialogo della salute,* "the more he needs to talk; the more he lacks the real knowledge of his actions . . . the more he needs to speak in order to state it. . . . A good chess player plays in silence, since in every move he enjoys his plan; he who deludes himself about having a plan, speaks" (*Dialoghi*, 56).

In a letter to Rico, dated June 29, Carlo had clearly expressed his feeling of uneasiness in writing his dissertation, his fear of being caught in the traps of *rettorica*.

> That voice that comes from free life, that I needed in order to write my work as I wanted; I had fooled myself into thinking I could find it, and, instead, I found myself only wishing to remain silent, and lacking any interest in doing what I had planned to say with great enthusiasm. Yet it is a necessity that I finish my dissertation in order to get out of this abominable condition. . . . But to write empty words without conviction only for the sake of presenting a written paper, this to me was still impossible. (*Ep.*, 441)

Michelstaedter seems here to be fully conscious of the impasse in which he is caught. Words fail him in his attempt to express *persuasione;* by now he is aware of this. This is not the life he wishes for himself. He wants a "free life." Yet in order to obtain it, he must at least finish his piece of *rettorica*. We also know from Paula's brief biography of her brother that he had decided to live at sea and become a sailor. After his profound crisis he could not have undertaken a professional career.[22]

Michelstaedter seems here to be advocating an age of silence where communication will be achieved through actions alone. It is, of course, another of his dramatic and extreme statements that must be read as a demand for absolute sincerity, honesty, and authenticity among individuals. But it could also be read in line with Wittgenstein's idea that the absolute cannot be expressed through language. Thus silence can be seen as the only form of expression for it. It is precisely in this light that Pieri interprets Michelstaedter's suicide: the choice of absolute silence for a message of absolute truth.[23]

There was nothing more to be said, comments Pieri. Pointing out the connection between the end of a work and the choice of silence in other writers—Mainländer and Weininger, for example, who killed themselves after the publication of their works, and Stirner, who after *Der Einzige und sein Eigentum* published nothing more—Pieri interprets the choice of silence as the only possible way to avoid *rettorica*. Once everything has been said, any further discourse would become mere rhetorical exercise. Such choice is by no means limited to the philosophers. Already Hölderlin at the age of thirty had written almost his entire poetical work. His choice of silence was not the rejection of the poetic word; it stood "for the word's surpassing of itself, for its realization not in another medium but in that which is its echoing antithesis and defining negation."[24] Rimbaud, too, chose silence but for a different reason. His was a statement about the priority of action over words, just as Michelstaedter had believed.

"The political inhumanity of the twentieth century which followed the erosion of European bourgeois values has done injury to language," wrote George Steiner in *Language and Silence*. "A writer who feels that the very condition of language is in question, that the word may be losing something of human genius, might very well 'choose' the suicidal rhetoric of silence."[25] The lack of a linguistic identity was, naturally, felt more by those writers from *Mitteleuropa,* many of whom were of Jewish origin, who were brought up in a varied linguistic milieu. Michelstaedter, as had Kafka or Svevo, had that experience. Yet "an estrangement from language was, presumably, a part of a more general abandonment of confidence in the stabilities and expressive authority of central European civilization."[26] The work of writers like Hofmannsthal, Kafka, Wittgenstein, Broch, but also Beckett, was determined and nourished by this critical awareness. In this light the attempts of many artists to wander amid different media in the desperate attempt to find the authentic, pristine means of expression, is fully understandable.

Plunged into the isolation of his tragic discovery Michelstaedter did not only "choose the suicidal rhetoric of silence," but also the rhetorical silence of suicide.

His philosophical discourse that ended in suicide, although it passed almost unknown and unnoticed, was the pioneer voice of much contemporary thought about language and literature. It is not too farfetched to state that Blanchot's *L'écriture du désastre* and even Bataille's central idea of the insuperable *différence* of the negative had their conscious sacrificial victim in Carlo Michelstaedter.

NOTES

INTRODUCTION

1. Giovanni Gentile's review appeared in *La Critica*, 20, no. 4 (1922): 332–36. A complete list of the scholarship on Michelstaedter is Sergio Campailla's *Quaderno bibliografico* (Genova: Università degli studi, 1976). For the most recent studies, see the new edition of Marco Cerruti's *Carlo Michelstaedter* (Milan: Mursia, 1967–87) and Francesco Muzzioli's *Michelstaedter* (Lecce: Milella, 1987). The entire second half of Muzzioli's book is a detailed survey of all major critical works of Michelstaedter from his death up to 1987.

2. Piero Pieri, *La differenza ebraica. Ebraismo e grecità in Michelstaedter* (Bologna: Cappelli, 1984), 59–60. All translations are mine unless otherwise stated.

3. For a detailed study of the Jewish population in Gorizia see O. Altieri's *La comunità ebraica di Gorizia: caratteristiche demografiche, economiche e sociali (1778–1900)* (Udine: Del Bianco, 1985). Two essays on Hebraism in Michelstaedter's family have recently appeared in the volume edited by Sergio Campailla, *Dialoghi intorno a Michelstaedter* (Gorizia: Biblioteca Statale Isontina, 1988). They are Orietta Altieri's "La famiglia Michelstaedter e l'ebraismo goriziano," 35–41; and Ada Neiger's "Michelstaedter e la sindrome ebraica," 43–57. The only biographical study of Michelstaedter is Sergio Campailla's *A ferri corti con la vita* (Gorizia: Campestrini, 1974–81).

4. Michelstaedter was a compulsive letter writer, as will be shown at the end of Chapter 1. Sergio Campailla has recently edited two hundred letters that remain. The volume is part of a major project to publish the entire work of Michelstaedter. Four volumes have already been published by Adelphi in Milan. They are *La persuasione e la rettorica* (1982), *Epistolario* (1983), *Poesie* (1987), and *Il dialogo della salute e altri*

dialoghi (1988). They will be referred to in the text as *Persuasione, Ep., Poesie,* and *Dialoghi*. For Michelstaedter's other writings I shall use the 1958 edition by his friend Gaetano Chiavacci (Sansoni); unfortunately this edition has been out of print for years. Thus Campailla's enterprise is doubly praiseworthy. The Chiavacci edition, titled *Opere di Carlo Michelstaedter,* will be hereafter referred to as *Opere.*

Writing to his sister Paula in January 1906, he called Hebraism "a general aberration" and the Jewish, "people who do not live in our world" (91). A couple of months later, telling his father of having gone to a Jewish party "in spite of his antipathy toward" the Zionist milieu, he admitted that he had enjoyed himself because no one at the party had any Zionist ideas (112). More than a year and a half later, writing home and describing a visit he paid to a Jewish family of a common friend, he used hard and sarcastic words in describing their religious practices and rituals (248). The same sarcasm appears in another letter to his family written the following year (295).

5. Guido Fubini's "Sui contenuti d'una cultura ebraica" in *Ebrei e Mitteleuropa,* edited by Quirino Principe (Brescia: Shakespeare and Company, 1984), 414–17 (415). This rich volume is a collection of papers given at the Conference Ebrei e Mitteleuropa that took place in Gorizia in December 1982.

6. Piromalli well saw this quality of Michelstaedter's personality. He and many other scholars, however, have thought that Michelstaedter spent some time in Vienna, as he enrolled at the University there to study mathematics. No records are left, however, to prove any sojourn in the capital, and it is safe to say that he must never have gone there. Michelstaedter finished his last school year in the summer of 1905. His first letter after that event is dated October 22. It was written on his way to Florence, and was the beginning of an intense correspondence—in the first year, daily—that he kept up while away from home. Antonio Piromalli, *Carlo Michelstaedter* (Florence: La Nuova Italia, 1974), 11.

7. Carlo Salinari was the first to mention the name of Michelstaedter in connection with Pirandello in his fundamental book *Miti e coscienza del Decadentismo italiano,* 9th ed. (Milan: Feltrinelli, 1973), 274. The observation was then taken up by Marco Cerruti in his important monographic study mentioned in note 1; by Campailla in *Pensiero e poesia di Carlo Michelstaedter* (Bologna: Pàtron, 1973), 132; by Piromalli in the work cited above (18); and by Gian Paolo Biasin in his original book *Literary Diseases. Theme and Metaphor in the Italian Novel* (Austin: University of Texas Press, 1975), 101.

8. These are Gianni Vattimo's words in a short article by the title "C'è una sola verità: il dolore" that appeared in *Tutto libri* (*La Stampa*) on April 23, 1983, on the occasion of an exhibit of Michelstaedter's art in Milan. It was this short article that introduced me to Carlo Michelstaedter. To Gianni Vattimo, whom I have never met, goes my first thanks. The quote is on page 3.

9. Vattimo, "C'è una sola verità: il dolore," 3.

10. "C'è una sola verità," 3.

11. With the exception of a few minor articles none of Michelstaedter's works were published during his lifetime. The first edition of his work was compiled by his

friend Vladimiro Arangio Ruiz in 1912. It included in one volume *Il dialogo della salute* and *Poesie*. The following year a second volume was published with *La persuasione e la rettorica* (Genova: Formiggini). The *Appendici critiche* to the dissertation were published for the first time only in 1922 (Vallecchi), thanks to Michelstaedter's cousin, Emilio Michelstaedter. For a complete chronological bibliography see Muzzioli, 181–83.

12. Sergio Campailla published with an enlightening introductory essay about 150 drawings, sketches and paintings; unfortunately the volume has been out of print for years. Carlo Michelstaedter, *Opera grafica e pittorica* (Gorizia: Istituto per gli Incontri Culturali Mitteleuropei, Arti grafiche Campestrini, 1975).

13. The passage, still unpublished, is in the *Fondo Carlo Michelstaedter*, abbreviated *FCM* in the *Taccuino* (notebook) 6, p. 7, in the Civic Library of Gorizia.

14. Moretti Costanzi's article is in *L'esistenzialismo*, edited by L. Pelloux (Rome: Studium, 1943), 159–72.

15. Giuseppe Catalfamo, "L'esistenzialismo di Carlo Michelstaedter," *Teoresi*, 1, no. 1 (1946): 150–68, and nos. 2–3 (1946), 126–34. Reprinted in *Berdiaeff. Il Metafisico della libertà e altri saggi sull'esistenzialismo* (Messina: Edizioni Ferrara, 1953), 234, 235.

16. Jean-Paul Sartre, *Nausea*, translated by Lloyd Alexander (New Directions, 1964), 131. The verb "consistere" that Michelstaedter uses constantly in his writings, and which is a basic attribute of "il persuaso" (he who achieves *persuasione*), is his translation from the Greek *méno* (to persevere, to remain). It conveys the sense of stability, constancy; the sense of the Parmenidean being.

17. On his inertia he writes also on pages 336, 341, 436, 440, 442. Italo Svevo often uses the word "inertia" in his novel *Senilità* to characterize his antihero, Emilio Brentani.

18. Catalfamo, 247.

19. Ioachim Ranke, "Il pensiero di Michelstaedter. Un contributo allo studio dell'esistenzialismo italiano," first published in *Zeitschrift für philosophische Forschung* 15, no. 1 (1961), then in Italian in *Giornale critico della filosofia italiana* 41, no. 4 (1962): 518–39; 520.

20. Giorgio Brianese, "Essere per il nulla. Note su Michelstaedter e Heidegger," *Studi Goriziani* 59 (January–June 1984): 7–44; 16. Brianese is also the author of one of the best extensive works on Michelstaedter, *L'arco e il destino. Interpretazione di Carlo Michelstaedter* (Abano Terme: Francisci, 1985), from which I shall quote extensively. Also on Michelstaedter and Heidegger is the essay by Carlo Arata, "Il rapporto esistenza-trascendenza e la non assurdità della speranza," *La filosofia della Mitteleuropa* (Gorizia: Istituto per gli Incontri Culturali Mitteleuropei, 1981), proceedings of the conference held in Gorizia, September 28–October 1, 1974, pp. 263–73. Another scholar who sees Michelstaedter as a forerunner of Heidegger (and Wittgenstein) is Claudio La Rocca in *Nichilismo e retorica. Il pensiero di Carlo Michelstaedter* (Pisa: ETS, 1983), 104–10.

21. Brianese, "Essere per il nulla," 34.

22. Carlo Cattaneo, "La rivolta impossibile di Carlo Michelstaedter," *Aut-Aut,* no. 37 (January 1957): 85–92; 91.

23. Muzzioli's essay "Il confronto delle interpretazioni: Michelstaedter tra simbolismo e allegoria" was presented at the International Conference, "Michelstaedter: il coraggio dell'impossibile," which took place in Gorizia on October 1–3, 1987. The publication of the proceedings of the conference, undertaken by the City of Gorizia, is forthcoming.

24. Cristina Benussi wrote an extremely valuable study, *Negazione e integrazione nella dialettica di Carlo Michelstaedter* (Rome: Edizioni dell'Ateneo e Bizzarri, 1980), to which we will have occasion to return. Alberto Abbruzzese collected his various essays in *Svevo, Slataper, Michelstaedter: lo stile e il viaggio* (Venice: Marsilio, 1979). Romano Luperini's essays are in *Il Novecento,* vol. 1 (Turin: Loescher, 1981).

25. This sharp diagnosis is in Giorgio Brianese's "Essere per il nulla," 30. Brianese gives credit for a more restrained reading to Campailla.

26. It is certain that he knew Stirner's philosophy, as he quotes him extensively in a letter to Iolanda, a schoolfriend with whom he fell in love when studying in Florence. See *Epistolario,* 202. The same passage he had copied in his notes (*Opere,* 632–33).

27. This passage published here for the first time is in *FCM, Taccuino* 6, p. 9.

28. It is actually a short page where Michelstaedter wrote down the difference between *worth* and *value* with the obvious purpose of remembering and understanding it better. The page was published only by Cerruti in his *Carlo Michelstaedter,* 167–68. No comments accompanied the notes.

CHAPTER 1

1. Emile Cioran, *The Trouble with Being Born,* translated by Richard Howard (New York: Viking, 1976), 36.

2. The *Appendici* to *La persuasione e la rettorica* were published for the first time in the 1922 Vallecchi edition of *La persuasione e la rettorica.* The editor was Carlo's cousin, Emilio Michelstaedter. They were published again by Sansoni in Chiavacci's edition of 1958 and finally by Marzorati in 1972 together with *La persuasione e la rettorica* edited by Maria Adelaide Raschini, who contributed extensive, valuable footnotes. Campailla's edition of 1981 does not have the *Appendici.* Raschini is also the author of one of the first book-length studies of Michelstaedter's philosophy, *Carlo Michelstaedter* (Milan: Marzorati, 1965). The *Scritti vari* were published only in Chiavacci's edition and are therefore now available only in a few libraries. A new edition of them is part of Campailla's large project. For both the *Appendici* and the *Scritti vari,* Chiavacci's edition will be used. They will be referred to in the text as *Opere.*

3. Carlo must have become interested in the issue of language very early in his life. A high school composition (schoolyear 1903–4) was entitled "La lingua è il più utile e pericoloso organo dell'uomo." See Carlo Luigi Bozzi, "Carlo Michelstaedter studente ginnasiale," *Studi Goriziani* 40 (July–December 1966): 3–13, 11. In the

same article we find the titles of literary and philosophical compositions the students were writing in those years. One cannot but be impressed by the complexity and difficulty of many topics. Already before enrolling at the University Carlo was writing on Socrates, Buddha, and Leopardi, subjects that remained of interest for the rest of his life. It should be pointed out that, although the Michelstaedter family spoke Italian, the school was part of the state system and instruction was in German. Italian was merely one of the subjects in the curriculum.

4. Platone [Plato], *Opere*, 2 vols. (Bari: Laterza, 1966), 790–93. (*Phaedrus* 275e–276a).

5. Platone [Plato], 790. (*Phaedrus* 275a).

6. Christopher Norris, *Derrida* (Cambridge: Harvard University Press, 1987), 35.

7. Norris, 37–38.

8. Gabriele Giannantoni, *La filosofia prearistotelica* (Rome: Edizioni dell' Ateneo, 1962), 107.

9. Giorgio Brianese, *L'arco e il destino*, 12.

10. Heraclitus, fragment 88, in *Presocratici. Testimonianze e frammenti*, edited by G. Giannantoni (Bari: Laterza, n.d.), 214. Giannantoni follows the Diels edition.

11. Giannantoni, 119.

12. Parmenides, fragment 3, *Presocratici*, 271.

13. *Presocratici*, 276.

14. FCM 2:6.

15. Emanuele Severino discussed this issue in *La Strada* (Milan: Rizzoli, 1983). Brianese, *L'arco e il destino*, 75.

16. Francesco Fratta, *Il dovere dell'essere. Critica della metafisica e istanza etica in Carlo Michelstaedter* (Milan: Unicopli, 1986), 41. According to Fratta, *persuasione* is a mystical state, not a theoretical experience.

17. Fragment 4 in Giannantoni, *La filosofia prearistotelica*, 242.

18. Fragment 1, *La filosofia prearistotelica*, 242.

19. Fratta, 69.

20. Italo Calvino, *Six Memos for the Next Millennium*, translated by Peter Creagh (Cambridge: Harvard University Press, 1988), 56.

21. Luigi Pirandello, *The Old and the Young*, 2 vols., translated by C. K. Scott-Moncrieff (New York: Dutton, 1928) 1:74.

22. Umberto Eco, *Foucault's Pendulum*, translated by William Weaver (San Diego: Harcourt Brace Jovanovich, 1989), 50.

23. Italo Calvino, *Mr. Palomar*, translated by William Weaver (San Diego: Harcourt Brace Jovanovich, 1985), 55.

24. Antonio Devetag wrote *Michelstaedter: La grande trasgressione*. It was produced by Il Piccolo Teatro "Città di Gorizia" V.G.G. in Gorizia on December 9 and 10, 1982. Franco Ferranti is the author of *Il peso al gancio. Vita e morte di Carlo Michelstaedter* (Trieste: Edizioni Italo Svevo, 1983).

25. I would like to thank Giulio Nerini for talking to me about his music, and for

giving me a tape of his piece. His electronic music forms the background for a male voice that recites the poem. We will return to the piece in Chapter 2. Of the poem "All'Isonzo" there is a musical score for piano and soprano voice by Mario Zafred (edited by De Sanctis, 1953) in *FCM*.

26. Calvino, *Mr. Palomar*, 98; Umberto Eco, "Intentio Lectoris. The State of the Art," *Differentia. Review of Italian Thought* 2 (Spring 1988): 147–68; 164. Borges called interpreting "the normal respiration of the intelligence." The phrase was quoted by Victor Brombert in "Mediating the Work: Or the Legitimate Aims of Criticism," *PMLA* (May 1990): 391–97; 396.

27. Eco, *The Name of the Rose,* translated by William Weaver (New York: Harcourt Brace Jovanovich, 1983), 500.

28. Eco, *Foucault's Pendulum,* 641.

29. Ferdinando Adornato's interview with Umberto Eco: "Il mio piano," *L'Espresso* 40 (October 9, 1988): 102.

30. Adornato, 102.

31. Eco, "L'antiporfirio," in *Il pensiero debole,* edited by Gianni Vattimo and Pier Aldo Rovatti (Milan: Feltrinelli, 1983), 52–80; 74. The translation of this passage is by Peter Carravetta in his essay "Repositioning Interpretative Discourse. From 'Crisis of Reason' to 'Weak Thought'" in *Differentia* 2 (Spring 1988): 109. Carravetta points out the evolution of Eco's thought from his *Trattato di Semiotica.*

32. Eco, *The Name of the Rose,* 492.

33. In his essay "Carlo Michelstaedter o della razionalità del dolore," written as an introduction to a recent edition of *Il dialogo della salute* (Bologna: Agalev Soc. Coop a.r.l., 1988), Gian Andrea Franchi develops the idea that *persuasione* cannot be given a "precise conceptual meaning," and this "inconceivability is part of the very experience of *persuasione* . . . which does not make it at all irrational" (23).

34. The translation of this passage is Thomas Harrison's, in "Carlo Michelstaedter and the Metaphysics of Will," forthcoming in *Modern Language Notes*. Many thanks go to the author for having made his essay available to me before publication.

35. Brianese, *L'arco e il destino,* 25.

36. *Presocratici,* 276. See note 12, this chapter.

37. Fratta, 32.

38. In trying to underrate the existentialist interpretation of Michelstaedter, Fratta instead brings out a similarity between some of his ideas and the philosophy of empiriocriticism, in particular that of Mach and its linguistic development in Wittgenstein's *Tractatus*. Michelstaedter's attack against the pretense of absolute knowledge finds an echo in Mach's polemics against concepts that, rather than as signs of absolute knowledge, must be taken simply as means for organizing the material of our experience. As for Wittgenstein, he too did not believe it possible for the world to contain any intrinsic value. Any meaning of the world, in order to exist, must reside outside it. Fratta, 43. Michelstaedter's criticism of the Aristotelian concepts is in *Appendice* 4, especially 243–245.

39. Brianese, *L'arco e il destino,* 32.

40. Inevitably the bitter irony of Pirandello comes to mind. His masterpiece aims to show the impossibility of living without ties, without relations. As Mattia Pascal must kill himself in order to do so, so will Adriano Meis very shortly after having started his new life. Whether or not Michelstaedter had read the novel cannot be proved, although we know that he must have been familiar with some of Pirandello's stories. At the end of a letter home dated February 2, 1907, he wrote: "I just wrote today a letter to Gino and included in it a story by Pirandello" (*Ep.*, 182). His older brother Gino was then living in the United States and did not have access to contemporary publications of Italian literature.

41. Brianese, *L'arco e il destino,* 72. Echoing Severino (*La Strada,* 247), Brianese sees this position as very close to the Kantian postulates of Practical Reason (73).

42. Fratta, 144.

43. Fratta, 159, understood it well: "Being and existence are for Michelstaedter antinomic terms and that, therefore, as long as the latter lasts, the affirmation of the former can never be accomplished" (159). Brianese writes: "The finite subject wants himself infinite, but it cannot be it, unless it destroys itself as subject, annulling . . . its own empirical finiteness" and "The life of the persuaso is death," *L'arco e il destino,* 80, 81.

44. The image of the flame is recurrent. See *Dialoghi,* 80–81; *Opere,* 663, 687; *Poesie,* 74. The flame is, of course, also a basic element in Eastern religions.

45. Fratta and Gianni Carchia give a definite mystical connotation to *persuasione:* Fratta, 168–69; Gianni Carchia, "Linguaggio e mistica in Carlo Michelstaedter," *Rivista d'estetica* 9 (1981): 126–32.

46. Lucia Polisena (as Campailla) has underlined the closeness of the image of the flame to that of light in St. John. Pointing out Michelstaedter's familiarity with pre-Socratic thought, she sees in Empedocles an obvious source for inspiration. Michelstaedter, in fact, left several pages of notes on Empedocles. See Polisena, "Il Tramonto—aurora di Nietzsche e di Michelstaedter," *Letteratura italiana contemporanea* 7 (1986): 289–313.

47. Eugenio Montale, *Tutte le poesie* (Milan: Mondadori, 1977), 54, 53.

48. Brianese, *L'arco e il destino,* 86.

49. Gianni Vattimo, *Al di là del soggetto* (Milan: Feltrinelli, 1984), 11, 12.

50. There is a long passage in his *Scritti vari* that well exemplifies the process of *rettorica*. Here Michelstaedter shows how words are created to camouflage men's weaknesses and fears. "I go to church in order to put a poultice on my remorse—I am not a coward, a hypocrite, I am 'a saint.' I linger in boredom all over the place. . . . I am not an idle individual who is always bored, but I am 'a melancholic youth,' 'a pessimist.' I write all the stupidities that wine and vice inspire me. I am not an impotent idiot, I am an original artist, in fact I am 'a Futurist.' I corrupt others and myself with degenerate pleasures, I am not a perverted swine, I am a 'refined being,' in fact I am 'a D'Annunziano.' I am the artist, the creator of my pleasure" (*Opere,* 702). Thus meaningless words keep men away from painful truths, and society progresses under the banner of *rettorica*.

51. Quoted by Claudio Magris in *L'anello di Clarisse. Grande stile e Nichilismo nella letteratura moderna* (Turin: Einaudi, 1984), 5.

52. The passage against Croce continues and becomes yet more ferocious. "But one cannot make systems, and B.C. after having absorbed all the books of philosophy, squeezes himself and says: 'You see this water of such unspeakable color is the product of all these other waters, if one were to be missing, it could not be the way it is; in it there is only the addition of my own water, and my anxiety is the thirst of all the waters that are missing and that will be coming out of the rags of the future. So I squeeze myself desperately because it is the duty of every rag of a philosopher to squeeze himself down to the last drop of his own water and of that of the others, so that others can then absorb and squeeze again with the addition of their own water and so on . . . by absorbing and squeezing mankind will live forever, ad infinitum, the product will never be the same, yet it will always be perfect and not dirty bath water, as malicious minds say, but the absolute spirit." (*Opere*, 661–62; see also 837).

53. Luigi Pirandello, *Novelle per un anno*, 2 vols. (Milan: Mondadori, 1957), 2:718.

54. Giacomo Leopardi, "Palinodia al marchese Gino Capponi," *Poesie e prose*, 1:114; lines 203–5.

55. Michelstaedter had a good musical ear. Sounds as verses would catch his senses and remain in the back of his mind only to pop up at unpredictable times, prompted by an external assonance. The same phenomenon happened with lines of operas, which he often reused and varied to suit his own situations—always, of course, in a light humorous context. In one of his first letters home, written from Venice, he begins by saying "as you can see, my pen is awful [*la penna è infame*] and I am forced to use the pencil" (*Ep.*, 15) where one can hear the echo of the famous duet between Rodolfo and Marcello ("che penna infame! . . . Che infame pennello!") in the opening scene of *La Bohème*, act 4. Perhaps Carlo did empathize with the misunderstood painter and poet of *Bohème*. In a letter home written three years later, he used *Bohème* again (act 1), but this time he quoted Mimi's words. After having recounted his days to his family, he concluded: "Altro di me non vi saprei narrare" ("I could not tell you anything else of me") (*Ep.*, 293). There is an unpublished page in the *FCM* that begins with "O dolci treni e languidi ritardi, mentre io fremente per la fiacca del treno mi rodea, È già fuggito il treno di Trieste, l'ora è passata e resto disperato e non ho amato mai così Gorizia" ("Oh sweet trains, and languid delays, while I, impatient, was consumed by anger at the weariness of the train; and the train from Trieste has already vanished, the hour has fled and I remain desperate, and I have never loved Gorizia so much." In the translation, unfortunately, the sound and rhythm are lost.) At the station, probably either on a train to Trieste or watching the departure of one, Carlo sings his own version of "Lucean le Stelle" ("The Stars Were Shining"), the aria the painter Mario Cavaradossi sings in prison the night before his execution in the last act of *Tosca*. It is interesting to note that Michelstaedter prefers Puccini's painters or poets. *FCM, Taccuino* 4, 14.

56. Giacomo Leopardi, *Operette morali, Essays and Dialogues*, translated and

edited by Giovanni Cecchetti (Berkeley and Los Angeles: University of California Press, 1982), 489 (hereafter referred to as *Operette*).

57. Michelstaedter left an edition of Leopardi's *Canti* with many notes in the margin. Campailla examines these notes, pointing out the themes and the images that were particularly close to Michelstaedter's, in "Postille leopardiane," discussed further in Chapter 2.

58. Giacomo Leopardi, *Operette,* 495–97, and *Tutte le opere,* 5 vols. (Verona: Mondadori, 1973); *Poesie e prose,* 2 vols., 1:1024. *Poesie e prose* will be cited in the text as *PP* 1, *PP* 2; the *Zibaldone,* also in two volumes, will be referred to as Z 1, Z 2.

59. At times Michelstaedter seems very close to Svevo's opposition of body and mind, whereby the well-being of the former is achieved at the expense of the latter. The following, written to his friend Gaetano Chiavacci, echoes similar expressions in Svevo's *Diario per la fidanzata:* "My spirit fluctuates deliciously in a sea of good things . . . so that I feel every day that I am becoming stupider and stupider . . . and progressively more and more a bourgeois" (*Ep.,* 265–66).

60. It is also possible that Michelstaedter might have developed a bone disease; in various letters he complains about pains in his limbs and about the treatments he endured that did not help him. See *Ep.,* 321, 379, 390. In a letter to Paula written in June 1909 he talked about the pain in his foot which was still the same, as well as the pain and the enlargement in his finger and hip that he had had since January.

61. *FCM,* 3, p. 8. The page is still unpublished.

62. This passage in *FCM,* 4, p. 14, was first published by Campailla in *A ferri corti,* 28–29.

63. R. D. Laing, *The Divided Self* (Penguin, 1960), 65.

64. Elio Gioanola's book is a reading of most of Pirandello's production through the psychoanalytical laws of R. D. Laing: *Pirandello la follia* (Genova: Il melangolo, 1983). On this topic see in particular, 127, 136–37.

65. This letter was quoted by Claudio Vicentini in his *L'estetica di Pirandello* (Milan: Mursia, 1970–85), 16.

66. Luigi Pirandello, "Pirandello parla di Pirandello," *Quadrivio* (November 15, 1936):3.

67. The suicide in 1903 of Otto Weininger (at the age of twenty-three, the same age as Michelstaedter when he killed himself), author of *Sex and Character,* had made a strong impact among the Mitteleuropean intellectuals of the time. Weininger chose for his final act the house where Beethoven had died. Beethoven was also one of Michelstaedter's models. The famous and fiery pen of Karl Kraus contributed to the posthumous fame of Weininger's *Sex and Character.* The book immediately became a bestseller and was translated into Hungarian, Russian, Polish, and Hebrew. For more on Weininger, see Alberto Cavaglion's "Otto Weininger e la cultura ebraica triestina," in *Ebrei e Mitteleuropa,* edited by Quirino Principe (Brescia: Shakespeare and Company, 1984), 267–76. In his recent extensive study *La scienza del tragico. Saggio su Carlo Michelstaedter* (Bologna: Cappelli, 1989), Pieri examines in detail the similarities between Michelstaedter and Weininger. In particular see pp. 100–101, 336–40.

68. Luigi Pirandello, *Saggi, poesie, scritti varii* (Milan: Mondadori, 1960), 900 (hereafter referred to as *Saggi*). Luigi Pirandello, *The Late Mattia Pascal,* translated by William Weaver (Hygiene, Colorado: Eridanos, 1964), 164.

69. Gioanola, 117.

70. Gioanola, 124.

71. Luigi Pirandello, *On Humor,* Translated by A. Illiano and D. P. Testa (Chapel Hill: University of North Carolina Press, 1974), 137.

72. Luigi Pirandello, *One, No One, and a Hundred Thousand,* translated by William Weaver (Boston: Eridanos, 1990), 156.

73. And in "Arte e coscienza d'oggi": "I am amazed that today we call God that which after all is pitch darkness." *Saggi,* 893.

74. Emile Cioran, 7.

75. As Antonio Verri recognized, Michelstaedter's attack was not against a particular philosophical system or school. It was against thought itself, at its roots, as "through its constructions we detach ourselves from the immediacy of existence." *Michelstaedter e il suo tempo* (Ravenna: Edizioni A. Longo, 1969), 55. Michelstaedter was well aware of his own vulnerability. He wrote to his dear friend Rico who had had the courage to sail to the New World, "It has been almost a year that we shook hands here in my house. . . . since then how much you have done, and how *your words have become action!* I instead still feed myself on words and I feel ashamed" (*Ep.,* 442). The emphasis is Michelstaedter's. I shall discuss this letter in greater detail later.

76. "La leggenda del San Valentin" was published by Sergio Campailla with a short introductory essay in *Studi Goriziani* (January–June 1975): 31–44. Campailla's introductory essay was published again in *Scrittori giuliani,* 93–101, 95.

77. Eco, *Foucault's Pendulum,* 44.

78. Ibid., 641.

79. Italo Svevo, *Confessions of Zeno* (1930), translated by Beryl De Zoete (New York: Vintage, 1958), 398.

80. The poetic language of this passage cannot be fully rendered in English. The original reads: "e del mondo intero, e delle infinite vicende e calamità delle cose create, non rimarrà pure un vestigio; ma un silenzio nudo e una quiete altissima, empieranno lo spazio immenso. Così questo arcano mirabile e spaventoso dell'esistenza universale innanzi di essere dichiarato nè inteso, si dileguerà e perderassi." G. Leopardi, "Cantico del gallo silvestre," *PP* 1, 971.

81. Cioran, *A Short History of Decay,* translated by Richard Howard (New York: Viking, 1975), 48.

82. The entire questionnaire of the game was published by Campailla in *A ferri corti,* 46–47.

83. *A ferri corti,* 47.

84. Montale could watch young Esterina dive into the sea and, being aware of his belonging, instead, to the race of those who think and do not act, accept it. Michelstaedter could not. "Esterina" in *Tutte le poesie* (Milan: Mondadori, 1977), 23.

85. Between 1948 and 1950 Umberto Saba wrote many letters to Michelstaedter's dear friend Vladimiro Arangio Ruiz. In them he expressed his existential crisis in words, as Rosita Tordi has pointed out, very similar to those Michelstaedter used in his famous letter to his sister. Furthermore, Saba, as did Michelstaedter, had a strong ethical view of the artist, who must be first an authentic human being. In one of the letters Saba mentioned the meeting with Michelstaedter that took place in Florence, at the same time that Michelstaedter must have met Vlado for the first time. He remarked: "As far as I can remember we were both a little 'crazy' and we did not like each other."

Michelstaedter and Umberto Saba must have seen each other in Florence more than once, as Michelstaedter drew a portrait of him with the epigraph: "Everything is beautiful, even man with his suffering. From Beethoven: Umberto da Montereale." Saba was then twenty-five, but Michelstaedter portrayed him as an older man. According to Tordi, in the portrait Michelstaedter "was making palpable an aversion that could not derive from aesthetic or philosophical evaluations." Yet Tordi's judgment might be challenged if we keep in mind that Michelstaedter was not much more magnanimous in his self-portraits. As will be shown in Chapter 3, one of his last self-portraits shows a very aged and suffering face, almost unrecognizable when placed next to the others and to the few photographs of him left. (It must be pointed out that for Michelstaedter a face aged through suffering was a positive rather than negative feature of a being. It was the sign of a struggle to achieve *persuasione*.) In this unclear relationship Saba, of course, had the upper hand. He survived Michelstaedter and judged him a posteriori, many years later after having become acquainted with psychoanalysis and psychotic studies. He denied, in fact, the thesis of a philosophical suicide; according to psychoanalysis, there is no such thing. Furthermore, he denied any value to either Michelstaedter's philosophical or poetical work. (He had done the same with the poetry of Dino Campana.) "Crazy, only crazy," he wrote of Michelstaedter to Vlado. As Tordi notes, such an outburst can only be explained as the consequence of irreducible hatred toward him.

Tordi's short essay ends thus with a question mark, but with a clear, justifiable judgment of Saba's *mauvaise foi*. For us it is inexplicable without more information about their relationship in Florence. Rosita Tordi, "U. Saba e C. Michelstaedter: Dalle lettere inedite di Saba a V. Arangio Ruiz," *Letteratura italiana contemporanea* 4, no. 9 (May–August 1983): 285–91; 289, 291. Maybe the two writers had more in common than either wanted to admit. Carlo's last letter to his mother has many echoes from Saba's poem "A mamma," which Saba wrote and rewrote throughout his life. Perhaps Michelstaedter had heard Saba reciting this poem in one of his poetry readings in Florence. See *Per conoscere Saba,* edited by M. Lavagetto (Milan: Mondadori, 1981), 117–31.

86. "The habit of measure," writes Alberto to his son, "will give you, I hope, that restraint that is so hard for you to impose upon yourself—the restraint against the impulse of rage, that awful adviser that takes away from us our conscience and veils justice, turning us over blindly to our wicked instinct that pushes us to the search of a

brutal outlet, leaving us unarmed, tired, and disappointed with ourselves." It is a rhetorical piece, undoubtedly, but it shows Alberto's knowledge of Carlo's nature. "It does not help you to be right, if you have proclaimed that with an act of violence. . . . Believe me, Carlo, it is worthy of strong men to achieve a victory over oneself, to control one's temperament, to win against our passions." It is obvious that Alberto was extremely concerned about Michelstaedter's mercurial nature, and his fears were not unfounded (*Dialoghi intorno a Michelstaedter,* 11).

87. Michelstaedter had concluded the last letter to Paula before the long pause with the following statement: "At the moment there is a beautiful young lady at the Institute who interests me" (*Ep.,* 183). At this time, it must be noted, Nadia was still alive.

88. The twenty-page biographical sketch written by Paula Michelstaedter Winteler was published by Campailla as an appendix to the first valuable book-length study of Michelstaedter that pointed out the unity of the philosopher and the poet. *Pensiero e poesia di Carlo Michelstaedter* (Bologna: Pàtron, 1973), 147–64.

89. Michelstaedter, who knew Aeschylus's tragedies, might very well have had in mind Celissa's (Orestes' nurse) monologue in *The Libation Bearers,* lines 749–762. Celissa, who must bring Aegistus the news of Orestes' death (pretended, of course), recalls the days when she cared about all the basic needs of that beloved baby. Aeschylus, *The Complete Greek Tragedies,* 4 vols., ed. by David Grene and Richmond Lattimore (University of Chicago Press, 1953) 1:119.

90. The letter was published by Campailla in *Dialoghi intorno a Michelstaedter,* 34.

91. Michelstaedter never mentions "Longinus" as far as I was able to find, perhaps because he was not familiar with it or perhaps because it would have contradicted his pessimistic view of rhetoric as progressively deteriorating after Aristotle. Yet the pseudo-Longinus words agree with Michelstaedter's belief in the identity between ideas and expression, between content and form. When "Longinus" insists that great style is produced by a great mind, that it is a gift of nature and that "sublimity is the echo of a noble mind," a discourse is developing that Michelstaedter could not but agree with. See Longinus, "On the Sublime" in Aristotle, Horace, Longinus, *Classical Literary Criticism* (New York: Penguin, 1965), 109. The figures of speech were to "Longinus" not "arbitrary devices invented by rhetoricians; but rather a natural means of giving to style an element of true surprise, something rooted in genuine emotion." J. W. H. Atkins, *Literary Criticism in Antiquity,* 2 vols. (Gloucester, Mass.: Peter Smith, 1961), 2:225. Asyndeton, hyperbaton, rhetorical question, repetition and accumulation are all figures present in Michelstaedter's letter. Yet, as "Longinus" said, they are used because the topic invites it, because they are the stylistic devices prompted by an intense psychological state.

92. In his recurrent use of the images of the mountain and the sea, he recalls Nietzsche's *Zarathustra,* in particular the chapter entitled "The Wanderer" (*Thus Spoke Zarathustra,* translated by Walter Kaufman [New York: Penguin, 1978] 152–55).

93. *A Nietzsche Reader,* selected and translated by R. J. Hollingdale (Harmonds-

worth: Penguin, 1977), 55–56. Pieri has dealt extensively with Nietzsche's influence on Michelstaedter, but he places the emphasis on the *Übermensch (La scienza del tragico,* especially pp. 33–55 and 443–65). Pieri's book was published after this study was completed.

94. Robert Musil, *Young Törless,* translated by Eithne Wilkins and Ernst Kaiser (New York: Pantheon, 1955), 91.

95. Musil, 90.

96. Martin Heidegger, "A Dialogue on Language," in *On the Way to Language,* translated by Peter D. Hertz (New York: Harper, 1982), 15, 77.

97. Heidegger, 70. The citation from Nietzsche is quoted by Heidegger on the same page.

CHAPTER 2

1. Claudio Magris, "Things Near and Far: Nietzsche and the Great Triestine Generation of the Early Twentieth Century," *Stanford Italian Review* 6, nos. 1–2 (1986): 293–99; 299.

2. Benussi, *Negazione e integrazione,* 91.

3. Benussi, 119.

4. Gianni Vattimo, *La fine della modernità. Nichilismo ed ermeneutica nella cultura postmoderna* (Milan: Garzanti, 1985), 84, 88.

5. Sergio Campailla, *L'agnizione tragica. Studi sulla cultura di Slataper* (Bologna: Pàtron, 1976), 77–78. Campailla, who pointed out the fascination with the mountain, the high ideals of purity and authenticity in the two writers, notes, however, that their similarity stops here. Slataper's "positive mentality" makes him soon realize that the "top" must be reached in modest, daily life, by fulfilling one's moral duties. Michelstaedter, instead, remains much closer to Ibsen's characters, trying to realize in full their ideals of the absolute.

6. "In alto," in Ruggero Jacobbi's *Ibsen* (Milan: Edizioni Accademia, 1972), 215.

7. S. Campailla, "Michelstaedter lettore di Ibsen," first published in *Lettere italiane* 1 (1974): 46–63, now in Campailla's *Scrittori giuliani,* 65–91; 82.

8. Henrik Ibsen, *The Complete Major Prose Plays,* translated and with introduction by Rolf Fjelde (New York: Farrar, Straus, and Giroux, 1965), 772.

9. Luigi Pirandello, *Novelle,* 1:717.

10. Pirandello, *Novelle,* 1:717.

11. A. Devetag's *La grande trasgressione,* 4.

12. Franco Ferranti, *Il peso al gancio,* 11.

13. Ferranti, 30.

14. Ferranti, 39.

15. Campailla, *Pensiero e poesia,* 53. By far the most complete study of Michelstaedter's poetry is Campailla's "La poesia della salute," first published in *Prospetti* 35–36 (September–December 1974): 27–51, now in *Pensiero e poesia.*

16. *Pensiero e poesia,* 46.

17. Not much has been written on Michelstaedter's poetry. Gilberto Lonardi's "Mito e accecamento in Michelstaedter," *Lettere italiane* 19 (1967): 291-317, is one of the best essays on this topic. Lonardi sees in Michelstaedter's "Leopardism of the twentieth century" an original voice that finds an equivalent only in that of Clemente Rebora, the other poet whose language is founded in "a densely philosophical background" (309). Lonardi also examines the theme of Orpheus in the work of Michelstaedter as well as in that of Dino Campana and in Rilke. For Michelstaedter, in fact, not even poetry is capable of salvation. On the comparison between Michelstaedter and Rebora, see Lucilio Giovanni Mussini's "Clemente Rebora e Carlo Michelstaedter: rapporti interpretativí" in *In ricordo di Cesare Angelini* (Milan: Il Saggiatore, 1979), 320-42. On Michelstaedter's poetry see also Alberto Savini's "Dodici note a Michelstaedter poeta," in *Aut-Aut* 26 (March 1955): 150-55. Silvio Ramat in his *Storia della poesia italiana del Novecento* (Milan: Mursia, 1976): 65-69, speaks of Michelstaedter's poetry as "the threshold of the poetical system of the twentieth century" (69). He points out the presence of themes that were to be developed by poets like Saba, Sbarbaro, and even Zanzotto. Vittorio Enzo Alfieri in "Michelstaedter poeta" underlines the similarity between his poetry, that of German Romanticism, and above all that of Leopardi; *Letterature moderne* 12 (March–June 1962): 133-47. Another short essay on the topic is Maurizio Pistelli's "Appunti su Michelstaedter poeta," *Otto/Novecento* 7, nos. 3–4 (May–August 1983): 139-49, where once more it is Leopardi's name that is mentioned. Similarities with Hölderlin and Rilke are briefly drawn by Rosita Tordi in "Volontà come rischio. La poesia della logica di Carlo Michelstaedter," *Galleria* 35, nos. 5–6 (September–December 1985): 227-42. At the International Conference of 1987 there were two presentations on this topic: Antonio Piromalli's "La poesia di Carlo Michelstaedter," which emphasized the theme of alienation; and Erika Kanduth's "Dal tu all'io nella poesia di Carlo Michelstaedter."

In his recent book Pieri examines D'Annunzio's presence not so much in Michelstaedter's poetry as in his conception of the heroic intellectual. In this examination Pieri also points out, for the first time, the influence of the Florentine journal *Il Leonardo* on Michelstaedter, in particular the writers Papini and Prezzolini (*La scienza del tragico*, 17–75, 91–109, 351–417).

18. Sergio Campailla's "Postille leopardiane di Michelstaedter" was first published in *Studi e problemi di critica testuale* 7 (October 1973): 242-52, and reprinted in *Scrittori giuliani*, 51-64. The theme that was already in Lucretius is developed by Leopardi in Z 1:1548-49.

19. For a detailed stylistic comparison between Leopardi and Michelstaedter, see Campailla's "Postille leopardiane," *Pensiero e poesia*, 64-74, and his first critical edition of *Poesie* (Bologna: Pàtron, 1974), 25-30.

20. B. Marin, "Ricordo di Carlo Michelstaedter," *Studi Goriziani* 32 (1962): 101-7.

21. Campailla, *Pensiero e poesia*, 60-61.

22. Cerruti, *Carlo Michelstaedter*, 31.

23. Ibsen, 639. Examining the influence of music on Michelstaedter, Pieri quotes a

long passage from Wagner in which the composer uses the image of the sea "to characterize the nature of music" (*La scienza del tragico*, 455).

24. Montale, 22–23.

25. Ibsen, 626.

26. Cerruti, *Carlo Michelstaedter*, 37.

27. Brianese, *L'arco e il destino*, 156–57.

28. Quoted by Alessandra Comini in *The Changing Image of Beethoven* (New York: Rizzoli, 1987), 390.

29. Though it could be attractive to draw a parallel between Michelstaedter and Weininger, there is no precise reference to the latter in Michelstaedter's writings. The two names were mentioned together by Scipio Slataper in his review of Michelstaedter's poems (*La Voce*, 39, September 26, 1912). He began a trend continued by G. Papini and S. Benco in their articles on Carlo's suicide (see Epilogue). Michelstaedter and Weininger were considered kindred spirits mainly on the basis of their suicides at age 23. The popularity reached rapidly by *Sex and Character* contributed to the idea that Michelstaedter must have been influenced by the book. Pieri dwells extensively on this topic in *La scienza del tragico*, 100–101, 116–17, 147–48, 338–40.

30. The letter was first published by Campailla in *A ferri corti*, 77–78; and recently in *Dialoghi intorno a Michelstaedter*, 21.

31. *Dialoghi intorno a Michelstaedter*, 22.

32. Campailla, *A ferri corti*, 102–3.

33. It is a translation from Sanskrit by Ludwig Fritze Drossen (Reclam, 1880). See *Ep.*, 403 n.

34. Campailla, *Pensiero e poesia*, 66–67.

35. Montale, *Tutte le poesie*, 54. In his collection called, fortuitously, "Xenia," there is a poem entitled "I falchi" ("The Hawks"); these hawks "are always too far from your sight" (358).

36. Eugenio Montale, *The Bones of Cuttlefish*, translated by Antonino Mazza (Ontario: Mosaic, 1983), 36. I prefer to translate "il male" and "il bene" as "the evil" and "the good" rather than "the pain" and "the well-being." The first choice maintains the metaphysical connotation that, I think, Montale gave to these two words. In *L'arco e il destino*, Brianese, commenting on Campailla's definition of Michelstaedter's "philosophical poetry," sees this trend as beginning with Leopardi, then continuing in Montale.

37. Friedrich Nietzsche, *Thus Spoke Zarathustra*, 103. Pieri in his presentation "Per una dialettica storica del silenzio" at the 1987 conference spoke of the theme of the desert and the sea, relating it not only to Nietzsche, but also to the Judaic faith.

38. Montale, *Tutte le poesie*, 53.

39. The poem is part of "Mediterraneo," in *Tutte le poesie*, 85.

40. Giuseppe Gioacchino Belli, *Sonetti* (Milan: Mondadori, 1984), 211. See also the sonnet "La vita dell'omo," 208.

41. Cerruti, *Carlo Michelstaedter*, 126.

42. Campailla, *Pensiero e poesia,* 82. In his dissertation Michelstaedter explains the symbology of the fish (*Persuasione,* 103–5).

43. *Pensiero e poesia,* 83.

44. G. Brianese, "Il silenzio e i richiami. Per una rilettura de 'I figli del mare' di Carlo Michelstaedter," *Studi Goriziani* 65 (January–June 1987): 7–22; 17–18.

45. Hugo Friedrich, *The Structure of Modern Poetry* (Evanston: Northwestern University Press, 1974), 3–4.

46. Brianese, "Il silenzio e i richiami," 21.

47. Campailla, *L'agnizione tragica,* 74.

48. Ibsen, 671. Michelstaedter quotes this verb in *Opere,* 804.

49. Campailla, "Michelstaedter lettore di Ibsen," *Lettere italiane* 1 (1974): 46–63, reprinted in *Scrittori giuliani,* 65–91; 89.

50. Lonardi sees some similarity between the image of Orpheus in Michelstaedter and in Dino Campana. In both conceptions, Orpheus "symbolizes the attempt to integrate . . . the painfully severed terms of 'I' and nature"; Lonardi concludes, however, "Michelstaedter's Orpheus is blind and mute, it is a poet without lyre, a stoic hero . . . who from a gesture filled with action, not from the poetic singing, hopes in the light that would break through darkness" ("Mito e accecamento," 305). Orpheus is also present in *La Persuasione e la rettorica,* 106.

51. In Campailla, *Pensiero e poesia,* 161.

52. Campailla, *Pensiero e poesia,* 162.

53. More than with Dino Campana this poem could be associated with Clemente Rebora's "Notturno," where poetic expression is given to the negative concept of love, "Amore era d'intorno quanto men si scopriva" ("Love was around with more force, the less it would reveal itself"). *Lirica del Novecento,* edited by L. Anceschi and S. Antonielli (Florence: Vallecchi, 1961), 198.

54. Michelstaedter, *Poesie,* introduction and notes by S. Campailla (Bologna: Pàtron, 1974), 36, 37.

55. Michelstaedter, *Poesie,* 41. These are Campailla's words.

56. Dino Campana, *Canti Orfici e altri scritti* (Florence: Vallecchi, 1966), 286.

57. Campailla, *A ferri corti,* 137.

58. V. E. Alfieri, "Michelstaedter poeta," 136.

59. The expression was borrowed from Frank Kermode's *The Sense of an Ending. Studies in the Theory of Fiction* (Oxford: Oxford University Press, 1966).

60. Silvio Ramat, *Storia della Poesia italiana del Novecento,* 69.

61. The quote was taken from G. P. Biasin's *Il vento di Debussy* (Bologna: Il Mulino, 1985), 17.

62. Biasin, 20.

63. It was Pieri who pointed out the influence of Wagner on Michelstaedter. He sees it especially in a letter Carlo wrote home from Venice after hearing Wagner's music played in San Marco Cathedral. In my view, however, the echo of Wagner is even louder in the first poem to Senia. See Pieri, *La scienza del tragico,* 455.

64. Cerruti, *Carlo Michelstaedter,* 112.

65. Folco Portinari, "Michelstaedter: deserto con poesia," *La Stampa. Tutto libri* (October 3, 1987).

CHAPTER 3

1. Quotations are from Italo Calvino's *Six Memos for the Next Millennium*, 78.

2. Paraphrased by Hugo Friedrich in *The Structure of Modern Poetry*, 156.

3. In the introduction to Michelstaedter's *Opera grafica e pittorica*, edited by Sergio Campailla (Gorizia: Campestrini, 1975), xi. The painter Fulvio Monai also spoke of an Expressionism *ante litteram* in "L'opera grafica di Michelstaedter," *Trieste*, 20, no. 100 (January 1976): 22–23. He had already written on this topic in "Validità dei 'Taccuini pittorici'" in *Il Piccolo* (September 7, 1974), and on October 3 in "Nei disegni del pensatore goriziano voci annunciano l'espressionismo," 3.

4. Paul Vogt, introduction to the catalogue *Expressionism. A German Institution 1905–1920* (New York: S.R.E. Guggenheim Foundation, 1980), 18.

5. Vogt, 17.

6. In Ladislao Mittner, *L'espressionismo* (Bari, 1965), quoted by Campailla in "Espressionismo e filosofia della contestazione," in *Scrittori giuliani* (Bologna: Pàtron, 1980), 106.

7. Michelstaedter, *Opera grafica*, xii.

8. Campailla, "Espressionismo e filosofia," 116–17. For the quote from Leonardo, see the epigraph at the beginning of this chapter.

9. Graziella Corsinovi, *Pirandello e l'Espressionismo. Analogie culturali e antici-pazioni espressive nella prima narrativa* (Genova: Tilgher, 1979), 87. Corsinovi ana-lyzes the new Expressionist technique employed by Pirandello in his description of scenes as far back as in 1884 (89 ff.). In her analysis she concentrates on the formal aspects of his narration, pointing out the use of brevity, essentiality, almost isolated brief sentences and the powerful play of light and darkness (91). The landscape is clearly analyzed with the interior eye of the protagonist (94).

10. Michelstaedter's *Marina* is in *FCM*, Album G, sheet 3. Pirandello's is in the private collection of Dr. Pietro D'Alessandro, reproduced in Antonio Alessio's *Piran-dello Pittore* (Agrigento: Edizioni del Centro Nazionale di Studi Pirandelliani, 1984), 108.

11. Antonio Alessio, "Tra pittura e narrativa nella novella di Pirandello," *Le Novelle di Pirandello*, Atti del 6° Convegno internazionale di studi pirandelliani (Agrigento, 1980): 173–90. Alessio's *Pirandello pittore* reproduces, for the first time, most of what is left of Pirandello's paintings. With the exception of a few portraits of his family members they are landscapes, done in a rather traditional style. As the painter Longaretti (interviewed by Alessio, 41–45) said, Pirandello's pictorial style is in line with late nineteenth-century artists such as the Tuscan *Macchiaioli* and the French Impressionists. The art critic Mascherpa, on the other hand, does not agree with this interpretation. He sees Pirandello's last paintings in their substance rather than in their form, in the light of Expressionism.

Although I tend to agree with Longaretti, one cannot deny the presence of an Expressionist spirit in some of Pirandello's paintings. After all, he continued to paint until he died, and he could not have been completely unaware of the revolution created by the Expressionist movement. He was, however, a "summer painter" as his son remarked; he painted only when vacationing.

Alessio's essay on Pirandello's painting in his narrative and dramatic work (*Pirandello pittore,* 19–31) points to the large number of characters who are artists— insignificant, unsuccessful artists who try to fix life on canvas or marble. Perhaps in them Pirandello projected a part of himself, that of the failed painter. Yet if we follow his long debate on life and art, we could venture a hypothesis. If art had to win over life, it needed not to be only eternal but also alive. Only drama that could be reenacted over and over again had that characteristic.

12. Pirandello was familiar with A. Binet, *Les Altérations de la personalité* (1902) and with Giovanni Marchesini's *Le finzioni dell'anima.*

13. Rudolf Arnheim, "The Rationale of Deformation," in *Art Journal* 43, no. 4 (Winter 1983): 319–24; 323.

14. Arnheim, 323.

15. Daumier's lithograph is in Arnheim, 323. The definition of caricature is Olszewski's in "The New World of Pier Leone Ghezzi," *Art Journal* (Winter 1983): 325–30; 325, 324.

16. "Ciaula scopre la luna," *Novelle per un anno,* 2 vols. (Milano: Mondadori, 1956–57), 1:1272. There are other splendid lithographs by Daumier with the *Parisiens* looking up at the sky; *Effet de lune* and *Vain Search for "Leverrier's Planet,"* done in 1846, are among the most effective. The first represents a man and his wife in their night clothes, looking out of the window at the moon. The simplicity of their appearance is emphasized by the true emotion the moon provokes in their souls. *Honoré Daumier. A Century of Tribute,* edited by Andrew Stasik (New York: Pratt Graphics, 1980), 68. The famous *Vain Search for "Leverrier's Planet"* is L.D. no. 1531 in Roger Passeron's *Daumier* (New York: Rizzoli, 1981), 133.

17. Luigi Pirandello, *On Humor,* 155.

18. The sketch of the knights riding is reproduced in Arnheim, p. 324. The original is in the Metropolitan Museum of Art (no. 140). The paintings are in Passeron's *Daumier,* p. 253 (*Don Quixote and the Dead Mule,* no. 209, in the Louvre Museum) and p. 250 (*Don Quixote and Sancho Panza under a Tree,* no. 174, in the New York Carlsberg Glyptotek in Copenhagen).

19. E. H. Gombrich, *Art and Illusion* (Princeton University Press, 1956), 355.

20. Flaminio Gualdoni, "Diario tedesco," in *Espressionisti.* Catalogue of the exhibit at the Royal Palace in Milan. September 20–November 18, 1984 (Milan: Mazzotta, 1984): 17–22; 17.

21. Quoted by Frederick S. Levine in *The Apocalyptic Vision* (New York: Harper, 1979), 2.

22. Alessio, "Tra pittura e narrativa," 173–74.

23. Rosso di San Secondo, "Pirandello tra i castagni," *Almanacco letterario Bompiani* (1938): 96.

24. Alessio, "Tra pittura e narrativa," 181; Leone De Castris, *Storia di Pirandello* (Bari: Laterza, 1962), 115.

25. They are respectively plates 63 and 112 in the *Opera grafica e pittorica*. The titles of the figures are by Campailla who, when possible, used indications in the margin by Michelstaedter. The plates will subsequently be referred to in the text as figures and numbered in succession.

26. Commenting on this caricature Campailla rightly hypothesized a conscious satire against the Austrian officers. The moustache, in fact, has an obvious Habsburg quality. I shall refer to this work in discussing all Michelstaedter figures.

27. Luigi Pirandello, *Novelle*, 1:1247.

28. Pirandello, *Novelle*, 2:1127.

29. Ibid.

30. Ibid.

31. Campailla, "Psicologia del comico nei disegni di Michelstaedter," first published in the Atti del X convegno Mitteleuropeo in Gorizia, 1975, now in *Scrittori Giuliani*, 133–54.

32. Pirandello, *Novelle*, 2:366.

33. Pirandello, *On Humor*, 143.

34. Campailla, "Psicologia del comico," 137.

35. Campailla, "Psicologia del comico," 141.

36. Luigi Pirandello, *One, No One, and A Hundred Thousand*, 135.

37. Pirandello, *On Humor*, 142.

38. Pirandello, *On Humor*, 142–43.

39. Pirandello, *On Humor*, 144.

40. Beside a shocking self-portrait, made in 1905, Heckel drew many dramatic faces. See Alexander Dückers's *Graphik der "Brücke"* (Berlin: Gebr. Mann, 1984), 54–57 (Catalogue nos. 23, 20, 21, 32, 22, 33, 24). Nolde's self-portrait of 1907 is in *Expressionism*, 70. Schmidt-Rottluff's self-portrait of 1906 is in *Expressionism*, 154.

41. The reproduction of Klee's etching is in James P. Bednarz, "The Dual Vision of Paul Klee's Symbolic Language" in *Passion and Rebellion, The Expressionist Heritage*, edited by S. E. Bronner and Douglas Kellner (New York: Universe Books, 1983), 277.

42. Bednazy, 279.

43. Brianese, *L'arco e il destino*, 12–13.

44. *Expressionism*, 21.

45. Ibid.

46. For a more detailed treatment of this topic, see Campailla's introduction to *Opera grafica*, xxvi.

47. "I will try to get accepted in *Cyrano*, a weekly opposition journal that is widely read and that also publishes caricatures, naturally I will not be hired, . . . *sed quid temptare nocebit* [but what harm is there in trying]?" (*Ep.*, 42).

48. Reproduced in Ralph E. Shikes and Steven Heller's *The Art of Satire. Painters as Caricaturists and Cartoonists from Delacroix to Picasso* (New York: Pratt Graphic Center and Horizon Press, 1984), 29.

49. Reproduced in Giuseppe Gatt's *Kokoschka* (London: Hamlyn, 1971), 10. In the tradition of caricature that points out the similarities between man and animal are two beautiful heads of the same old man with a flowing mane of white hair and a similar flowing beard whose features slowly change from one caricature to the other—they should, in fact, be seen in a succession, as one sees Philippon's *Poire*—showing the obvious similarities with a baboon (*FCM*, Album N, sheet 12).

50. *FCM*, Album L, sheet 2. It is also interesting to point out the existence of another beautiful drawing of a sailor, also not yet published. It represents a middle-aged man with a similar hat and moustache. His head is erected on a strong large neck over a similarly powerful chest. The eyes that look to the left and the slant position of the head reveal a sense of sadness. Perhaps this still strong sailor is looking ahead at what he will shortly become (*FCM*, Album G, sheet 14).

51. In George Heard Hamilton, *Painting and Sculpture in Europe, 1880–1940*, The Pelican History of Art (New York: Penguin, 1981 [1967]), 198.

52. Heckel's portrait of his brother is plate 102 in *Expressionism*, 117. The self-portrait is in *Brücke: German Expressionist Prints*, exhibit catalog, Granvil and Marcia Specks collection, edited by Reinhold Heller (Northwestern University, Mary and Leigh Bloch Gallery, 1988), 105.

53. *Brücke: German Expressionist Prints*, 113, plate 39.

54. The drawing by Michelstaedter is in *FCM*, Album N, sheet 10.

55. In a letter to Kurt Valentin written in 1937 (Wolf-Dieter Dube, *L'Espressionismo*, translated by Gabriella Buora [Milan: Mazzotta, 1979], 38). For his Berlin scenes, see 44, 45, 51. The sharp, angular features of the face are also emphasized in the *Portrait of the Sick Woman, or Woman with Hat* (1913), where the sharpness of the lines is coupled with an exaggerated pale complexion that reveals the presence of an illness which is not only physical (plate 134, *Expressionism*, 131).

56. Quoted by Ernst Kris in *Psychoanalytic Explorations in Art* (New York: International Universities, 1952), 191.

57. Ibid.

58. George Grosz, *Ecce Homo* (New York: Dover, 1976), 59.

59. Grosz, *Ecce Homo*, respectively, 66, 4, 80. The portrait of Hermann-Neisse is in Hamilton, plate 280, p. 477.

60. Grosz, 19.

61. Quoted from Campailla in *A ferri corti*, 48.

62. Another letter from father to son remains. Although it is about Michelstaedter's petition to be exempted from university tuition which had been the subject of many letters, in its warm tone it still reveals the affection Alberto felt for his son. Alberto offers his son all the help he can. Even the so-called *sermone paterno*, examined in Chapter 1, appears tender once the formal, authoritarian veneer is removed. It is hard for a modern reader to accept that rhetoric; perhaps we tend to take it more seriously

than the receiver would have in those times. It was a formal letter written according to certain rhetorical schemata. But this formality was only its shell, not its content. Both letters are now in *Dialoghi intorno a Michelstaedter*, 10–14.

63. *A ferri corti*, 88–89.

64. Kris, 182.

65. Kris, 201.

66. Michelstaedter, *Opera grafica*, 68.

67. In *Expressionism*, plate 276, p. 254.

68. *Oskar Kokoschka, 1886–1980*, exhibit at the Galérie des Beaux-Arts, Bordeaux, May 6–September 1, 1983, catalogue 2, p. 2.

69. In Giuseppe Gatt's *Kokoschka*, plate 4, p. 12; plate 6, p. 14; plate 8, p. 16; plate 9, p. 17; plate 10, p. 18.

70. Ehrenstein is quoted in *Oskar Kokoschka, 1886–1980*, 82.

71. Hamilton, 491.

72. Ibid. The affinity between Michelstaedter and Kokoschka was clearest in the portraits, but went beyond them. One of the very few landscapes Michelstaedter drew of his mountains is very close in style to those of Kokoschka, for example, *Landscape in Montana*, an oil painting he did as late as 1947. Michelstaedter's is more desolate. There is no trace of human life in his drawing. By contrast, Kokoschka painted a village at the foot of the mountains. The human presence is threatened by the towering mountains that overpower the small houses in a juxtaposition that emphasizes the frailty and precariousness of human life. The mountain scene by Michelstaedter has never been published. It is in *FCM*, Album F, sheet 7. Kokoschka's mountain scene is plates 35–36 in *Kokoschka* by Giuseppe Gatt.

73. Campailla, *A ferri corti*, 133.

74. Reproduced in Alessandra Comini's *The Fantastic Art of Vienna* (New York: Knopf, 1978), plate 22.

75. See note 44, this chapter.

76. Nietzsche's view of Christ was commented on by Masao Abe in *Zen and Western Thought* (London: Macmillan 1985), 141.

77. Abe, 147.

78. Abe, 145.

79. *Persuasione*, 179; *Epistolario*, 396.

80. Campailla, who first saw the influence of Eastern thought in this self-portrait, tells us that Enrico Mreule as late as 1952 talked about his friend as the "Western Buddha" and that Arrigo Bongiorno, picking up his suggestion, entitled an article in the *Giorno* of Milan "The Suicidal Buddha"; *Opera grafica*, 126.

81. See plates 41a, 41b, 42, 43 in *Richard Gerstl (1883–1908)* (Vienna: Historisches Museums der Stadt Wien, 1984).

82. *Richard Gerstl*, plate 1. All my attempts to obtain permission to reproduce this painting were frustrated.

83. Jane Kallir's *Arnold Schoenberg's Vienna* (New York: Galérie St. Etienne and Rizzoli, 1984), plate 24. See also the pastel self-portrait in the same book (fig. 35, p. 56).

84. *Gaze* is plate 25 in Kallir, *Arnold Schoenberg's Vienna. The Red Glance* is plate 21 in Alessandra Comini's *The Fantastic Art of Vienna.*

85. Max Beckmann's self-portrait is plate 9, p. 209, of Gualdoni's *Espressionisti.* His portrait is similar to another one by Michelstaedter: *Autoritratto tenebroso* (*Opera grafica,* 76).

86. Ladislao Mittner, *Storia della letteratura tedesca,* 3 parts and 7 vols. (Torino: Einaudi, 1971), part 3, 2:1023.

87. This drawing is reproduced at the beginning of the introduction to this volume.

EPILOGUE

1. Nietzsche, *Thus Spoke Zarathustra,* 221. Translation slightly revised.

2. Sigmund Freud, *Al di là del principio del piacere* (Rome: Newton Compton, 1976), 64–65, 84.

3. Published in Massimo Cacciari, *Dallo Steinhof. Prospettive viennesi del primo Novecento* (Milan: Adelphi, 1980), plate 14.

4. Schiele's message could not be more explicit than in several portraits of mother with two children. In all of them the mother's face shows clear signs of death. He also left two paintings called *Dead Mother,* done in a much more dramatic and expressionistic style than Klinger's. In both works the child can be detected still in the womb. The womb, symbol of life, is here seen in its mysterious darkness as being also the source of death. The child is alive inside a dead body. The creative principle has ceased to be in order to create life. See figures 280, 287, 294, 158 and 168 in Gianfranco Malafarina, *Toute l'oeuvre peint de Schiele, Catalogue et documentation* (Paris: Flammarion, 1983).

5. For a detailed examination of this topic, see L. D. Hankoff and Bernice Einsidler's *Suicide. Theory and Clinical Aspects* (Littleton, Mass.: PSG, 1979). In particular see the essay by Edwin S. Shneidman, "An Overview: Personality, Motivation and Behavior Theories," 143–63.

6. Thomas S. Szasz, "A Critique of Professional Ethics," in Hankoff and Einsidler, *Suicide,* 59.

7. Joost Meerloo, *Suicide and Mass Suicide* (New York: Grune and Stratton, 1962), 63.

8. Shneidman, in Hankoff and Einsidler, *Suicide,* 144.

9. Giovanni Papini, "Un suicidio metafisico," in *Il resto del Carlino,* November 5, 1910. Reprinted as "Carlo Michelstaedter" in *Ventiquattro cervelli* (Florence: Vallecchi, 1924), 174–75. The crisis of the Hapsburg Empire that Musil had described so well in his masterpiece *The Man Without Qualities* brought about a high number of suicides at the turn of the century. Among the most distinguished individuals who committed suicide in that period were Otto Mahler, brother of Gustav; the poet Georg Trakl; and three of Ludwig Wittgenstein's older brothers. An analysis of this topic is in Allan Janik and Stephen Toulmin's *Wittgenstein's Vienna* (New York: Simon and Schuster, 1973); in particular, see the end of chapter 2.

10. Emilio Cecchi, "La vita nella morte: Carlo Michelstaedter," *La Tribuna*, November 12, 1912, reprinted in *La fiera letteraria*, July 13, 1952, and again in *Letteratura italiana del Novecento* (Milan, 1969) 2:764.

11. Vladimiro Arangio Ruiz, "Per Carlo Michelstaedter," *Il Convegno*, 3 (1922): 343–62; 352, 359.

12. Silvio Benco, "Il suicidio filosofico," *Il piccolo della sera*, August 10, 1913: 1–2; 1.

13. Thomas Harrison develops this idea in his intelligent essay "Carlo Michelstaedter and the Metaphysics of Will." See Chapter 1, note 34, this book; Brianese, *L'arco e il destino*, 84.

14. *L'arco e il destino*, 86.

15. Paula's biography of Carlo is in Campailla's *Pensiero e Poesia*, 147–64.

16. Meerloo, 70.

17. *Thus Spoke Zarathustra*, 71, 72.

18. These are also Hedda Gabler's words. Ibsen, *Complete Major Prose Plays*, 772.

19. Schopenhauer discusses the topic in his essay "On Suicide," *The Pessimist's Handbook. A Collection of Popular Essays* by Arthur Schopenhauer, translated by T. Bailey Saunders (Lincoln: University of Nebraska Press, 1964), 151–57. In order to explain Michelstaedter's suicide Harrison quotes Schopenhauer's statement that the suicide "wills life . . . and is only dissatisfied with the conditions under which it has presented itself to him. . . . Just because the suicide cannot give up willing, he gives up living" (20).

20. Sidney S. Furst and Mortimer Ostow, "The Psychodynamics of Suicide," in Hankoff and Einsidler, *Suicide*, 165–78; 171.

21. Giacomo Leopardi, *Operette morali*, 473.

22. Campailla, *Pensiero e poesia*, 164.

23. Piero Pieri, "Per una dialettica storica del silenzio." Paper given at the International Conference, "Michelstaedter: Il coraggio dell' impossibile," held in Gorizia on October 1–3, 1987. The proceedings are forthcoming.

24. George Steiner, *Language and Silence* (London: Faber and Faber, 1958), 67.

25. Steiner, 69. Paolo Valesio develops this idea in his book *Ascoltare il silenzio. La retorica come teoria* (Bologna: Il Mulino, 1986). In particular see section 5.4, "Rettorica e silenzio," 353–97. He considers silence an effective theoretical choice in a large part of social and artistic communication. Yet not even silence can escape *rettorica*.

26. Steiner, 70.

SELECTED BIBLIOGRAPHY

Abbruzzese, Alberto. *Svevo, Slataper e Michelstaedter: lo stile e il viaggio.* Venice: Marsilio, 1979.

Abe, Masao. *Zen and Western Thought.* London: Macmillan Press, Ltd., 1985.

Alessio, Antonio. *Pirandello pittore.* Agrigento: Edizioni del Centro Nazionale di Studi Pirandelliani, 1984.

———. "Pirandello pittore e critico d'arte." *Quaderni d'Italianistica* 2, no. 2 (1981): 192–203.

———. "Tra pittura e narrativa nella novella di Pirandello." In *Le Novelle di Pirandello. Atti del 6° Convegno internazionale di studi pirandelliani.* Agrigento, 1980.

Alfieri, Vittorio Enzo. "Michelstaedter poeta." *Letterature moderne* 12 (March–June 1962): 133–47.

Allen, Roy F. *Literary Life in German Expressionism and the Berlin Circles.* Ann Arbor, Mich.: UMI Research Press, 1972.

Altieri, Orietta. *La comunità ebraica di Gorizia: Caratteristiche demografiche, economiche e sociali (1778-1900).* Udine: Del Bianco, 1985.

———. "La famiglia Michelstaedter e l'ebraismo goriziano." In *Dialoghi intorno a Michelstaedter,* edited by S. Campailla, 35–41. Gorizia: Biblioteca Isontina, 1988.

Anceschi, L., and S. Antonielli, eds. *Lirica del Novecento.* Florence: Vallecchi, 1961.

Arangio Ruiz, Vladimiro. "Per Carlo Michelstaedter." *Il Convegno* 3 (1922): 343–62.

Arata, C. *La filosofia della Mitteleuropa. Atti del IX Convegno culturale Mitteleuropeo* (Gorizia 1974). Gorizia: Istituto per gli incontri culturali mitteleuropei, 1981.

Aristotle, Horace, and Longinus. *Classical Literary Criticism.* New York: Penguin, 1965.

Arnheim, Rudolf. "The Rationale of Deformation." *Art Journal* 43, no. 4 (Winter 1983): 317–24.

Atkins, J. W. H. *Literary Criticism in Antiquity.* 2 vols. Gloucester, Mass.: Peter Smith, 1961.

Barilli, Renato. *Retorica.* Milan: Isedi, 1979; Mondadori, 1983.

Bednarz, James P. "The Dual Vision of Paul Klee's Symbolic Language." In *Passion and Rebellion.* New York: Universe Books, 1983.

Belli, Giuseppe Gioacchino. *Sonetti.* Milan: Mondadori, 1984.

Benco, Silvio. "Il suicidio filosofico." *Il piccolo della sera* (Aug. 10, 1913): 1–2.

Benussi, Cristina. *Negazione e integrazione nella dialettica di Carlo Michelstaedter.* Rome: Edizioni dell'Ateneo e Bizzarri, 1980.

Bergamaschi, Giuliano. *Linguaggio Persuasione Verità.* Padova: Cedam, 1984.

———. "Dell'attimo come Kairos. Aspetti del problema del tempo nell'Epistolario di Michelstaedter." In *Dialoghi intorno a Michelstaedter,* edited by S. Campailla, 97–119. Gorizia: Biblioteca Isontina, 1988.

Bernardini, Paolo. "Il tempo e le tenebre. Saggio su Carlo Michelstaedter." *L'Erbaspada* 1, no. 1 (1984): 21–51.

Biasin, Gian Paolo. *Il vento di Debussy. La poesia di Montale nella cultura del Novecento.* Bologna: Il Mulino, 1985.

———. *Literary Diseases.* Austin and London: University of Texas Press, 1975.

Bini, Daniela. "Carlo Michelstaedter: The Tragedy of Thought." *Differentia. Review of Italian Thought* 2 (Spring 1988): 185–94.

———. "Il peso e il pendolo: The Precarious Balance between Life and Thought." *Romance Languages Annual,* Purdue University (1989): 87–93.

———. "Leopardi e Michelstaedter tra autenticità e inautenticità." *Italiana,* Rosary College (1988): 219–27.

———. "Michelstaedter, Pirandello and Folly." *Italian Culture* (1990): 363–76.

———. "Michelstaedter tra persuasione e rettorica." *Italica* 4 (Winter, 1986): 346–60.

Bozzi, Carlo Luigi. "C. Michelstaedter studente ginnasiale." *Studi goriziani* 40 (1966): 3–13.

Brianese, Giorgio. "Michelstaedter e la Retorica." In *Dialoghi intorno a Michelstaedter,* edited by S. Campailla, 121–35. Gorizia: Biblioteca Isontina, 1988.

———. *L'arco e il destino. Interpretazione di Carlo Michelstaedter.* Abano Terme: Francisci, 1985.

———. "Essere per il nulla. Note su Michelstaedter e Heidegger." *Studi goriziani* 59 (January–June 1984): 7–44.

———. "Il silencio e i richiami. Per una rilettura de 'I figli del mare' di Carlo Michelstaedter." *Studi Goriziani* 65 (January–June 1987): 7–22.

Bronner, S.E., and D. Kellner, eds. *Passion and Rebellion.* New York: Universe Books, 1983.

Buscaroli, Silvano. "Sacralità ed essere del linguaggio e del silenzio, tra Heidegger e Michelstaedter." In *Sull' Essere del linguaggio e dell'analogia: oltre la metafisiche,* 13–34. Bologna: Tipografia Negri, 1984.

Cacciari, Massimo. *Dallo Steinhof. Prospettive viennesi del primo Novecento.* Milan: Adelphi, 1980.

Calvino, Italo. *Mr. Palomar.* Translated by William Weaver. San Diego: Harcourt Brace Jovanovich, 1985.

———. *Six Memos for the Next Millennium.* Translated by Peter Creagh. Cambridge: Harvard University Press, 1988.

Campailla, Sergio. *A ferri corti con la vita.* Gorizia: Arti grafiche Campestrini, 1974.

———, ed. *Dialoghi intorno a Michelstaedter.* Gorizia: Biblioteca Isontina, 1988.

———. "Ebraismo e letteratura." In *Ebrei e Mitteleuropa,* 24–35. Brescia: Shakespeare & Co., 1984.

———. *L'Agnizione tragica. Studi sulla cultura di Slataper.* Bologna: Pàtron, 1976.

———. *Pensiero e poesia di Carlo Michelstaedter.* Bologna: Pàtron, 1973.

———. "Postille leopardiane di Michelstaedter." *Studi e problemi di critica testuale* 7 (October 1973): 242–52.

———. "Psicologia del comico nei disegni di Michelstaedter," *La pittura nella Mitteleuropa.* Atti del X Convegno, 25–34 (Gorizia, September 27–30, 1975). Gorizia: Istituto per gli incontri culturali Mitteleuropei, 1981.

———. *Quaderno bibliografico.* Genoa: Università degli studi, 1976.

———. *Scrittori giuliani.* Bologna: Pàtron, 1980.

Campana, Dino. *Canti orfici.* Florence: Vallecchi, 1966.

Camus, Albert. *The Myth of Sisyphus and Other Essays.* New York: Vintage Books, 1955.

Cannata, Roberto. *Il fauvismo e l'Espressionismo.* Milan: Fabbri, 1976.

Carchia, Gianni. "Linguaggio e mistica in Carlo Michelstaedter." *Rivista d'estetica* 9 (1981–1983?): 126–32.

Carravetta, Peter. "Repositioning Interpretative Discourse. From 'Crisis of Reason' to 'Weak Thought'." *Differentia. Review of Italian Thought* 2 (Spring 1988): 83–126.

Catalfamo, Giuseppe. "L'esistenzialismo di Carlo Michelstaedter." *Teoresi* 1 (1946): 150–68, and 2–3: 126–34. Reprinted in *Berdiaeff.* Messina: Edizioni Ferrara, 1953.

Cattaneo, Carlo. "La rivolta impossibile." *Aut-Aut* 37 (January 1957): 85–92.

Cecchi, Emilio. "La vita nella morte: Carlo Michelstaedter." In *Letteratura italiana del Novecento,* vol. 2. Milan: Mondadori, 1969.

———. "Michelstaedter precursore dell'esistenzialismo." In *Letteratura italiana del Novecento,* vol. 2. Milan: Mondadori, 1969.

Cerruti, Marco. *Carlo Michelstaedter.* Milan: Mursia, 1967–87.

Chiavacci, Gaetano. "Carlo Michelstaedter e il problema della persuasione." *Il Leonardo* 16 (June–August 1947): 129–46.

———. "Il pensiero di Carlo Michelstaedter." *Giornale critico della filosofia italiana* 5 (1924): 1, 2.

Cioran, Emile. *A Short History of Decay.* New York: Viking, 1975.

———. *The Trouble with Being Born.* New York: Viking, 1976.

Comini, Alessandra. *The Changing Image of Beethoven.* New York: Rizzoli, 1987.

———. *The Fantastic Art of Vienna.* New York: Alfred A. Knopf, 1978.

Corsinovi, Graziella. *Pirandello e l'Espressionismo. Analogie culturali e anticipazioni espressive nella prima narrativa.* Genoa: Tilgher, 1979.

De Benedetti, Giacomo. *Il romanzo del Novecento.* Milan: Garzanti, 1971.

De Castris, Leone. *Storia di Pirandello.* Bari: Laterza, 1962.

Derrida, Jacques. "La pharmacie de Platon." In *La dissémination.* Paris: Editions du Seuil, 1972.

Devetag, Antonio. *Michelstaedter. La grande trasgressione.* Piccolo teatro "Città di Gorizia," U.G.G., December 9–10, 1981.

Dube, Wolf-Dieter. *L'Espressionismo.* Translated by Gabriella Buora. Milan: Mazzotta, 1979.

Dückers, Alexander. *Graphik der Brücke.* Berlin: Gebr. Mann, 1984.

Durkheim, Emile. *Suicide. A Study in Sociology.* Translated by J.A. Spaulding and G. Simpson. New York: The Free Press, 1951.

Eco, Umberto. *Foucault's Pendulum.* Translated by William Weaver. San Diego: Harcourt Brace Jovanovich, 1989.

———. "Intentio Lectoris. The State of the Art." Translated by Peter Carravetta. *Differentia. Review of Italian Thought* 2 (Spring 1988): 147–68.

———. *The Name of the Rose.* San Diego, New York, London: Harcourt Brace Jovanovich, 1983.

Ferranti, Franco. *Il peso al gancio. Vita e morte di C. Michelstaedter.* Trieste: Edizioni Italo Svevo, 1983.

Franchi, Gian Andrea. "Carlo Michelstaedter o della razionalità del dolore." In Carlo Michelstaedter, *Il dialogo della salute,* edited by G. Franchi. Bologna: Agalev, 1988.

Fratta, Francesco. *Il dovere dell'essere. Critica della metafisica e istanza etica in Carlo Michelstaedter.* Milan: Unicopli, 1986.

Freud, Sigmund. *Al di là del principio del piacere.* Rome: Newton Compton, 1976.

Friedrich, Hugo. *The Structure of Modern Poetry.* Evanston, Ill.: Northwestern University Press, 1974.

Furst, Sidney D., and Mortimer Ostow, "The Psychodynamics of Suicide." In *Suicide. Theory and Clinical Aspects.* Littleton, Mass.: PSG Publishing Co., 1979.

Garcia-Pignide, Lucille. "Fantasmes et rationalisations dans l'oeuvre de C. Michelstaedter." In *Idéologies et politique. Contributions à l'histoire récente des intellectuels italiens.* Abbeville, France: Paillart, 1978.

Gatt, Giuseppe. *Kokoschka.* London: Hamlyn, 1971.

Gentile, Giovanni. "Review of *La persuasione e la rettorica* (Vallecchi)." *La Critica* 20, no. 4 (1922): 332–36.

Gerstl, Richard. *Richard Gerstl (1883–1908).* Vienna: Historisches Museums der Stadt Wien, 1984.

Giannantoni, Gabriele. *La filosofia prearistotelica.* Roma: Edizioni dell'Ateneo, 1962.

Gioanola, Elio. *Pirandello la follia.* Genoa: Il melangolo, 1983.

Gombrich, E. H. *Art and Illusion.* Princeton, N.J.: Princeton University Press, 1956.

Gopnik, Adam. "High and Low: Caricature, Primitivism, and the Cubist Portrait." *Art Journal* 43, no. 4 (Winter 1983): 371–76.

Grene, D., and R. Lattimore, eds. *The Complete Greek Tragedies.* 4 vols. University of Chicago Press, 1953.

Grosz, George. *Ecce Homo.* New York: Dover Publications, 1976.

Gualdoni, Flaminio. "Diario tedesco." In *Espressionisti*, edited by Gabriele Mazzotta. Milan: Mazzotta, 1984.

Hamilton, George Heard. *Painting and Sculpture in Europe, 1880–1940*. Harmondsworth: Penguin Books, 1981.

Hankoff, L. D., and Bernice Einsidler. *Suicide. Theory and Clinical Aspects*. Littleton, Mass.: PSG Publishing Co., 1979.

Harrison, Thomas. "Carlo Michelstaedter and the Metaphysics of Will." Forthcoming in *Modern Language Notes*.

Heidegger, Martin. *On the Way to Language*. Harper and Row, 1982.

Heller, Reinhold, ed. *Brücke: German Expressionist Prints*, from the Granvil and Marcia Specks Collection. Evanston, Ill.: Northwestern University, Mary and Leigh Block Gallery, 1988.

Ibsen, Henrik. *The Complete Major Prose Plays*. New York: Farrar, Strauss, Giroux, 1965.

Janik, Allan, and Stephen Toulmin. *Wittgenstein's Vienna*. New York: Simon and Schuster, 1973.

Kallir, Jane. *Arnold Schoenberg's Vienna*. New York: Galérie St. Etienne and Rizzoli, 1984.

Kermode, Frank. *The Sense of an Ending. Studies in the Theory of Fiction*. Oxford: Oxford University Press, 1966.

Kokoschka, Oskar. *Oskar Kokoschka, 1886–1980*. Exhibit at the Galérie des Beaux-Arts, Bordeaux, May 6–September 1, 1983.

Kris, Ernst. *Psychoanalytic Explorations in Art*. New York: International Universities Press, 1952.

Laing, R. D. *The Divided Self*. New York: Penguin Books, 1960.

La Rocca, Claudio. *Nichilismo e retorica. Il pensiero di Carlo Michelstaedter*. Pisa: ETS, 1983.

Lavagetto, M., ed. *Per conoscere Saba*. Milan: Mondadori, 1981.

Leopardi, Giacomo. *Operette Morali. Essays and Dialogues*. Translated and edited by Giovanni Cecchetti. Berkeley: University of California Press, 1982.

———. *Tutte le opere*. 5 vols. Verona: Mondadori, 1973.

Levine, Fredrick S. *The Apocalyptic Vision*. New York: Harper and Row, 1979.

Lonardi, Gilberto. "Mito e accecamento in Michelstaedter." *Lettere italiane* 19 (1967): 291–317.

Luperini, Romano. *Il Novecento*, vol. 1. Turin: Loescher, 1981.

Magris, Claudio. *L'anello di Clarisse. Grande stile e nichilismo nella letteratura moderna*. Turin: Einaudi, 1984.

———. "Things Near and Far: Nietzsche and the Great Triestine Generation." *Stanford Italian Review* 6, nos. 1–2 (1986): 293–99.

Magris, Claudio, and Angelo Ara. *Trieste un'identità di frontiera*. Turin: Einaudi, 1982.

Maier, Bruno. "La letteratura triestina del Novecento." In *Scrittori triestini del Novecento*, 97–102. Trieste: LINT, 1968.

Malafarina, Gianfranco. *Toute l'oeuvre peint de Schiele*. Paris: Flammarion, 1983.

Marin, Biagio. "Ricordo di Carlo Michelstaedter." *Studi Goriziani* 32 (1962): 101–7.

Mazzotta, Gabriele, ed. *Espressionisti*. Milan: Gabriele Mazzotta, 1984.

Meerloo, Joost. *Suicide and Mass Suicide*. New York and London: Greene & Stratton, 1962.

Menninger, Karl A. *Man against Himself.* New York: Harcourt, Brace & World, 1938.

Meyers, Bernard S. *The German Expressionists. A Generation in Revolt.* New York: Frederick A. Praeger, 1956.

Michelstaedter, Carlo. *Epistolario*. Edited by Sergio Campailla. Milan: Adelphi, 1983.

———. *Il dialogo della salute e altri dialoghi.* Edited by Sergio Campailla. Milan: Adelphi, 1988.

———. *La persuasione e la rettorica.* Edited by Sergio Campailla. Milan: Adelphi, 1982.

———. *Opera grafica e pittorica.* Edited with an introduction by Sergio Campailla. Gorizia: Campestrini, 1975.

———. *Opere.* Edited by Giovanni Chiavacci. Florence: Sansoni, 1958.

———. *Poesie.* Edited by Sergio Campailla. Bologna: Pàtron, 1974. Rev. ed., Milan: Adelphi, 1987.

Mittner, Ladislao. *Storia della letteratura tedesca.* Turin: Einaudi, 1971.

Monai, Fulvio. "L'opera grafica di Michelstaedter." *Trieste* 20, no. 100 (January 1976): 22–23.

———. "Nei disegni del pensatore goriziano voci annunciano l'espressionismo." *Il Piccolo* (October 3, 1974): 3.

Moretti Costanzi, Teodorico. "Un esistenzialista ante litteram: Carlo Michelstaedter." In *L'Esistenzialismo,* 159–72. Rome: Studium, 1943.

Musil, Robert. *Young Törless.* Translated by E. Wilkins and E. Kaiser. New York: Pantheon, 1955.

Mussini, Lucilio G. "Clemente Rebora e Carlo Michelstaedter: rapporti interpretativi." In A.A.V.V. *In ricordo di Cesare Angelini,* 320–47. Milan: Il Saggiatore, 1979.

Muzzioli, Francesco. *Michelstaedter.* Lecce: Milella, 1987.

Nietzsche, Friedrich. *A Nietzsche Reader.* Translated by R. J. Hollingdale. New York: Penguin, 1977.

———. *L'Anticristo.* Rome: Newton Compton Editori, 1984.

———. *Thus Spoke Zarathustra.* Translated by Walter Kaufman. New York: Penguin Books, 1978.

Norris, Christopher. *Derrida.* Cambridge: Harvard University Press, 1987.

Ottonello, Pier Paolo. *Irrazionalismo e Scetticismo.* Milan: Marzorati, 1974.

Papini, Giovanni. "Un suicidio metafisico." *Il resto del Carlino,* November 5, 1910. Reprinted as "Carlo Michelstaedter," in *Ventiquattro Cervelli.* Florence: Vallecchi, 1924.

Passeron, Roger. *Daumier.* New York: Rizzoli, 1981.

Paterson, R. W. K. *The Nihilistic Egoist. Max Stirner.* Oxford: Oxford University Press, 1971.

Perniola, Mario. "Carlo Michelstaedter. La conquista del presente." *Mondo operaio* 4 (April 1984): 108–9.

Pieri, Piero. *La differenza ebraica. Ebraismo e grecità in Michelstaedter.* Bologna: Cappelli, 1984.

———. *La scienza del tragico. Saggio su Carlo Michelstaedter.* Bologna: Cappelli, 1989.

Pirandello, Luigi. *Novelle per un anno.* 2 vols. Milan: Mondadori, 1956–57.

———. *One, No One, and A Hundred Thousand.* Translated by William Weaver. Boston: Eridanos, 1990.

———. *On Humor.* Translated by A. Illiano and D. P. Testa. Chapel Hill: University of North Carolina Press, 1974.

———. *Saggi poesie, scritti varii.* Milan: Mondadori, 1960.

———. *The Late Mattia Pascal.* Translated by William Weaver. Hygiene, Colo.: Eridanos, 1964.

———. *Tutti i romanzi.* 2 vols. Milan: Mondadori, 1973.

Piromalli, Antonio. *Carlo Michelstaedter.* Bologna: La Nuova Italia, 1974.

Pistelli, Maurizio. "Appunti su Michelstaedter poeta," *Otto / Novecento* 3/4 (May–June 1983): 139–49.

Platone [Plato]. *Opere.* 2 vols. Bari: Laterza, 1966.

Polisena, Lucia. "Il tramonto-aurora di Nietzsche e di Michelstaedter." *Letteratura italiana contemporanea* 7, no. 18 (1986): 289–313.

Pontiggia, Elena. "Il grande postumo. Carlo Michelstaedter, pensatore e artista." In *Catalogue of the Exhibit,* April 22–May 23, 1983, Padiglione d'Arte Contemporanea, Milan.

Portinari, Folco. "Michelstaedter: deserto con poesia." *La Stampa. Tutto libri* (October 3, 1987).

Presocratici. Testimonianze e frammenti. Edited by G. Giannantoni. Bari: Laterza, n.d.

Principe, Quirino, ed. *Ebrei e Mitteleuropa.* Brescia: Shakespeare & Co., 1984.

Raabe Paul, ed. *The Era of German Expressionism.* Translated by J. M. Ritchie. London: Calder and Boyars, 1974.

Ramat, Silvio. *Storia della poesia italiana del Novecento.* Milano: Mursia, 1976.

Ranke, Ioachim. "Il pensiero di Michelstaedter. Un contributo allo studio dell'esistenzialismo italiano." *Giornale critico della filosofia italiana* 41, no. 4 (1962): 518–39.

Raschini, Maria A. *Carlo Michelstaedter.* Milan: Marzorati, 1965.

Rilke, Rainer Maria. *On Love and Other Difficulties.* Translated by John J. L. Mood. New York: W. W. Norton, 1975.

Rosso di San Secondo. "Pirandello tra i castagni." *Almanacco letterario Bompiani* (1938).

Salinari, Carlo. *Miti e coscienza del Decadentismo italiano.* Milan: Feltrinelli, 1980.

Sartre, Jean-Paul. *Nausea.* Translated by Lloyd Alexander. New York: New Directions, 1964.

Savini, Alberto. "Dodici note a Michelstaedter poeta." *Aut-Aut* 26 (March 1955): 150–55.

Schopenhauer, Arthur. *The Pessimist's Handbook. A Collection of Popular Essays.* Translated by T. Bailey Saunders. Lincoln: University of Nebraska Press, 1964.

Semeraro, Licia. *Lo svuotamento del futuro*. Lecce: Milella, 1986.

Severino, Emanuele. "Discepolo infedele di Parmenide." Interview by Angelo Mainardi, in *Mondo operaio* 4 (April, 1987).

———. *La Strada*. Milan: Rizzoli, 1983.

Shikes, Ralph E., and Steven Heller. *The Art of Satire. Painters as Caricaturists and Cartoonists from Delacroix to Picasso*. New York: Pratt Graphic Center and Horizon Press, 1984.

Shneidman, Edwin S. "An Overview: Personality, Motivation and Behavior Theories." In *Suicide—Theory and Clinical Aspects*. Littleton, Mass.: PSG Publishing Co., 1979.

Stasik, Andrew, ed. *Honoré Daumier. A Century of Tribute*. New York: Pratt Graphics, 1980.

Steiner, George. *Language and Silence*. London: Faber and Faber, 1958.

Stirner, Max. *Der Einzige und sein Eigenthum (The Ego and His Own)*. Translated by Stephen T. Byington. New York, 1907.

Svevo, Italo. *Confessions of Zeno*. 1930. Translated by Beryl De Zoete. New York: Vintage, 1958.

Szasz, Thomas S. "A Critique of Professional Ethics." In *Suicide. Theory and Clinical Aspects*. Littleton, Mass.: PSG Publishing Co., 1979.

Tordi, Rosita. "Michelstaedter—Trakl Volontà come rischio." *Mondo operaio* 14 (April 1987): 116–19.

———. "Volontà come rischio: La poesia della logica di Carlo Michelstaedter," *Galleria* 5–6 (Sept.–Dec. 1985): 227–42.

———. "Umberto Saba e Carlo Michelstaedter: Dalle lettere inedite di Saba a Vladimiro Arangio Ruiz." *Letteratura italiana contemporanea* 4, no. 9 (May–Aug. 1983): 285–91.

Valesio, Paolo. *Ascoltare il silenzio. La retorica come teoria*. Bologna: Il Mulino, 1986.

Vattimo, Gianni. *Al di là del soggetto. Nietzsche, Heidegger e l'ermeneutica*. Milan: Feltrinelli, 1984.

———. "C'è una sola verità: il dolore." *Tutto libri. La Stampa* (April 23, 1983).

———. *La fine della modernità. Nichilismo ed ermeneutica nella cultura postmoderna*. Milan: Garzanti, 1985.

———, and P. A. Rovatti. *Il pensiero debole*. Milan: Feltrinelli, 1983.

Verri, Antonio. *Michelstaedter e il suo tempo*. Ravenna: Longo, 1969.

———. "Michelstaedter oggi." *L'Albero* 38, nos. 71–72 (1984): 33–55.

Vicentini, Claudio. *L'estetica di Pirandello*. Milan: Mursia, 1970–1985.

Vogt, Paul. *Expressionism. A German Institution 1905–1920*. New York: S.R.E. Guggenheim Foundation, 1980.

Weininger, Otto. *Sex and Character*. London: Heinemann; New York: G. P. Putnam's Sons, 1906.

INDEX